ST. METHODIUS

THE SYMPOSIUM
A TREATISE ON CHASTITY

ΣΥΜΠΟΣΙΟΝ Η ΠΕΡΙ ΑΓΝΕΙΑΣ

ANCIENT CHRISTIAN WRITERS

THE WORKS OF THE FATHERS IN TRANSLATION

EDITED BY

JOHANNES QUASTEN, S. T. D.
Catholic University of America
Washington, D.C.

JOSEPH C. PLUMPE, PH.D.
Pontifical College Josephinum
Worthington, O.

No. 27

ST. METHODIUS

THE SYMPOSIUM
A TREATISE ON CHASTITY

TRANSLATED AND ANNOTATED
BY

HERBERT MUSURILLO, S.J., D.Phil.(Oxon.)

Professor of Classics
Bellarmine College and Fordham University
New York

NEWMAN PRESS

New York, N.Y./Ramsey, N.J.

De Licentia Superioris S.J.
Nihil Obstat
J. Quasten
Cens. Dep.

Imprimatur:
Patricius A. O'Boyle, D.D.
Archiep. Washingtonen.
die 6 Maii 1955

Library of Congress
Catalog Card Number: 58-7775

ISBN: 0-8091-0143-2

PUBLISHED BY PAULIST PRESS
Editorial Office: 1865 Broadway, New York, N.Y. 10023
Business Office: 545 Island Road, Ramsey, N.J. 07446

PRINTED AND BOUND IN THE UNITED STATES OF AMERICA

CONTENTS

CONTENTS

ST. METHODIUS

THE SYMPOSIUM

A TREATISE ON CHASTITY

INTRODUCTION

1. Life

'Methodius, otherwise known as Eubulius,' as Epiphanius refers to him,[1] is one of the most interesting as well as the most mysterious of the Greek Fathers who wrote before the peace of the Church. No other ecclesiastical writer has sprinkled his pages so liberally with quotations and reminiscences from the works of Plato. Methodius' *Symposium*, the only authentic work of his that is preserved completely in Greek, has had a profound influence on the stream of ascetical thought in both the East and the West.[2] And yet his life is veiled in such obscurity that it is hardly possible to make any statements about it with absolute certainty.

Eusebius does not mention him in his extant works (although Jerome knew of a reference[3]); yet he quotes a long section from Methodius' *De autexusio* (5–7), attributing it to a certain Maximus.[4] So too the fourth-century dialogue, *De recta in Deum fide*, attributed to Adamantius, copies from the *De autexusio* as well as the *De resurrectione* of Methodius without acknowledging their author.[5]

Our first clear—perhaps misleadingly clear—references occur in Jerome. He refers to Methodius several times[6] as *episcopus et martyr*; and in *De viris illustribus* 83 (Richardson) we have the following entry:

> Methodius, Olympi Lyciae et postea Tyri episcopus, nitidi compositique sermonis adversus Porphyrium confecit libros, et Symposium decem virginum, de resurrectione opus egregium contra Origenem, et adversus eumdem de Pythonissa, et de αὐτεξουσίῳ, in

> Genesin quoque et in Cantica Canticorum commentarios, et multa alia quae vulgo lectitantur. Et ad extremum novissimae persecutionis, sive, ut alii affirmant, sub Decio et Valeriano, in Chalcide Graeciae martyrio coronatus est.

Socrates, in his *Ecclesiastical History* 6.13, mentions Methodius in passing as 'bishop of the city in Lycia named Olympus.' So too, about the year 435, John of Antioch in a letter to Proclus of Constantinople, included in the Acts of the Council of Ephesus,[7] mentions Methodius as one of the early Fathers who flourished 'in Greece and Illyricum.' Finally we have the following entry in Suidas (Adler *s.v.*):

> Methodius, bishop of Olympus in Lycia or of Patara and afterwards of Tyre. [There follows a list of books in the same order as Jerome's.] . . . And at length he was crowned with martyrdom in the persecution under Decius and Valerian in Chalcis of the East.

It looks very much as though we have here a contamination of several traditions, the one reflected in Jerome and at least one other. But Jerome's information is itself the result of contradictory accounts: for Porphyry's *Adversus Christianos* is generally dated to about the year 270,[8] and if we accept Methodius' authorship of a tract *Against Porphyry*, he could hardly have been martyred under Decius (249/50) or in the persecution of Valerian which ended about the year 259. And if this were not sufficiently confused, there still remains the meaning of Jerome's *ad extremum novissimae persecutionis*, 'towards the end of the last persecution.' Does this mean, as most suppose, the persecution of Diocletian (311/12) or, as the Bollandist Jean Stiltinck suggested,[9] the brief persecution under Licinius about the year 320?

Further, even if we pass over the problem of Tyre, there is the question as to which Chalcis Jerome intended. There were at least five fairly important centers of this name:

Chalcis in Euboea; an island of this name near Lesbos; towns in Elis, Aetolia, and Ionia.[10] It seems clear that Jerome did not critically scrutinize his materials; and I cannot see how F. Diekamp, in his otherwise brilliant article,[11] can say that Jerome's testimony, at least as to the place of the martyrdom, must be respected. Holding fast to this single detail in the *De viris illustribus* Diekamp rejects the claims of Olympus, Patara (and, of course, of Side, Tyre and Myra) to be the seat of Methodius' bishopric, and casts his vote in favor of Philippi, although he admits that the *Symposium* and part at least of the *De resurrectione* might have been composed in Lycia. But the evidence remains nothing less than ambiguous; and even if Stiltinck's suspicion, that there were several Methodii,[12] seems today somewhat extreme, a certain skepticism would seem advisable until clearer evidence should be forthcoming. The author of the *Symposium* was undoubtedly a Christian teacher, and perhaps a bishop and martyr, who was familiar with certain localities in Lycia (such as Patara, Olympus and Termessus) and flourished in the latter half of the third century. Beyond this meager statement, I feel, it is very difficult to go.

2. Works

The study of Methodius' works must begin with the edition of G. Nathanael Bonwetsch (=Bo), GCS 27 (Leipzig 1917), although his Greek text at times leaves much to be desired from the viewpoint of modern textual criticism, and the Palaeoslavic (or Old Church Slavonic) fragments which he publishes are merely presented in German translation. The Methodian corpus, so far as we know it today, is as follows:[13]

1. *The Banquet, or a Treatise on Chastity* is the only work preserved (more or less) completely in the Greek: Bo 3–141.[14]

2. *Free Will* (=*De autexusio*) is Methodius' reply to the Gnostic and Neoplatonic theory of the origin of moral evil, written in the form of a dialogue; the speakers are Orthodoxus (representing Methodius' point of view), a certain Valerius, and a friend (named Aglaophon in some MSS). As an orthodox Christian, Methodius attacks the theory of the eternity of matter and that matter is the ultimate cause of evil. Sin, he teaches, arises from man's misuse of his power of free choice, though the idea of committing sin was first introduced into the world by the suggestion of the devil.

Of this work (or Aristotelian 'demonstration' as Vaillant calls it) we have a more or less complete Slavonic version: see A. Vaillant PO 22.5 (1930) 631–889. There are also selections in an Armenian paraphrase by Eznik (about A.D. 450); and Greek quotations in Eusebius (*Praep. evang.* 7.22, where he attributes the work to a certain Maximus, otherwise unknown), in a MS of the tenth century (Codex Laurentianus Plut. 9.23), in the *Sacra Parallela*, and in Photius (*Bibl.* cod. 236 Bekker). The text in Bo 145–206 must be checked against the results of Vaillant; there is a good French translation of Vaillant's text by J. Farges, *Méthode d'Olympe: Du libre arbitre* (Paris 1929).

The treatise on *Free Will* gives us a most important clue to Methodius' theology and theory of asceticism. 'Man, I say, is free. And this not in the sense that he had the power, if he wished, to choose some pre-ordained evil, but that he is the sole cause of his obeying or disobeying God.'[15] It is by this power, Methodius teaches, that man was made in God's image; and thus the entire history of the world, from God's point of view, revolves about the restoration of a state of equilibrium between good and evil, that balance which Adam had before the fall, a state that is particularly demonstrated by man's ability to be chaste. Not only did Christ redeem man by His life and death, but He has furnished him with a λόγος, a spiritual doctrine, communicated by Mother Church, by which God's image in man can be restored. Thus Methodius' voluntarism or libertarianism is at the very heart of his theological thought; and the tract *Free Will* clearly shows that Methodius' main philosophic direction was Aristotelian, as Vaillant has suggested,[16] and not Platonic.

3. *Life and Rational Activity* (=*De vita*). This is a fragment of an exhortation on rational hope and trust in God, preserved only in a Slavonic version. There is the impression of a stronger Stoic influence in this piece than elsewhere in Methodius, but as Bardenhewer says, 'Its authenticity should not be doubted.'[17] See Bo 209–216.

4. *Aglaophon, or a Treatise on the Resurrection of the Body* (=*De resurrectione*). This was in three books, now preserved in a Slavonic version (which abridges books 2 and 3) and in fairly extensive Greek fragments (e.g., in Epiphanius, *Haer.* 64; Photius, *Bibl.* cod. 234; the dialogue *De recta in Deum fide*; the *Sacra Parallela* and a few other quotations); there are also quotations from Syriac florilegia: Bo 219–424.

The *Aglaophon* is an anti-Origenist dialogue whose scene is laid in the home of a physician named Aglaophon in the city of Patara. The other characters in the dialogue are Eubulius (=Methodius), Proclus (or Proculus) of Miletus who defends Origenism along with Aglaophon, Theophilus, Sistelius, Auxentius and Mem(m)ianus. Against the Origenist theory of the 'pneumatic body' Methodius argues firmly for the traditional view of the risen body; he also defends the orthodox doctrine of Adam's fall and the salutary effects of Christ's Atonement.

It is interesting to note that in *De res.* 2.23.1 (Bo 377) he mentions Mt. Olympus with its chaste-trees or the so-called agnus-castus; again, he makes repeated use of the image of melting down and casting bronze statues (particularly in connection with the doctrine of the Atonement)—symbolism which is very important in the *Symposium*.

5. *The Jewish Foods and the Red Heifer* (=*De cibis et de vacca rufa*) is a short and somewhat fragmentary tract in the form of a letter addressed to a Christian woman whom Methodius in the beginning calls Phrenope and afterwards Chilonia. (She had perhaps a double name, Chilonia Phrenope; there is no evidence otherwise that the tract is addressed to two women, as most commentators, including Bardenhewer, have presumed.) This work, preserved only in a Slavonic version, puts forward an allegorical interpretation of the Jewish food laws (a subject which is also touched on in the *Symposium*), as well as the sacrifice of the red heifer in Num. 19: see Bo 427–447.

From *De cib.* 1–2 it is clear that Methodius, despite his involvement in controversy, has already completed his *Symposium* and is engaged in writing the *De res.* It is with this text in mind that Vaillant, arguing convincingly that Methodius became progressively more bitter towards the Origenists, postulated the following order of composition:[18] *De autex., Symp., De cib., De res.* Further, Jerome tells us[19] that Eusebius criticized Methodius for changing his attitude towards Origen; and if, as seems likely, the work of Eusebius (and Pamphilus), the *Apologia Origenis*, to which Jerome attributes this criticism, may be dated to about 309/10, it would follow that the *De res.*, which reflects Methodius' sharpest attack on Origen, ought to be dated to a period not long before. We may thus plausibly arrive at good terminal dates for the major part of Methodius' literary activity: between 270 (the date of Porphyry's *Adversus Christianos*) and 309.

6. *To Sistelius on Leprosy* (=*De lepra*) is a short dialogue between Sistelius and Eubulius on the spiritual meaning of the Jewish laws concerning leprosy in Lev. 13. Various kinds of leprosy are distinguished; and the mention of 'green leprosy,' or cowardice in time of persecution (*De lepra* 6.1, Bo 457) would date the work perhaps after A.D. 303. The text is in an abridged Slavonic version, with some Greek fragments from a florilegium (Coislinianus, 11/12th cent.). See Bo 451–474.

7. *The Leech and the Verse 'The Heavens Proclaim the Glory of God'* (=*De sanguisuga*) is a short tract in the form of an epistle to a certain Eustachius, who had requested Methodius for the spiritual interpretation of the leech of Prov. 30.15 ff. and a verse of Psalm 18. It is preserved only in the Slavonic: Bo 477–489.

8. *Creatures* (=*De creatis*), most probably identical with the *Xenon* mentioned by Socrates, *Hist. eccl.* 6.13, is represented only by fragments in Photius, *Bibl.* cod. 235 (Bekker): see Bo 493–500. In this dialogue (probably late, if Vaillant's chronology is accepted), Methodius sharply attempts to refute Origen's theory on the eternity of the world, here defended by a certain Xenon and a man called 'the Centaur' (=Origen?).

9. *Against Porphyry*, highly praised in antiquity, for example, by Jerome, is represented only by a few fragments in Greek (from the *Sacra Parallela* and from a piece

once called Methodius' *Homily on Christ's Cross and Passion*) and Syriac. The work must have been composed as a counterthesis to Porphyry's fifteen books *Adversus Christianos*, published about A.D. 270. See Bo 503–507.

10. *Fragments:* (a) from a commentary on the book of Job, our knowledge of which is derived from scattered quotations in Old Testament *Catenae*; (b) from *The Martyrs* (quoted by Theodoretus Eranistes and the *Sacra Parallela*), perhaps to be dated to the period after 303; (c) four Greek fragments which cannot be certainly identified. See Bo 511 ff. and xxxix f.[20]

11. *Lost works*: (a) *Commentary on Genesis*; (b) *Commentary on the Canticle of Canticles*; (c) *Adversus Origenem de pythonissa.*

12. *Certainly Spurious works*: (a) *De Simeone et Anna* (*PG* 18.347–82), a sermon which may be as late as the ninth century; (b) *In ramos palmarum* (*PG* 18.383–98), reflecting later Christological controversies; (c) *Sermon on the Ascension*, extant only in an Armenian version; (d) *The Revelations of St. Methodius*, an apocalypse which may have originated in Syria in the seventh century. It was extremely popular in a Latin version in the middle ages.[21] But its authenticity was suspect even to Robert Bellarmine, *De scriptoribus ecclesiasticis* (1613). (e) Two sermons *On the Presentation*, attributed to Methodius in a MS in the Bibliothèque Nationale, Paris, are referred to by Stiltinck.[22]

3. The Symposium—The Banquet: A Treatise on Chastity

Interest in the *Symposium* as an imitation of Plato's dialogue has tended to obscure the fact that it is actually a manual of Christian doctrine, of philosophy and thelogy, unified under the concept of chastity, and dedicated apparently to Methodius' patroness Telmesiake (or, as I should prefer, 'the Lady from Termessus'). It is clear that in the course of the eleven great discourses with prelude, interludes and epilogue, Methodius is not only discussing the place of celibacy in the Christian scheme of life; he is also giving practical instruction, for example, on the allegorical interpretation of the Scriptures (e.g., on the numerological and 'botanical' methods of exegesis), on the nature of the Millennium and the hereafter, on the divinity of Christ, on the fallacy of astrology, on the freedom of the will, on the meaning of world history, on prayer, and on the method of combating temptations. In fact, as the dialogue unfolds, we learn that the chastity in question is nothing less than the perfect practice of Christian virtue, without which we cannot enter heaven.

Methodius' patroness was perhaps herself unmarried or a widow; further, she may have encouraged a number of young ladies to embrace a life of virginity and live within her household; and it is for these women, perhaps, that the work was primarily written. If so, it is not unlikely that Methodius would have used the actual names of some of these women for his characters: they are certainly of the kind that turn up not infrequently among the Greek inscriptions of imperial Asia Minor.[23] At any rate, in this comparatively short work—I have estimated that it would take about four to five hours to complete in a single public reading—Methodius poured a concentrate of his own readings and reflections,[24] the results of contemporary controversies, concluding with a hymn which he probably composed, with music, for his patroness' actual use. The absence of any reference to urgent persecution[25] suggests a period of comparative peace for the Church. Since the great bulk of Methodius' works are not later than A.D. 309/10, we may place the *Symposium*—composition and publication—during the generation of peace that lasted from the suspension of the anti-Christian edicts of Valerian (in 260) till the resumption of persecution by Diocletian (in 303); and a date around 270/90 would probably not be far from the truth.

4. Outline of the Symposium

Characters of the Dialogue. (a) Outside the Narrative: the two ladies Eubulion and Gregorion (with special reference to Methodius and his pupil, 'the Lady from Termessus'). (b) Within the Narrative:

Arete, daughter of Philosophia
Marcella, the oldest
Theophila
Thalia
Theopatra
Thallusa
Agathe
Procilla
Thecla, disciple of St. Paul
Tusiane
Domnina, the youngest

Dramatic Date: in the days of Thecla, companion of St. Paul.

Place: (a) At the house of Eubulion (?). (b) For the banquet, at Arete's estate high up in the mountains (perhaps near Mt. Olympus), with the table set in a garden facing the east under the shade of a chaste-tree.

* * *

Prelude: Gregorion tells Eubulion of the banquet at Arete's estate. Description of the approach to estate; Arete's beauty; the garden.

Logos 1: MARCELLA—The place of Chastity in the history of Redemption.

1. The 'Ascent of the Soul'; external practices of the virgin.

2–4. 'World history': evolution from incest, through polygamy, monogamy (and continence within marriage) to the virginity of the Christian era.

5. Virginity is the true likeness to God and to Christ: Christ the Leader of the choir of virgins.

Logos 2: THEOPHILA—A defense of Marriage.

1–2. Procreation of children is good and willed by God.

3. Marcella's interruption: Does God approve of illegitimate children?

4–6. Theophila's reply: the Myth of the Craftsman's Cave.

7. Because virginity is more excellent, this does not make marriage evil.

Logos 3: THALIA—Methodius' Christology. Pauline doctrine on virginity.

1. Defense of a spiritual interpretation of the union of Adam and Eve.

2. Excursus on Paul's style.

3–5. In what sense Christ may be called Adam.

6. The significance of the Atonement: to destroy the state of sin and to prevent men from being overwhelmed by the deception of pleasure; to give life as Adam gave death.

7. Methodius' Christian doctrine of Platonic participation: man, midway between corruption

and incorruption, can partake of sin-death or resurrection-life.

8. The sleep of Adam foreshadows the sleep and ecstasy of Christ on the Cross (His marriage to the Church). The Church is divided into two classes:
   (1) The perfect, who collaborate with Christ—the Church in the strict sense;
   (2) The imperfect, who are yet to be born in Christ.

9. Transitional: application of the previous distinction to Paul.

10–14. Pauline doctrine on virginity and marriage in 1 Corinthians: marriage is only by way of dispensation from the general law because of weakness (12).

Interlude 1

Logos 4: THEOPATRA—The Flood of Sin.

1. Exordium.
2. Man's ship in the floodtide of the world.

3–5. Spiritual exegesis of Psalm 136, 'Upon the rivers of Babylon.'

5–6. Generalizations on the practice of chastity and self-discipline.

Logos 5: THALLUSA—Allegorical variations on virginity.

1–3. Various allegorical interpretations (the heifer, goat and ram; the three night watches; the yoke and the horseman).

4–6. The 'Nazarite Vow' applied (spiritually) to consecrated virgins.

4. Consecration of the senses and powers to God.

5–6. Two types of wine and their effects.

6–8. Community of virgins compared to the altar (or ark) of the Temple. The distinction of shadow, image and reality (7–8).

Logos 6: AGATHE—Chiefly on the Parable of the Wise and Foolish Virgins.

1. Exordium. The devil's plot against the beauty of the soul made in God's image.

2–4. Application of the Parable of the Ten Virgins.

5. Mystical processional of the virgin choir to meet Christ with their lamps: the 144,000 virgins of the Apocalypse.

Logos 7: PROCILLA—The application of the Canticle of Canticles.

1–7. The allegorical interpretation of the Canticle.

8–9. The Lord's 'Bride' is His spotless flesh, and with this virginity is associated.

Logos 8: THECLA—The ascent of the soul. Exegesis of Apocalypse 12. The refutation of astrology and determinism.

1. Virginity = 'Next-to-God-ness' (*parthenia* = *partheia*).

2. The ascent of the soul: the virgins rise in spirit to the heavenly meadows.

3. The heavenly vision of the essential Virtues.

4–12. Exegesis of Apoc. 12. Introduction to numerological exegesis (§ 11).

13. Transition to the tract on astrology.
14–16. A treatise *adversus astrologos*, with a refutation of determinism (§ 16).

Interlude 2

Logos 9: TUSIANE—Allegorical interpretation of the Feast of Tabernacles.

1–5. The Seventh Day and the Seventh Month signifies the rebuilding of our bodily tabernacles at the resurrection. It is the beginning of the Millennium of Christ, and only the chaste shall enter heaven, and hence the married must also be chaste.

Interlude 3

Logos 10: DOMNINA—Methodius' 'Botanical Exegesis': the symbolism of trees (1–6).

[*Logos 11*:] The Discourse of Arete. The conclusion of the Contest. General summary. The warning against pride in the practice of chastity. Exhortation to practice all the virtues. Awarding of a special chaplet to Thecla.

Thecla's Hymn: an acrostic epithalamium on the mystical marriage of Christ and the Church.

Epilogue: Dialogue between Eubulion and Gregorion on the place of concupiscence in the practice of virtue. The essence of virtue.

5. The Doctrines of the Symposium

It is difficult to give any unified impression of the various doctrines of the *Symposium*; for, as we have said, it seems to have been intended not only as a protreptic, an exhortation to the practice of chastity, but also as a handbook against Encratism and Gnosticism, and, further, as a manual of Christian doctrine which would serve as a guide in Trinitarian and Christological dogma, in the technique of allegorical exegesis, in what Methodius regarded as necessary information in psychology and even physiology,[26] and, finally, in asceticism and the manner of prayer.[27] And what is particularly odd about this doctrine is that Methodius thought it necessary to set it down in a dialogue which is, especially in some places, a veritable cento of Platonic vocabulary and phraseology. The *Symposium* stands, therefore, as one of the most peculiar phenomena in patristic literature: for despite the vast wealth of Platonic quotation and allusion, one has the definite impression that even where Methodius has not positively misunderstood Plato and failed to comprehend the complexities of his system, he was not really interested in its doctrinal content. Was it purely, then, as some have said, an infatuation with form and language? I do not think so. Methodius writes rather like the 'self-taught' Platonist, and it is my view that his aim was much more subtle and it is perhaps connected with the paradox that he, one of the first to write against the Neoplatonist Porphyry and the allegorist Origen, should make extensive use of both Platonism and allegory. In both cases perhaps it was a question of invading the adversary's armory for weapons to turn against him. Methodius would show how Plato's doctrines could be more fittingly harmonized with the traditional Christianity that had been attacked by Porphyry and his teacher Plotinus (of whose labors at least Methodius must have heard). It is all the more interesting, too, to find parallels, however faint, in the *Symposium* which remind one of the *Corpus Hermeticum*, Plotinus, Proclus and Pseudo-Dionysius the Areopagite;[28] these parallels, of course, are hardly to be pressed and do little more than illustrate the general syncretist atmosphere, at least in certain areas, of the late third century.

The core of Methodius' theology is the supernatural history of man on earth, and hence it revolves entirely about the creation, the Fall, and man's consequent restoration. But his anthropology is at the opposite pole from Origenism; in Methodius' extant works there is no trace of the Origenist doctrine of the pre-existence of the soul or the doctrine of final Restoration (ἀποκατάστασις) in the Alexandrian sense. Even though Methodius is closest to Origen in his allegorism, even here, as we shall see, he clearly parts company. For the external history of man's Fall, Methodius closely follows the Scriptural account; for the internal psychology of sin, however, his explanation is not far removed from the Aristotelian theory of free choice. Adam, created in God's image[29] and typifying in his creation and subsequent sleep the birth and death of Christ,[30] participated, by his nature in both life and death, placed halfway between corruption and incorruptibility. Endowed with the power of self-determination, the first man nonetheless chose to follow the suggestions of the Evil One[31] who was jealous of man's perfection.[32] Adam was thus expelled from the Garden of Paradise, and condemned to death (and all mankind with him); although, as Methodius holds, the penalty of death was somehow intended to prevent man's sin from becoming everlasting.[33]

Because of this initial fall all men are more prone to be deceived by pleasure,[34] and their senses are more easily disturbed by the flood of external impressions. And one of the greatest losses of the human race, in Methodius' view, was its inability, until the time of Christ, to be perfectly chaste. By God's providence, man evolved through a period when incest was allowed, through polygamy to monogamy. But only through Christ were men able to embrace virginity.[35] Christ by His death brought life to men; and it is by this life that His bride, Mother Church, brings forth her children (that is, the 'perfect' collaborate with Christ to bring forth the less perfect[36]). Through her teachings men at last come to know the Trinity,[37] and listen to that instruction which will help them to control their passions.[38] For it is thus, after baptism, that God wishes them to grow up with the features of Christ, that is, that men may become like to God.[39]

Methodius' language, when speaking of the mystery of the God-Man, is sometimes obscure, and sometimes very clear. In his clearest passage, Methodius explicitly states that Christ, who had been in the beginning with God was Himself God, God received in man.[40] And developing to an extent the Pauline doctrine, He is at pains to explain how Christ was in some sense Adam.[41] Not that there was any substantial union between the Word and the first man at the beginning of time; but rather that just as Adam was taken from the virgin earth at the creation of the world, so too Christ was born of a virgin mother when the world was re-created and re-fashioned. Again, Christ is the Archvirgin, and His virginal flesh is the bride that the Canticle and the forty-fourth Psalm speak of.[42] Yet on another level this bride is the Church, our Mother, and she is attended by the community of virgins on earth as she will be one day in heaven.[43] So too, the virgin, like Mother Church, is espoused and consecrated to the Lord, and she remains faithful by keeping her senses pure for Him.[44]

All men are commanded to embrace a life of chastity; only by way of dispensation from the law, in virtue of weakness of the flesh, are they permitted to marry (just as the infirm are dispensed from fasting).[45] But even in marriage they must be chaste; they must not abuse their marital privileges by lack of moderation.[46] For only the chaste can enter heaven.[47]

The practice of chastity requires a certain austerity in diet[48] and apparel,[49] self-discipline in thought and imagination.[50] But it elevates us high above the world, to the meadows of heaven where all the flowers and trees of virtue grow; for virtues on earth are only shadows of the reality we shall see 'there.'[51] There our food will be the fruit of the virtues, our drink, the waters of immortality; for we shall see the Godhead Itself, and immortality welling up from His bosom in an eternal stream.[52] This is a vision that the chaste might perhaps enjoy, though afar off, even in this life.[53]

Living thus chastely, we are to prepare for the final coming of Christ; but if we take advantage of the spiritual doctrines of Mother Church, control our passions, and persevere in the practice of virtue—which consists largely in a struggle against concupiscence—we shall be able to join the group who will celebrate the great Feast of Tabernacles on the day of the Resurrection. For the age of the world is as six days, six millennia; on the seventh day, the great Seventh Millennium, Christ will restore the world; and only those who are sealed with His blood[54] will come to the Promised Land escorted by angels to celebrate with Christ the Millennium of Rest. Only after this is consummated will the bodies of the just be changed from their 'human and corruptible appearance to angelic shape and beauty.'[55] Then the time of shadow and symbol will be over, and we shall pass 'into the heavenly assemblage,' of which the Church, and the garden of Arete with its banquet, were only images.[56] The real drama which we shall enact there at the doors of the Bridal Chamber can be rehearsed even in this life as a kind of celebration of the mysteries;[57] and, finally, Methodius composes a hymn by which the virgin can, in spirit, participate in the great nuptials of heaven, ever reminding herself that in order to enter the Bridal Chamber she must guard her senses like a lamp of five flames.[58]

Such, then, is the apocalyptic conception of the *Symposium*. It cannot be appreciated by toning down, as some scholars have done,[59] the less orthodox or the chiliastic aspects of Methodius' thought. Harnack, who did not perhaps read his Methodius carefully, was nonetheless accurate in his intuition of the Greek Father's position in patristic literature: it was Methodius, in Harnack's view, who inaugurated the union of the objective, dogmatic aspects of the Church's teaching with the subjective, mystical, monastic aspirations of the ἀσκηταί at the turn of the fourth century.[60] But the words 'objective, dogmatic,' hide a serious over-generalization: for Methodius' work at times reflects the cobwebbed, cluttered mind of the pedant, never profound enough to be satisfying, full of good intentions but deeply illogical and emotional. His theological outlook, despite its range, is profoundly anthropocentric; his asceticism self-centered and meticulous. For all his protestations, his own view of matter and the material world smacks of Neoplatonism: we live in a land of shadows, in the midst of a floodtide, constantly swept, like a foundering ship, by the waves of disturbing sense impressions. It is a dull, humorless world that Methodius paints. True, this drabness is relieved by the profound meaning he attaches to marriage as well as virginity, and, as Plumpe in *Mater Ecclesia* has well brought out,[61] to the concept of the Church as Bride and Virgin Mother. But apart from the strictly apostolic relationship the faithful have with one another (for the 'perfect' preach to the 'imperfect'), Methodius' world seems almost devoid of normal interpersonal relationships; and his voluntarism on the question of sin gives the impression that he had little of the sympathy for human nature that we find, for example, in Plotinus. Methodius' message is austerely eschatological and anchoretic.

Bonwetsch's judgment, that Methodius was '*kein grosser Geist*,'[62] though excessive, does contain an element of truth. Methodius' anthropology and Christology is basically Irenaean;[63] but in translating it into a kind of Platonic poetry, what he gains in charm he loses in theological clarity and depth. Methodius' Origenism,[64] again, is rather an Asiatic form of Alexandrianism: by temperament, perhaps, and education, Methodius inclined towards the more moderate school of allegorizers; and even his adaptation of the shadow-image allegorism should not be made to derive directly from Origen. In any case, all of these previously existing elements are poured into the one mould (to use one of Methodius' favorite images[65]); and his frank Millennarianism is heightened by an apocalyptic treatment of the imagery of the Canticle of Canticles.

In this connection it should perhaps be noted that, although the general use of the nuptial imagery of the Canticle for the relationship between Christ and the soul are usually traced back to Origen's *Commentary* and *Homilies on the Canticle of Canticles*, there seems no need to postulate any very close or direct dependence on the part of Methodius. For one thing, the symbolism seems to have become part of traditional Greek theology by the late third century; and one has the impression that there were many minor intermediary sources, now lost, in the stream of what Dölger has called 'the theology of Asia Minor,'[67] from which Methodius must have drawn—as he surely seems to have done in his tracts on astrology, on numerology, on botanical exegesis, and on the divisions of world history. But until further evidence on these last sources is forthcoming, there is much that must remain speculative.

6. The Text of the Symposium

There is little doubt but that Bonwetsch had an incomparable knowledge of Methodius' doctrine as well as its sources and the various testimonies; but his edition has remained unsatisfactory. He does not seem to have understood the stemmatic relationships among the various MSS and indirect witnesses; he too often neglected to collate the readings of Ottobonianus (O) on the grounds that his photograph was illegible; and, finally, his treatment of the quotations from Andreas and Arethas leaves something to be desired; for he often misquoted their readings as well as those of the Photian MSS.

These faults were first pointed out by Heseler in two articles published in 1928 and 1933,[68] although their significance has been largely overlooked. Again, in view of the controversy which, as Photius seems to suggest, revolved about the Trinitarian doctrines of the *Symposium*, neither Bonwetsch nor Heseler were sufficiently aware of the possibility of post-Methodian deletions and interpolations. Lastly, though this is indeed a minor flaw, Bonwetsch made little effort to divide the text accurately into sense paragraphs or to number the units for convenience of quotation.[69]

After the partial edition of the *Symposium* (from Photius) by François Combefis, O.P. (Paris 1644), Leo Allacci (Allatius) the Vatican librarian, published the complete text (Rome 1656), based chiefly on a MS in his own possession (undoubtedly now Codex Vallicellianus 119.2).[70] Allatius' MS was a copy of the defective M, and hence a MS twice removed from O; but he also used two other Roman MSS, which most probably were Barberinus gr. 463 and the MS V. A French Jesuit, Pierre Poussines (or Possinus) with the help of the scholar H. Valesius (Henri de Valois) attempted to rival Allatius' edition by using another Vatican MS, B, a copy of which was sent him by Lukas Holste (Holstenius);[71] and before publication (Paris 1657), Possinus' text was checked against the Paris MS M, apparently by Valesius. Some years later Combefis published the complete text in his *Auctarium novissimum* (vol. 1, Paris 1672) relying particularly on Possinus, though he also used Allatius and made a number of emendations himself. Finally the Oratorian Andrea Gallandi reprinted Combefis' text and notes, with some notes of his own, in his *Bibliotheca veterum patrum . . . graeco-latina* (14 vols., Venice 1765–81), in vol. 3 (1767) 663–832. Thus it was that Migne, in reprinting Gallandi (PG 18.27–240) reprinted Combefis' text, translation and notes, together with some additional notes of Gallandi's and an appendix taken from Allatius' edition. Finally, A. Jahn's edition (Halle 1865), as Heseler has shown, leaned very heavily on Combefis, including some erroneous readings ultimately coming from Possinus.

Now Heseler has made clear,[72] once and for all, the interrelationships of the MSS: O and P are the earliest branches of the manuscript tradition, and all the extant MSS are copies of them, as will be clear from our stemma.

All the MSS ultimately derive from a single archetype which omitted a passage (due to homoioteleuton) near the beginning of Thecla's speech in *Symp*. 8.14, preserved only in the quotations in the *Sacra Parallela* and already restored properly by Combefis. Further, it seems clear that the tradition from which the MSS OP and the *Sacra Parallela* descend is quite different from that from which Photius derived his quotations. In his *Bibliotheca*, cod. 237 (Bekker 313a), Photius tells us that the dialogue 'has been extensively tampered with: you can find Arian passages interpolated in it as well as sections inserted from other authors.' Certainly Photius has preserved many lines which do not fit into the *Symposium* as we have it today; but he quotes nothing that could be stigmatized as definitely of Arian provenance, and our problem is made all the more complicated by the suspicion that Photius may have been quoting from two different editions of the text, one the Arian and the other the 'Orthodox.' As for the relationship of the quotations from Andreas of Caesarea's *Commentary on the Apocalypse* (about A.D. 614), with its derivatives (Arethas' *Commentary*, about A.D. 895, and the excerpts attributed to Oecumenius),[73] I can only say that they seem to follow the manuscript tradition quite closely, and I should incline, though perhaps on insufficient evidence, to place them closer to the Orthodox tradition than to Photius.

The following are the chief sources for the text:

A. *Manuscripts*

O Ottobonianus graecus 59, probably 14th century (late 13th cannot be excluded; but the 15th seems too late), in the Vatican Library. It becomes illegible at the word 'Theopatra' at the beginning of *Symp.* 9 and soon breaks off. It has several good marginal notes and contains a verbose defence of Methodius' orthodoxy inserted in the text at *Symp.* 2.5 (transcribed by Allatius from the margin of Vall., PG 18.223).

P — Patmiacus graecus 202, 11th century, in the monastery of St. John Theologus on the island of Patmos.

B — Barberinus graecus 427, 16/17th cent., in the Vatican Library, formerly belonging to Holstenius. A copy of P, it contains corrections which may derive from contamination.

M — Parisinus graecus 946 (formerly Mazarinus Reg. 2906), 16th cent., in the Bibliothèque Nationale, Paris. Copied from O when O had had already become illegible in many places, it abounds in poor guesses and defective readings. Some of the marginal notes are of interest. It breaks off at the end of *Symp.* 8.

V — Vaticanus graecus 1451, 15/16th cent., in the Vatican Library. It is derived from P and seems to have been contaminated with the tradition of O.

Sin. — Sinaiticus graecus 1139, 17th cent., a late copy of P which is only interesting for its marginal variants and conjectures (transcribed by Heseler, *loc. cit.*, II.326 f.).

Barb. — Barberinus graecus 463, A.D. 1623/44, in the Vatican Library, a copy of V.

Ath. — Atheniensis Bib. Nat. 391, 17th cent., in the National Library at Athens. This is a copy of the Possinus-Valesius text.

Vall. Vallicellianus 119.2, 16/17th cent., in the library of S. Maria in Vallicello, Rome.

B. *Quotations from the 8th-century Damascene* Sacra Parallela, *as cited by Bonwetsch, chiefly from:*

C Coislinianus 276, 10th cent., Paris.

K Vaticanus graecus 1553, 12/13th cent., Rome.

C. *Quotations from Photius,* Bibliotheca, *cod. 237 (Bekker 1824):*

Ph[a] Marcianus graecus 450, 10th cent., in Venice.

Ph[b] Marcianus graecus 451, 12th cent., in Venice.

D. *Quotations from Andreas and Arethas:*

Andreas Ed. princ. of F. Sylburg, 1596 (=Migne, PG 106.215–458) based on two MSS: Augustanus and Palatinus (both of the 12th cent.). A paragraph of the text of Andreas as in Sylburg (PG 106.320BC) is given by H. C. Hoskier, *The Complete Commentary of Oecumenius on the Apocalypse* (Ann Arbor 1928) 12 f., as it appears in Patmiacus 179.

Arethas In the ed. of J. A. Cramer, *Catenae graecae patrum in N.T.* 8 (Oxford 1840) 181–496 (=PG 106.499–786), based chiefly on two MSS: Coislin. 224 and Barocc. 3 (as cited in his notes): Arethas' quotations of Methodius seem to have been derived solely from Andreas' quotations.

PsOecum The so-called Pseudo-Oecumenius on the Apocalypse represents merely an abridgment of Andreas' *Commentary,* and thus is another source for Andreas' quotations of Methodius: in J. A. Cramer, *op. cit.* 497–582. (This is to be distinguished from the genuine *Commentary on the Apocalypse* by Oecumenius, of the 6th century, edited by H. C. Hoskier, *op. cit.*, which does not quote Methodius.)

E. *Syriac Fragment*: from Brit. Mus. Add. 14532 and several other Syriac MSS. The fragment merely covers a few lines, *Symp.* 6.1: Bo 64.14–20 (cf. the apparatus of Bo); but the variant it reflects is not useful: 'without need, dwelling among inexpressible and unapproachable lights.' Attention was first called to the fragment by J. B. Pitra, *Analecta sacra* 4 (1883) 438 f., where a Latin translation is given.

The diagram on page 29 gives a tentative stemma of the sources and MSS.

As can be seen from our stemma, the problem of reconstructing Methodius' text is a very difficult one, even if we rely on the earliest extant sources and manuscripts leaving all copies out of account. Further, how far can we be sure that the 'Orthodox Edition' which must be reconstructed from manuscripts OP and the testimonies SacParall and Andreas-Arethas, represents the original work of Methodius in all substantials? In any case, this is the only edition which we can be legitimately expected to restore. I have attempted to avoid some of the mistakes made by Bonwetsch, and have based my text chiefly on O, so far as it goes; to this end I have completely re-collated O, checking it with its direct copy, M; and I have attempted to place slightly more weight upon the early quotations contained in Photius, Andreas and Arethas according to the intensive studies of Heseler.[74]

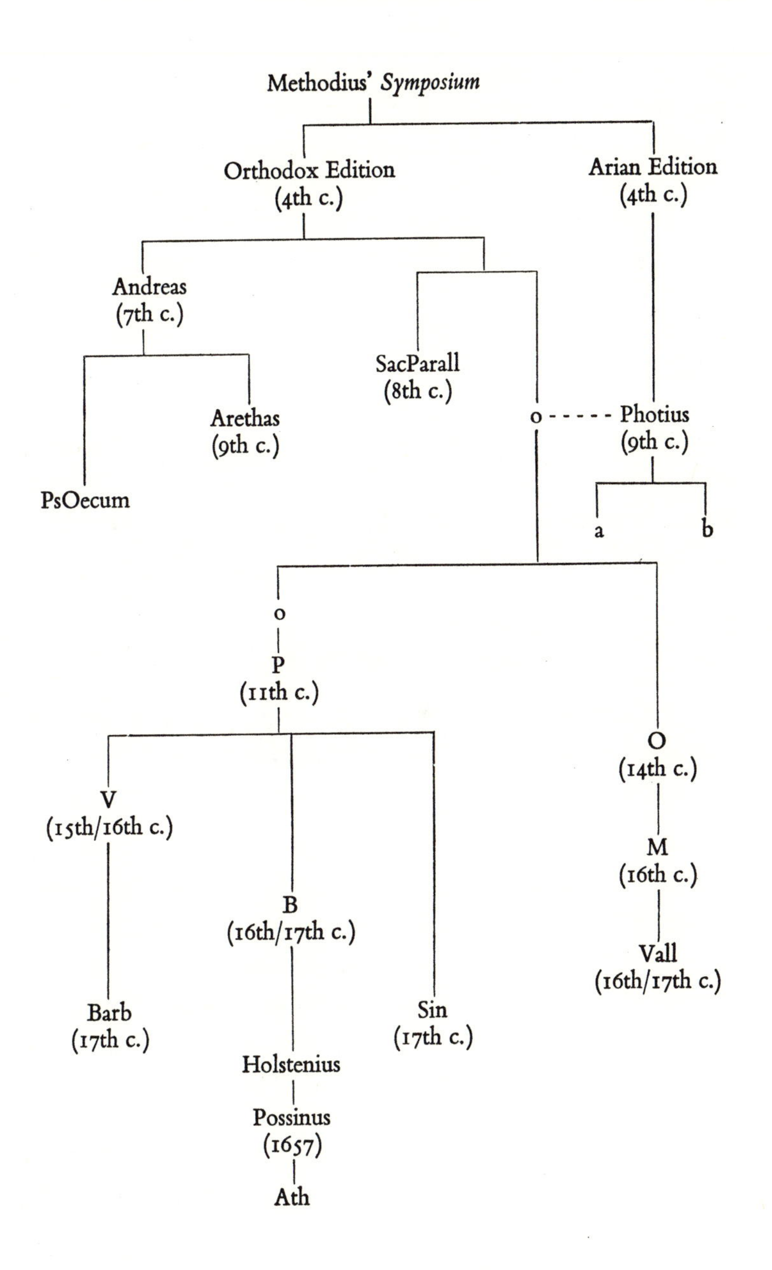
Methodius' *Symposium*
Orthodox Edition (4th c.)
Arian Edition (4th c.)
Andreas (7th c.)
SacParall (8th c.)
Arethas (9th c.)
o
Photius (9th c.)
PsOecum
a
b
o
P (11th c.)
O (14th c.)
V (15th/16th c.)
M (16th c.)
B (16th/17th c.)
Vall (16th/17th c.)
Barb (17th c.)
Sin (17th c.)
Holstenius
Possinus (1657)
Ath

Of the existing translations, the finest are undoubtedly the French by J. Farges (Paris 1932), based on Bonwetsch's text, and the German by L. Fendt (Bibliothek der Kirchenväter, Kempten 1911) based on Jahn. The first English version, by W. R. Clark (Ante-Nicene Christian Library, vol. 16, Edinburgh 1869=Ante-Nicene Fathers ed. by A. C. Coxe, vol. 16, Buffalo 1886), has a rugged primitive beauty, but was made from the Migne text and was heavily influenced by the Latin of Combefis. There are two Italian versions, one by P. Ubaldi (Turin 1925), and another by A. Zeoli, *S. Metodio. Il banchetto delle dieci virgini* (Testi cristiani N. S. 2, Florence 1952); a Spanish version by B. Vizmanos in *Las vírgenes cristianas* (Madrid 1949) 989–1088; and a Russian version by Evgraph Lovjagin (St. Petersburg 1877).

7. The Problem of the Orthodox Edition

There are in our present text seven places where our manuscript tradition is not entirely satisfactory. They are as follows:

(i) Prelude, *Symp.*: Bo 4.16. Eubulion merely asks for information—'where you held the meeting, what you had to eat,' and then quotes a Homeric verse. Gregorion does not reply to this, but praises her hostess: 'You are always so clever in discussions....' Unless the dialogue is here very carelessly written, it would seem that something has dropped out of the text.

(ii) *Symp.* 2.1: Bo 15.8. Theophila praises the first discourse but adds that she cannot say the same for Marcella's suggestion that 'from henceforth men are not to procreate children' (τὸ δὲ μηκέτι χρῆναι . . . τεκνογονεῖν). This strong unqualified language, especially in maidens who are so careful not to speak imprudently, suggests that Marcella, the first speaker, must have made a remark somewhere to this effect. But of this we have no trace. Here it seems very likely that a later redactor, misunderstanding Methodius' style of debate, deleted some such remark, thinking that it smacked too much of Encratism.

(iii) *Symp.* 3.4: Bo 30.22–31.2. 'This was Christ . . .': here the theologically precise assertion of the divinity of Christ stands in strange contrast with the preceding and the following contexts; and the grammar, especially the use of the infinitive (εἶναι) for the indicative, is suspect. In any case, the direct statement is out of place, for the context demands a sequence of phrases such as 'It was fitting that,' etc.

(iv) *Symp.* 8.6: Bo 88.13 f. 'For just as a woman receives the unformed seed of her husband and after a period of time brings forth a perfect human being, so too the Church, one might say, constantly conceiving *those who take refuge in the Word* and forming them. . . .' The words italicized are present in OP, but wanting in Andreas.[75] This surely cannot be right; and although elsewhere Methodius speaks of doctrine as 'sowed' by the Word (*Symp.* 7.4: Bo 75.14 f.), here suddenly the text avoids the stronger expression; in fact the entire comparison seems to be missing from the *Commentary* of Andreas.

(v) *Symp.* 8.9: Bo 91.4–14. This entire passage, as we shall have occasion to note, interrupts the trend of the exegesis; it is stronger language than Methodius ever uses elsewhere—in fact, J. Lebreton quotes[76] precisely this passage to defend Methodius from all suspicion of Subordinationism; again, the technical words it employs are not found elsewhere in Methodius' extant works, and are of the sort that would be more suitable in a debate against the Arians. It should of course be noted that Photius was particularly careful to excerpt precisely this passage, though his text contains some minor variants, twice agreeing with O against P. Here, obviously, we cannot exclude the possibility that Methodius himself, at some time after he had completed the *Symposium*, added this passage himself, in order to make clear once and for all the doctrine he held on the generation of the Word.

(vi) *Symp.* 8.10: Bo 93.2–8. Although this heresy-catalogue is in the MSS, it is omitted by Andreas who quotes the passage from 'one of the numbers of the Trinity' down into the following section. The passage interrupts the development of the allegory, and it is difficult to see how the heretics mentioned, with the exception perhaps of Sabellius, were, even in Methodius' day, of more than academic interest. On the other hand, it would be an entirely expected insert or gloss in an Orthodox edition prepared for a polemic purpose.

(vii) *Symp.* 8.13: Bo 98.16–99.1. This entire passage, beginning with the word ἡμέτερον up to βιώσει is a *locus desperatus*, and it is odd that Bonwetsch should not have given it more attention. With the sentence which begins, 'But, if with the help of Christ, you tear them [the dragon's horns] out by the roots,' Methodius apparently concludes his explanation of Apocalypse 12. Then without transition we read: 'Now [*or* 'For'] it is possible for us to determine

> beforehand ...' This is followed by an apparently dangling purpose clause stressing the imitation of Christ. The next sentence, beginning with an attack on the doctrine of the astrologers, indicates the topic sentence or the proposition of the entire section following, and it ties up not with the immediately preceding purpose clause, but rather with the transitional sentence, 'Now it is possible for us to determine beforehand, etc.'
>
> If the confusion at this point was not the result of incomplete revision by the author himself, it would surely look as though the sentence on the imitation of Christ is a later interpolation. In any case, the transition from the discussion on the Apocalypse to the proposition on astrology seems too abrupt even for Methodius, and something must have fallen out of the text. It is interesting to note that the excerpt in the *Sacra Parallela* begins merely with the sentence containing the proposition, 'For of all the evils that have been implanted.'

To sum up, of the seven cases we have mentioned, two (i and vi) may merely be due to poor textual transmission; one (iv) to a tendency to soften Methodius' language; one (ii) may be attributed to a redactor suspicious of Encratism; and three (iii, v, vii), if pressed, might possibly be evidence of an attempt, on the part of a later editor, to shield the author from all taint of Subordinationism. But the evidence is obviously not clear; and though it would be tempting to postulate a special edition of Methodius made to counteract the Arian edition mentioned by Photius, such a theory must in the present state of our knowledge remain in the realm of pure hypothesis.

8. Methodius and the Scriptures

The text used by Methodius in the New Testament (presuming it has not been 'harmonized' by scribes) is essentially eclectic: in the Pauline epistles and the Apocalypse, for example, at times he comes close to P^{46} (the Chester Beatty papyrus);[77] in other cases he reflects the extremely poor text of what is now called the 'Lucianic recension.' Very often he manifests variants not attested elsewhere; and in such cases there is always the suspicion that he is quoting from memory or paraphrasing.

In the Old Testament the picture is much clearer. His text is basically Alexandrian, with a certain percentage of unattested readings as well as some eclecticism.

In his allegorical exegesis, Methodius points out that we should be prepared to look for a meaning that is loftier (ὑψηλότερον) than the literal meaning (τῆς ἱστορίας), without denying that the literal meaning is also important.[78] In fact, in his exegesis of St. Paul Methodius adheres very closely to what he believes is the Apostle's meaning, even going so far as to study the elements of his style.[79] However, in his treatment of the Old Testament Methodius for the most part ignores the literal sense—although we may except certain obvious apothegms from Wisdom and Proverbs. In his Old Testament allegorizing we may notice two levels: (i) where he is concerned to establish the relationship of 'shadow-image-reality' in certain elements from the Old Law, the New Law, and Heaven. These are invariably on a more universal and wider plane of application. Then in level (ii) we have certain *ad hoc* allegorical exegeses which, at least in many cases, seem to be invented *currente calamo* and applied to the topic on hand—here, mainly virginity. Methodius is also at pains to explain the technique of exegesis based on, for instance, the meaning of trees and plants, as well as numerology. In fact there is a running numerological scheme throughout the entire *Symposium*:

(Days 1–7=7 millennia; Day 8=eternity)

Days 1–5	Period of the Temple: Dogmas and virtues exist only in shadow—in the ritual prescriptions and the development of man from incest to monogamy	shadow
Day 6	Period of the Church in the World (6, the symbol of the perfect Christ): Dogmas and virtues as taught by the Church; symbolized by the banquet of Arete	image
Day 7	Period of the Millennium of Rest: Celebration of the Feast of Tabernacles with Christ after the resurrection	reality
Day 8	Heaven: Vision of immortality, the heavenly meadows with the trees of truth	

Although Methodius gives no clear criteria as to how we should apply the various senses, one point of practice seems to emerge: the ritual laws of the Jews do not refer to material structures (tabernacles, etc.), real animals or rites, but rather to the wealth of good things to come. Thus the Jews are accused of hovering about the bare letter of the Scriptures like butterflies[80] precisely because they have failed to recognize the hidden sense of the Law, that is, the relationship of shadow to image and, ultimately, to transcendental truth.

9. Summary

There is truth in L. Fendt's remark[81] that we must not look for anti-Origenism in the *Symposium*; rather,

Methodius' exegesis attempts to combine an outright, though moderate, Alexandrianism with the Platonic distinction between the Here and There, between Shadow and Reality. Virginity becomes a means of achieving the Platonic ascent of the soul, whereby the chaste rise to behold the heavenly realities, of which the doctrines of the Church here below are but the images. The march of history that culminated in the Second Adam, the Archvirgin who brought chastity to earth, must finally close with His second Coming and the reign of the Thousand Years. On the mystical eighth day, those who are sealed with His blood, and particularly the chaste, will go in a solemn procession to the Gates of Life. All others are to be punished by fire and the divine penalties.

Such, then, is Methodius' brilliant, poetic doctrine in all its eschatological vividness, at least so far we are able to reconstruct it through the haze of a controversial textual transmission. He has much that is good, much that is uninspired and derivative. But the *Symposium* cannot be understood except in a tightly interwoven historical context; and yet by the peculiar selectivity of history, its noblest thoughts were to become the permanent heritage of Christian asceticism and mysticism. He anticipated much that we find in John of the Cross and in later Byzantine and Russian eschatological spirituality. Methodius' doctrine on chastity must be seen as part of his stark apocalyptic message; but his profoundest vision is of the transitoriness of man and the transcendence of God, of the incompleteness of all human knowledge, and of man's power to transcend the limitations of the flesh if he would but rise to the attraction of Christ the Bridegroom. That it should be developed within the framework of millennarianism ought not to blind us to the importance of his message and the character of his testimony to the theology of the early Church. Later centuries, it is true, were to retain of the *Symposium* only those elements which were more easily conformable to the orthodox stream of Christian monastic asceticism. For an appreciation of this selective process, constantly at work in the history of Christian literature, Methodius' work is a most instructive document. But it is more: it is perhaps the most beautiful symbolic prose-poem of the early patristic period.[82]

THE SYMPOSIUM: OR A TREATISE ON VIRGINITY

Prelude

The scene is apparently laid in the home of the lady Eubulion.[1]

Eubulion. You are just in time, Gregorion. I had just been looking for you. I wanted to find out about the meeting Marcella and Theopatra had with the other girls who attended the dinner party, and what they had to say on the subject of chastity. From what I hear, they argued so vigorously and so brilliantly that there was nothing left to be said on the topic. So if you had anything else on your mind in coming here, do put it off and hurry and give me[2] a complete and orderly account of everything that has to do with our request.

Gregorion. So I am to be disappointed, it seems! Someone else has been here before me to tell you what you wanted to know. And I had thought that you would have heard nothing at all about it; and I was greatly flattering and complimenting myself that I should be the first to tell you! That was why I hurried so to get here to see you: I was afraid that another might beat me to it.

Eub. You need not worry. As a matter of fact, my dear, we did not go into any of the details. Our informant could only tell us that certain discussions took place. When we asked him to give us an account of them, he admitted he did not know.

Greg. Then, would you like to hear the whole story of the discussion right from the beginning? That is why I came here. Or would you rather not have me tell you everything, but only what I think were the more important points?

Eub. No, no, Gregorion. Tell us everything from the beginning—where you held the meeting, what you had to eat, how you yourself[3] served the wine:

> They in golden goblets
> Each other pledged, gazing upon the broad heavens.[4]

* * *[5]

Greg. Eubulion, you are always so clever in discussion, and argumentation is your speciality. You simply get the better of everyone!

Eub. Please, Gregorion, do not work yourself into an argument on that subject now. Do fall in with our request and tell us exactly what happened from the beginning.

Greg. I shall try my best. But first of all, let me ask you a question. Of course you know Arete, the daughter of Philosophia?

Eub. Yes—and?

Greg. It was to her garden, with its view to the east, that we were invited—so Theopatra told me, and I have the information from her—to enjoy the fruits of the season, myself, Procilla, and Tusiane. What a rough and difficult path it was, Eubulion, and uphill too! Well—so Theopatra said—when we got near the spot, we were met by a tall, lovely woman[6] walking quietly and gracefully. The garment she wore was as white as glistening snow. Her beauty was really preternatural and quite indescribable. Her face bloomed with deep modesty joined with dignity. I do not recall ever having seen a face that was such a pleasant blend of severity and gentleness. It was, moreover, completely without cosmetics and there was nothing artificial about it. At any rate, she came up to us and looked at us with great joy as though she were a mother seeing her children after a long separation. And she embraced and kissed each one of us, saying: My dear daughters, I have been most eager to lead you to the Meadow of Immortality. Now you have come to me with great difficulty along a path beset with all kinds of terrifying monsters. I watched you as you turned aside again and again, and I was frightened lest you would turn back and slip over the cliffs. But thanks be to the Bridegroom, to whom I have espoused you[7]—He has fully answered all my prayers.

While she was saying this, said Theopatra, we came to her estate. The doors were still open;[8] and, walking in, we found Thecla, Agathe, and Marcella already there, about to eat dinner. Then Arete said: Come now and sit down here next to these sisters of yours who are so very like yourselves. Now we were, I think said Theopatra, ten in all at table. The spot was extraordinarily beautiful and full of a profound peace.[9] The atmosphere that enveloped us was diffused with shafts of pure light in a gentle and regular pattern;[10] and in the very center was a spring from which there bubbled up, as gently as though it were oil, the most delicious water; and the crystal-clear water formed into little rivulets.[11] These, overflowing their banks, as rivers do, watered the ground all about with their abundant streams. And there were various kinds of trees there, laden with mellow, ripe fruit hanging gaily from their branches—a picture of beauty. The ever-blossoming meadows, too, were dotted with all kinds of sweet-scented flowers, and from them there was wafted a gentle breeze laden with perfume. Now a stately chaste-tree grew nearby; here under its far-spreading canopy we rested in the shade.[12]

Eub. Dear lady, you seem to be describing the vision of one abiding in the bliss of a new Eden.

Greg. Yes, that is true. Well, Theopatra went on, after we had enjoyed a richly laden banquet, with every kind of good cheer added so that no delight was lacking, Arete came in again and spoke to us as follows: My dear girls, you who are all my pride, fair virgins who tend the immaculate meads of Christ with unwedded hands, enough now of food and feasting. And indeed, we have had everything we wish in plenty and abundance. Now what shall we do next? What do you suppose I wish and look forward to? That each of you deliver a panegyric on virginity. Let Marcella begin. She is the eldest and reclines in the place of honor. Now I give you my word: whoever wins the contest, I should be ashamed of myself if I did not make her one to be envied; I shall crown her with an exquisite garland of wisdom.

LOGOS I: MARCELLA

1. Marcella then, if I mistake not, directly began her discourse as follows:

Virginity is something extraordinarily great, wonderful and glorious. To speak frankly in the manner of the Scriptures, this most beautiful, noble way of life alone is the Church's sustaining bosom,[1] her flower, her first fruits. This is the reason, too, why Our Lord, in that passage in the Gospels[2] in which He instructs us in the various ways in which men have become eunuchs, promises that all who make themselves virgins will enter the Kingdom of Heaven.

Chastity is rare indeed among humankind, and a goal difficult of attainment; it involves greater risks precisely because of its excellence and magnificence. Hence it demands strong and generous natures, that can completely divert[3] the stream of sensuality and guide aloft the chariot of their soul, straight and up and up, never losing sight of their goal—until, leaping easily over the world with the lightning speed of thought, they stand upon the very vault of heaven and gaze directly upon Immortality itself as it wells up from the pure bosom of the Almighty.[4] Such a draught cannot be produced on earth; it can issue only from the fountains of heaven.

Hence we should imagine Virginity as walking on earth but with her head touching the heavens. And some indeed have been eager to win her, but saw in her nothing but a goal to be attained. Imperfect and ignoble souls that they are, they approach her with unwashed feet[5] and have had to turn off the path; they were incapable of a single thought worthy of this way of life. For here it is not enough merely to keep our bodies undefiled, just as we should not display our temples[6] as more important than the statues in them; but we must also care for our souls, the images within our bodies, and adorn them with righteousness. And our souls receive this care and are adorned the more we strive constantly to hear the word of God and do not give up until we come to the gates of the wise and reach Truth itself.

Just as the bloody fluids of meat and all the elements which make for putrefaction are drawn off by salting it, so too all the irrational desires of the body are banished from a maiden by the pious instruction she receives. It is inevitable that the soul that has not been salted with Christ's words should begin to smell and breed worms. And thus surely it was that King David, tearfully confessing his sins on the mountains, cried out, *My sores are putrefied and corrupted*,[7] because he had not salted and cured himself by self-discipline, but giving himself instead to dalliance, he was seduced into passion and began to stink of adultery. Thus too it is forbidden in Leviticus[8] to offer any gift as a holocaust to the Lord God unless it be first seasoned with salt. In fact all our spiritual exercises in the Scriptures are given to us as a salt which purifies and stings for our improvement, and without it no soul can reasonably be led to God. *You are the salt of the earth*,[9] said the Lord to His apostles.

The virgin should therefore always love what is right and good, and distinguish herself among those who are superior in wisdom. She must not be given to laziness and softness; but her life should be one of extreme excellence. She should ever keep her mind occupied with thoughts that befit her state of virginity and with her thinking wipe away the foul humors of sensuality, lest some small spot of corruption, overlooked, breed the worm of incontinence.

Thus, as blessed Paul says, *the unmarried woman thinketh on the things of the Lord, how she may please God, that she may be holy both in body and in spirit.*[10] But there are many women who consider religious instruction a waste of time, and think they are doing something wonderful if they listen to it even for a short time. These we ought to exclude.[11] For it is not right to share the divine teachings with a creature that is petty, mean, and pretends to be wise. For would it not be ridiculous to go on talking to such who waste all their efforts on insignificant trifles, trying to fulfill their own desires down to the last detail, without ever a thought for the heroic efforts which are absolutely essential if the love of continence is to grow in them?

2. It was indeed a most extraordinary disposition that

the plant of virginity was sent down to mankind from heaven. Hence too, it was not revealed to the first generations: for in those days there were but few men, and it was necessary that their numbers be first increased and brought to perfection. Hence men of old did not bring disgrace upon themselves if they married their own sisters —until the Law came and separated them, forbidding and denouncing as sinful what had previously been thought to be virtuous, and calling him cursed who should uncover the nakedness of his sister.[12] In such wise did God in His goodness bring assistance to the human race in due season as do fathers to their children. For they do not at once put their children in charge of pedagogues, but they allow them during their early years to frisk about like little calves. First they send them to teachers who take them through their stammering period. Then, after they have shed the juvenile locks of the mind, they are introduced to the study of more serious subjects, and from there to still more important ones. In this way we should imagine that God the Father of all acted towards our forefathers. For the world while still unpopulated was in its infancy, as it were, and had first to be taken from this condition and grow to manhood.

But when later it had become populated from end to end overflowing with countless numbers, God did not suffer mankind to continue in its old ways any longer. He took thought how men might make progress and advance farther on the road to heaven, until at last they might become perfect by attaining to the most sublime goal of all, the science of virginity. To begin with, they were to advance from brother-sister unions to marriage with wives from other families. They they were to give up practicing, like brute beasts, multiple marriage (as though men were born merely for intercourse!). The next step was to take them from adultery; and the next, to advance them to continence, and from continence to virginity, in which state they train themselves to despise the flesh and come to anchor unafraid in the peaceful haven of immortality.

3. Now someone may have the hardihood to attack this account on the grounds that it has no Scriptural foundation. Very well, let us also bring forward the writings of the prophets and so demonstrate the truth of what has already been said. Surely Abraham, in being the first to receive the covenant of circumcision and in circumcising a member of his body, symbolizes nothing less that this: that one was no longer to procreate children with an offspring of the same parent. He teaches us that a man must cut off the pleasure of intercourse with his own sister, as with his own flesh. Hence from the time of Abraham men ceased the practice of living in marriage with their sisters.[13] Next, marriage with more than one wife is disallowed by the time of the prophets. *Go not after thy lusts,* we read, *but turn away from thy own will;*[14] for—*wine and women make wise men fall off.*[15] And in another passage: *Let thy fountain of water be thy own and rejoice with the wife of thy youth,*[16] obviously forbidding multiple marriage. Jeremias, too, frankly calls men who lust after different women *amorous stallions.*[17] Indeed we read: *The multiplied brood of the wicked shall not thrive, and bastard slips shall not take deep root.*[18]

But, not to spend too long a time citing the testimony of the prophets, let us further show how monogamy was succeeded by continence, and how continence little by little destroyed the sensuality of the flesh until it completely removed the habitual inclination to intercourse.

For presently we are introduced to one who clearly deprecates henceforth this same distracting emotion. He says: O *Lord, Father, and sovereign ruler of my life, leave me not to their counsel. . . . Take from me haughtiness of eyes. . . . Let not the greediness of the heart and lust of the flesh take hold of me.*[19] And in the book of Wisdom, that model of all virtue, the Holy Spirit clearly tries to draw those who hear Him to moderation and continence, singing as follows: *Better it is to have no children and to have virtue, for the memory thereof is immortal, because it is known both with God and with men. When it is present, they honor it, and they desire it when it hath withdrawn itself. And it triumpheth crowned forever, winning the reward of undefiled conflicts.*[20]

4. So much then for the ages of the human race, and how men advanced from brother-sister marriages to the practice of continence. Now we must consider virginity, and I shall make every effort to speak of it as well as I can. The first question to be answered is this: how is it that of the many prophets and righteous men[21] who spoke and taught so many noble things, not one of them praised or embraced the state of virginity? The answer is that it was reserved for the Lord alone to be the first to exalt this doctrine, just as He alone, coming into the world, taught men how to draw near to God. It was only fitting that He who was Archpriest, Archprophet, and Archangel, should also be called Archvirgin.[22]

Again, in antiquity man was not yet perfect and hence did not have the capacity to comprehend the perfect, that is, virginity. For being made in the image of God, man had yet to receive that which was according to His likeness.[23] And this was precisely what the Word was sent into the world to accomplish. He took upon himself our form, spotted and stained[24] as it was by our many sins, in order that we might be able to receive in turn the divine form which He bore for our sake. For then is it possible for us truly to fashion ourselves in the likeness of God when like skilled painters we express His features in ourselves [as on a panel],[25] and thus possess them in innocence, learning to follow the path He showed to us. This was why, although He was God, He chose to put on human flesh, that, by looking upon God's representation of our life as in a painting, we might be able to imitate Him who painted it. Thus there is no discrepancy between His thoughts and His actions, nor between what He thought to be right and what He actually taught us. He both taught and did those things which were truly both right and useful.[26]

5. What then did the Lord, the Truth and the Light, accomplish on coming down to the world? He preserved His flesh incorrupt in virginity with which He had adorned it. And so let us too, if we are to come to the likeness of God, endeavor to aspire to the virginity of Christ. For becoming like to God means to banish corruptibility.[27] Now we are told that the Word Incarnate became the Archvirgin as well as Archshepherd and Archprophet of His Church, by John in the book of the Apocalypse where, filled with Christ, he says: *And I beheld, and lo the Lamb stood upon Mount Sion, and with Him an hundred forty-four thousand, having His name, and the name of His Father, written on their foreheads. And I heard a voice from heaven, as the noise of many waters and as the voice of great thunder; and the voice which I heard was as the voice of harpers harping on their harps. And they were singing as it were a new canticle, before the throne, and before the four living creatures, and the ancients; and no man could say the canticle, but those hundred forty-four thousand, who were purchased from the earth. These*

are they who were not defiled with women; for they are virgins. These follow the Lamb whithersoever He goeth—thus showing that the Lord is the leader of the choir of virgins. And notice, again, how excellent is the dignity of virginity in God's sight. *These were purchased from among men, the first fruits to God and to the Lamb: and in their mouth was found no lie; they are without spot; these follow*, he says, *the Lamb whithersoever He goeth.*[28]

Here it is also clear that He wishes to teach us that the virgins were restricted to this number, that is, 144,000, from above,[29] whereas the multitude of the rest of the saints is beyond counting. Note what he teaches us as he considers the others: *I also saw a great multitude which no man could number, of every tongue and tribe and of every nation.*[30] Obviously, then, as I have said, he introduces an untold number in the case of the other saints, but only a very small number in the case of the virgins, as though he deliberately intended a contrast with the larger, uncounted number.[31]

There, my dear Arete, is my discourse on virginity, said Marcella. If I have left anything out, Theophila, who comes after me, can supply the omission.

Logos 2. THEOPHILA

1. Then, she said, Theophila spoke as follows:

Since Marcella has so well embarked on this discussion without adequately finishing it, I think I must try to complete the argument.[1] Now I think she has well explained the fact that man has made a slow and gradual progress towards chastity under the impulse that God has given him from time to time. But her suggestion that from henceforth men are not to procreate children is not well stated.[2] For I think I perceive clearly from the Scriptures that with the coming of virginity the Word[3] did not completely abolish procreation. The light of the stars is not extinguished simply because the moon is larger than the stars.

To give Scripture then its proper place,[4] let us begin with Genesis. God's declaration and ordinance with regard to the begetting of children is still being carried out accordingly up to the present day: the Creator is still fashioning men. For it is clear to everyone that God, like an artist, is still working on His universe, as indeed the Lord also taught when He said, *My Father worketh until now.*[5] But when the rivers rest from their emptying into the receptacle of the sea, and the light is perfectly separated from the darkness (at present the separation is still going on); and when the dry land ceases forever to bring forth fruit along with reptiles and beasts, and the predetermined number of men is completed, then must there also be no further procreation of children. But now man must cooperate in the production of God's image, so long as the universe still exists and continues to be formed. *Increase and multiply*[6] was the command, and we may not spurn the command of our Creator from whom we too, of course, have ourselves come into being.

Man's coming into existence begins with the sowing of the seed in the furrows of the maternal field: and thus bone from bone and flesh from flesh, taken in an invisible act of power and always by the same divine Craftsman, are fashioned into a new human being. In this way, we must believe, is fulfilled the saying, *This now is bone of my bones, and flesh of my flesh.*[7]

2. Moreover, this was perhaps the symbolism of that ecstatic sleep into which God put the first man, that it was

to be a type of man's enchantment in love, when in his thirst for children he falls into a trance, lulled to sleep by the pleasures of procreation, in order that a new person, as I have said, might be formed in turn from the material that is drawn from his flesh and bone. For under the stimulation of intercourse, the body's harmony—so we are told by those who have consummated the rites of marriage—is greatly disturbed, and all the marrow-like generative part of the blood, which is liquid bone, gathers from all parts of the body, curdled and worked into a foam, and then rushes through the generative organs into the living soil of the woman. Hence rightly is it said that *therefore a man leave his father and his mother:*[8] for man made one with woman in the embrace of love is overcome by a desire for children and completely forgets everything else; he offers his rib to his divine Creator, to be removed that he himself the father may appear once again in a son.

If then God is still fashioning human beings, would it not be insolent of us to loathe procreation, which the Almighty Himself is not ashamed to accomplish with His undefiled hands? For He says to Jeremias, *Before I formed thee in the womb of thy mother, I knew thee;*[9] and to Job, *Didst thou take clay and form a living creature, and make it speak upon the earth?*[10] And Job comes to Him in prayer, saying the celebrated words, *Thy hands have made me and fashioned me.*[11] And would it not be absurd to forbid marital unions, if we expect that there will still be witnesses[12] after us, and those who will array themselves against the Evil One; indeed it was for the sake of these that the Word promised that the days would be shortened.[13]

Now if it is true, as you said, that the procreation of

children is henceforth considered by God as something evil, on what plea could men be pleasing to God if they are born contrary to His divine plan and decree? Indeed, if children are produced like counterfeit coins, apart from the intention and decree of His authority, would they not of necessity be spurious and hated by God? Hence we must allow that men may procreate men.

3. Here Marcella interrupted: Theophila, you are clearly very much in error, and you even contradict yourself in what you have said; and do you imagine that we do not notice it because you have drawn such a cloud over it? Here is the objection, my very wise one, which might occur to anyone to put to you: what of the children illegally begotten in adultery? You claimed that it is utterly impossible for anyone to come into the world unless he be brought in by the will of the Almighty, with his bodily habitation prepared by God. And you must not try to take refuge, as it were, behind a wall by quoting as your proof the text, *The children of adulterers shall not come to perfection*;[14] you will be politely refuted and told that often we do see offspring who have thus been conceived in unlawful unions, appearing fully developed after normal childbirth.

And if you would quibble further and say: But look, by 'not coming to perfection' I mean not being perfected according to the righteousness taught by Christ, the reply will be made: Well, my dear, very many men who have been born out of wedlock are, notwithstanding, not only thought worthy of being counted among the flock of our brethren; they often are even chosen for positions of authority over them. Therefore, since it is clear and all testify to the fact that those who are conceived adulterously are permitted to develop to maturity, we must not imagine that the teaching of the Holy Spirit had anything to do with conception and birth; rather, He probably had in mind those who adulterate the truth, who corrupt the Scriptures with pseudo-scientific doctrine and beget an imperfect sort of wisdom, mixing in error with religion.

So now that this line of escape has been taken away from you, come, tell us whether the illegitimate are begotten with God's approval. You are claiming, remember, that it was impossible for man's offspring to come to maturity unless the Lord form it and give it life.

4. Now Theophila, although grasped around the waist by a sturdy opponent in the arena, began to grow dizzy, and recovering herself with great difficulty, she said: You are posing a question, my dear, which will have to be explained by an example, that you may understand still more clearly how the creative power of God that governs all things, is especially operative in the conception of human beings, giving growth to the seed that is planted in the productive soil. For we ought not to blame the seed that is sown, but rather the one who sows on another's field by a stolen act of marriage, shamelessly bartering his seed like a hireling in return for a brief pleasure.

Now imagine the process of our birth into this world to be something like a house with its entrance lying near to steep mountains; and further, that this house extends very far from the entrance; and that it has a great number of windows at the rear, and that in this part it is circular.[15]

Yes, said Marcella.

Well then, suppose there is a modeller sitting inside making many statues, and imagine that the material of clay is constantly being handed in to him through these windows from the outside by a number of men, none of whom see the artisan. Imagine, too, that the house is concealed by mist and clouds and that those outside can see nothing but the windows.

Let us suppose that too, said she.

And each of the men working together to supply the clay has assigned to him one special opening to which alone he must bring and deposit his clay; he must not touch the other openings. Should he, moreover, try to interfere and open one that is assigned to someone else, he is to be warned with threats of scourging and fire.[16] Now consider the sequel. The artisan within the house, going round to each of the windows in turn, takes the clay he finds there and separately moulds it in each case; and after a period of some months of modelling, he gives back the finished product through the respective windows to those on the outside. And his assignment is constantly the same, namely that he work indifferently on all clay that is capable of being moulded, even if someone should maliciously put some through another's window. The clay obviously has done no wrong, and being blameless it must be moulded and fashioned. But the one who, contrary to the command and ordinance, deposited the clay at the window belonging to another, is to be punished as a wretched transgressor. The clay is not to be blamed, but only the one who acted thus against the law; for by stealth and force he has taken and deposited his clay at another's window because of his want of self-control.

You are quite right.

5. So now that I have completed my picture, my wise lady, it remains for you to apply this entire image to what I have said before. The house stands for the invisible process of our generation; and the entrance lying near the mountains, for the descent of the soul from heaven and its

transfer into the body. The windows refer to the female sex; and the artisan stands for God's creative power which, under the veil of procreation, invisibly fashions human beings within us,[17] making garments for their souls, as I have said, by utilizing our natural processes. Those who bring the material of clay are the male sex who, desirous of offspring, are brought to deposit their seed in the woman's channels as provided by nature, just as the men above did with the clay in the windows. Thus the seed shares, so to say, the divine creative function, and is not to be thought guilty of the impulses of incontinence. Now an art always operates on the material submitted to it. And there is nothing that is to be considered evil of itself, but rather becomes such by the act of the men who use it.[18] For when a thing is dealt with in a good and prudent way, the result is good; and bad when it is treated improperly and disgracefully. Take iron, for example, which was discovered for the benefit of agriculture and the arts: did it do harm to those who have sharpened it for the purpose of murderous war?[19] And what harm did gold, silver, bronze, or, in short, the whole of the fallow earth do to those who, ungrateful to their own Creator, sinfully had recourse to glittering images that were made from these materials?

Similarly, if someone should present stolen wool to the craft of weaving, it will operate nonetheless on the material submitted to it, for this craft is interested merely in one thing, whether or not the material can take the artistic treatment involved, and does not reject whatever suits its purpose: the stolen material, being inanimate, is simply not responsible. Wherefore certainly it should receive artistic effort, while the man who absconded with it against the law should be punished. So too we certainly should inflict corporal punishment on those who ruin marriages and rend the bonds of life's harmony, men inflamed with insane lust and rousing passions for the purpose of adultery. They perpetrate the outrage of stealing from others' gardens the embraces of generation; but the seed itself, like the wool we spoke of, must be fashioned and given life.

6. But what need is there for me to prolong my discourse with such examples? Nature, it is clear, could not have accomplished so great a work in so short a time without divine assistance. Who, for instance, made bones solid, yet left their nature supple? Who was it that bound together the limbs with sinews so that they stretch and relax again as they turn at the joints? What god[20] but that Master Craftsman caused the humors to ferment by mixing them with the blood, and formed the soft flesh out of earth, devising and making man—ourselves—into the most rational and living images of Himself, and moulding us like wax within the womb from moist and infinitesimal seed? By whose providence is it that the fetus is not strangled by the pressure of the fluids that course over it in its narrow confines within? And after the child has been born and has come to light, who is it that transforms it from a weak and puny thing into a person of stature and strength and beauty? Is it not, as I said, this same Master Craftsman, God Himself, Who by His creative power transforms His archetypes and remodels[21] them according to the image of Christ?

It is for this reason that we have been taught by the divinely inspired Scriptures that all babies, even those from unlawful unions, are entrusted at birth to the keeping of guardian angels.[22] Whereas if they came into existence contrary to the will and ordinance of that blessed nature of

God, how could they be committed to angels to be brought up with great gentleness and indulgence? And if they are to accuse their own parents, how could they summon them before the judgment seat of Christ with bold confidence and say: 'Lord, You did not begrudge us this common light; but it was these who exposed us to die, they despised Thy commandment.[23] *For*, as it says, *the children that are born of unlawful beds are witnesses of wickedness against their parents in their trial*.'[24]

7. Now among such as lack intelligence and judgment it might be possible for me to defend the view that this fleshly garment of the soul, planted as it is by man, is formed by itself apart from God's disposition. But in any case one would not be believed if he were to teach that the soul's being, too, is sown together with the mortal body. For only the Almighty can infuse what is ageless and immortal, seeing that He alone is the Creator of the invisible and indestructible. Scripture says, He *breathed into his face the breath of life; and man became a living soul*.[25] So too the Word blames the artisans who, not recognizing their own Maker, fashion idols in human form for men's harm, saying in the most excellent Book of Wisdom: *For their heart is ashes and their hope more vain than earth and their life more base than clay: forasmuch as they knew not their Maker, and Him that inspired into them the soul that worketh, and that breathed into them a living spirit*,[26] that is, God the Maker of all men. Hence too, according to the Apostle, He *will have all men to be saved and to come to the knowledge of the truth*.[27]

And though our subject is hardly exhausted, a further point remains to be discussed: that is to say, when a person makes a thorough examination and study of all the things that happen to man in the course of nature, he will learn not to despise procreation, but he will also learn to praise and to prefer chastity. Honey is sweeter and more pleasant than all other things: yet, for all that, it would not be right to consider bitter whatever is blended in with the natural sweetness of fruit.

In support of what I have said I shall offer a trustworthy witness in Paul who says: *Therefore both he that giveth his virgin in marriage doth well; and he that giveth her not doth better.*[28] Surely his declaration, in which he proposed what is sweeter and better, was not intended to forbid or to take away the other: it merely arranges a hierarchy, assigning to each state its peculiar property and advantage. To some it has never been given to attain virginity, while for others it is His wish that they no longer defile themselves by lustful provocations, but that henceforth they strive to preoccupy their minds with that angelic transformation[29] of the body wherein *they neither marry nor are married*[30] according to the prophecies of the Lord which cannot deceive. For certainly the immaculate state of being a *eunuch for the kingdom of heaven*[31] is not entrusted to all, but obviously only to those who are able to preserve the undefiled and ever-blooming flower of virginity. Thus the prophetic Word can compare the Church with a meadow full of gay-colored flowers, adorned and garlanded not only with the blossoms of chastity, but also with those of continence and motherhood: for *on the right hand* of the Bridegroom *stands the queen ornate in a gold-embroidered gown.*[32]

This then, Arete, to the best of my ability, is my contribution to our discussion of chastity.

When Theophila had finished, Theopatra told me, there was a delightful burst of applause as the maidens complimented her on her discourse. And when all were quiet again, after a long silence, Thalia stood up. She had been given third place in the contest following Theophila.

LOGOS 3: THALIA

1. She then, picking up the discussion from there, I think, spoke as follows. Both in word and in deed, Theophila, she said, I think you are superior to all and are second to none in wisdom. Surely no one, no matter how contentious or contrary, would be able to criticize what you said.

But, while you discussed all the other points correctly, there is just one thing, my dear, that disturbs and distresses me: in my estimation it would have been pointless for that wise man who wrote under inspiration—I mean Paul—to apply the union of the first man and woman to Christ and the Church, if holy Scripture were referring to nothing loftier than the literal meaning of the words and to actual history. For if we are really to take Scripture merely as giving a representation of the union of man and woman, why then does Paul, in referring to it and, as I think, guiding us into the way of the Spirit, allegorize the story of Adam and Eve and apply it to Christ and the Church? The text in Genesis reads as follows: *And Adam said: This now is bone of my bones, and flesh of my flesh; she shall be called woman, because she was taken out of man. Wherefore a man shall leave father and mother and shall cleave to his wife, and they shall be two in one flesh.*[1]

The Apostle, then, in considering this same passage, does not now, as I have said, want it to be taken literally in a natural sense, as referring merely to the union of man and woman, as you do.[2] For you, studying the text too much on the natural level, have represented the Scriptures as speaking only of conception and birth: that bone is taken from bone to the end that another human being might be born; that for this reason, animals that they are, they come together, swell and are in travail, like trees,[3] at the hour of parturition. But the Apostle, teaching us to take the text in a more spiritual sense as referring to Christ, says: *He that loveth his wife loveth himself. For no man ever hateth his own flesh, but nourisheth and cherisheth it, as also Christ doth the church: because we are members of His body, of His flesh, and of His bones. For this cause shall a man leave his father and mother and shall cleave to his wife, and they shall be two in one flesh. This is a great sacrament; but I speak in Christ and in the Church.*[4]

2. You should not be disturbed by the shifts in Paul's discussions from one thing to another: this tends to give one the impression that he is confusing the point or bringing in material that is irrelevant to the issue, that he is wandering from the question, as for instance here. In his desire, it would seem, to support this discussion of chastity most carefully, he prepares his line of argumentation by first adopting a more persuasive form of speech.

You see, the style of his discourse is most varied and follows a climactic method of development: he begins with the more commonplace and advances to the more lofty and sublime. Then again, shifting to a profound level, he sometimes arrives at what is easier and simpler to grasp and sometimes at a point that is rather difficult and subtle. And yet in all these transitions he introduces nothing irrelevant to his subject; but encompassing all his ideas in a wonderful harmony, he makes them all tell on the single point at issue before him.

It is necessary for me, then, to explain more vigorously[5] the meaning of the Apostle's arguments without prejudice to anything we have said before. Certainly, Theophila, I think you have clearly and adequately discussed these points, working with a sure grasp on the words of the sacred text as they stand. For it is a precarious procedure to disregard utterly the actual meaning of the text as written,[6] particularly in the book of Genesis which contains God's immutable decrees on the constitution of the universe. It is in perfect harmony with these that the world is even now being perfectly directed; and it will so continue until the Legislator Himself who set it in order decides to reorganize it by a new disposition, and to destroy His first ordinances of nature by a new decree.

But I must not leave the exposition of my thesis go without any real proof and, as it were, limping on one side. Let us therefore inquire more deeply into the text and explain its corresponding spiritual sense. For when Paul goes beyond literal statement to apply a text to Christ and the Church, he is not to be passed over lightly.

3. Now, first of all, since it is only natural that various objections should be urged, we should investigate how it is that Adam can be compared with the Son of God—Adam, who was caught in the sin of the Fall and heard those words, *Earth thou art, and into earth thou shalt return.*[7] And just how is he to be considered *the firstborn of every creature*[8] who was first formed out of clay after the creation of the earth and the firmament? And how are we to grant that he too is *the tree of life,*[9] who was exiled from Paradise for his sin *that he might not again put forth his hand and eat of it, and live forever?*[10] Plainly a thing that is likened ought in many respects to be matched and compared with that of which it is a likeness, and its constitution must not be opposite and dissimilar to the other. For a person would not be thought rational who attempted to compare the

even with the uneven, harmony with disharmony; rather, the even goes with what is naturally even or practically so, and white with what is naturally white, even though it manifested but to a very small and moderate extent the whiteness by reason of which it is called white. Now it is surely clear to everyone that in our discussion of wisdom that which is even, ordered, and bright is sinlessness and incorruptibility; and that which is uneven and disordered is the sinful, the mortal, and all that is cast out by condemnation and is liable to penalty.

4. Such then, I think, are the objections urged by most people who, it is clear, think little of Paul's insight and do not like to compare the first man with Christ. But as for us, let us now consider how doctrinally correct he was in comparing Adam to Christ, inasmuch as he not only considers Adam as a type and image of Christ, but also that Christ became the very same as Adam through the descent of the Logos into Him.[11] It was only fitting, after all, that the first-born of God, His first and only-begotten offspring, should become man and be joined as His Wisdom to mankind's first man, first-formed and first-born. For this was Christ: man filled with the pure and perfect Godhead, and God comprehending man. Most fitting was it that the eldest of the Aeons,[12] the first among archangels,[13] when about to mingle with men, took up His abode in the first and eldest man of humankind—Adam. For thus, in remodelling what was from the beginning and moulding it all over again of the Virgin and the Spirit, He fashioned the same Man; just as in the beginning when the earth was virgin and untilled, God had taken dust from the earth and formed, without seed, the most rational being from it.

5. Now let there come to my support the prophet

Jeremias as a trustworthy and clear witness: *And I went down*, he says, *into the potter's house; and behold he was doing a work on the stones. And the vessel which he was making with his hands fell; and he made it again another vessel, as it seemed good in his eyes to make it.*[14]

So while Adam was still as it were on the potter's wheel, still soft and moist and not yet, like a finished vessel, strengthened and hardened in incorruptibility, he was ruined by sin dripping and falling on him like water. And so God, moistening His clay once again and modelling the same man again *unto honor*,[15] fixed and hardened it in the Virgin's womb,[16] united and mingled[17] it with the Word, and finally brought it forth dry and unbreakable into the world, that it might never again be drowned by the floods of external corruption and collapse into putrefaction.

And in His parable of the finding of the lost sheep my Lord teaches the same when he says to the bystanders: *What man is there among you that hath an hundred sheep, and if he shall lose one of them, doth he not leave the ninety-nine in the mountains, and going after that which was lost, seek it until he find it? And when he hath found it, he layeth it upon his shoulders, and coming home he calleth together his friends and neighbors, saying: Rejoice with me, because my sheep that was lost has been found.*[18]

6. For Christ really was and is, being *in the beginning with God*[19] and being Himself God, the Commander-in-Chief and the Shepherd of all that is in the heaven,[20] the while He marshals in orderly ranks and numbers the multitudes of the blessed angels, He to whom all rational creatures pay homage and obey.[21] Now this constituted the even and perfect number of immortal creatures, distributed by race and tribe, the fact that man was also

included in this flock; for he too had been created in incorruptibility that he might celebrate the King and Creator of all things in a song which would be an antiphon to the angelic voices wafted from heaven.[22] But then it happened that he transgressed the Commandment and suffered a terrible and destructive Fall and was transformed into death:[23] for this reason, the Lord tells us, He came from the heavens into the world, leaving the ranks and the hosts of the angels.

Thus the mountains are to symbolize the heavens, and the ninety-nine sheep the principalities and powers which the Shepherd and Commander left when He came down to look for His lost sheep.[24] Man remained to be included in this number and multitude: the Lord put him on Himself and carried him back, that he might not again, as I have said, be overwhelmed and submerged by the mounting waves and deceptions of pleasure. This was the reason why the Word assumed human nature, that He might through Himself defeat the Serpent and destroy the condemnation that existed for man's ruin. It was indeed fitting that the Evil One should be defeated by no one else but by him whom the Devil boasted he ruled since he first deceived him. For it was impossible otherwise to destroy the state of sin and condemnation unless the same man because of whom the words, *Earth thou art, and unto earth thou shalt return*, were spoken, should renew the contest and undo the sentence that had been passed against all men because of him. Thus, just as *in Adam all men die, so also in Christ*, who assumed Adam, *all were made to be alive.*[25]

7. Well, I think I have about finished with the subject of man's becoming an instrument and garment[26] of the Only-Begotten and being made the same as He who took

His abode in him. But that here there is no unevenness nor indeed disharmony is a question we must consider again briefly from the beginning. Now one would be correct in saying that what is essential goodness, essential holiness and justice, that on account of which all other things by participation become good—that this, second to God Himself, is Wisdom; and so too, that what is unholiness and injustice and wickedness is sin. Two elements which are utterly contradictory to each other are life and death, corruption and incorruptibility. Life is evenness; corruption is unevenness. And justice and prudence are harmony, while injustice and folly are disharmony.[27] Man himself, being between these two extremes, is neither absolute justice nor injustice; but placed midway between corruption and incorruptibility, to whichever he bends and inclines, he is said to turn to the nature of that which has gotten the upper hand of him. Inclining towards corruption he becomes corruptible and mortal; and incorruptible and immortal if he inclines towards incorruption. Placed midway between the tree of life and the tree of the knowledge of good and evil,[28] he was changed into the form of that whose fruit he had tasted; for he himself was neither the tree of life nor that of corruption, but became mortal because of the supervenience and presence of corruptibility, while by the fact that Life was domiciled with him and anointed him, he once more became immortal and incorrupt. This too is perhaps what Paul taught when he said, *neither shall corruption possess incorruption,*[29] nor death life: he fittingly defined corruption and death as that which of itself destroys and kills, not that which is destroyed and dies; and incorruptibility and life as that which of itself causes immortality and life, not that which is made immortal and living.

It follows, then, that man is not disharmony and unevenness, nor yet harmony and evenness. But when he took on disharmony, that is, transgression and sin, he became disharmonious and inacceptable; and when he took on harmony, that is, justice, he became an harmonious and acceptable instrument,[30] so that the Lord, Incorruptibility itself and the Conqueror of death, might mix in harmony the resurrection with the flesh, and never again suffer it to be claimed by incorruption. And so let this suffice on this point.

8. We have now established, by means of Scriptural arguments that are not to be ignored, the fact that the first man may properly be referred to Christ Himself inasmuch as he is not merely a figure and representation and image of the Only-Begotten, but precisely this has he become—Wisdom and the Word. For human nature, mingled like water with Wisdom and Life, has become one with that pure light which inundated it. Hence the Apostle could apply directly to Christ, as arrows to their mark, all that was said of Adam. Thus would it be in excellent accord[31] with this that the Church has been formed from His flesh and bone. For it was for her sake that the Word left His heavenly Father and came down to earth in order to cling to His Spouse,[32] and slept in the ecstasy of His Passion. Voluntarily did He die for her sake *that He might present her to Himself a glorious Church and without blemish, cleansing her by the laver*[33] for the reception of that blessed spiritual seed which He sows and plants by secret inspiration in the depths of the soul; and like a woman the Church conceives of this seed and forms it until the day she bears and nurtures it as virtue.

So too the word *Increase and multiply*[34] is duly fulfilled as the Church grows day by day in size and in beauty and numbers, thanks to the intimate union between her and the Word, coming down to us even now and continuing His ecstasy in the memorial of His Passion. For otherwise the Church could not conceive and bring forth the faithful *by the laver of regeneration*[35] unless Christ emptied Himself for them too for their conception of Him, as I have said, in the recapitulation[36] of His Passion, and came down from heaven to die again, and clung to His Spouse the Church, allowing to be removed from His side a power by which all may grow strong who are built upon Him, who have been born by the laver and receive of His flesh and bone, that is, of His holiness and glory. Correctly interpreted, the flesh and bone of Wisdom is understanding and virtue; and His side is the *Spirit of Truth*, the Advocate, from whom the illuminated[37] receive and by whom they are rightly begotten into immortality.

And it is impossible for anyone to participate in the Holy Spirit and to be counted a member of Christ unless again the Word has first descended upon him and fallen into the sleep of ecstasy, that he may rise from his own deep sleep[38] and, filled with the Spirit, receive a renewal and rejuvenation. Now the side of the Word may truly be called the Spirit of Truth which is septiform according to the prophet;[39] and God, taking from Christ's side during His ecstasy, that is, after His Incarnation and Passion, prepares for Him a helpmate, that is to say, all souls who are betrothed and wedded to Him. For in fact frequently the Scriptures thus refer to the Church[40] as the actual multitude and assembly of the faithful taken as a whole, while they also conceive of those who are more perfect in spiritual progress as the one person and body of the Church. Those who are more perfect and have embraced the truth with more perception, and thus, by their perfect faith and purification, have detached themselves from the absurdities of the flesh—these become the Church and the helpmate of Christ; they are the virgin, as the Apostle tells us,[41] espoused and wedded to Him that by receiving from Him the pure and fertile seed of doctrine they might collaborate with him in the preaching of the Gospel for the salvation of all the rest. But those who are still imperfect and have only begun their lessons in the way of salvation,[42] are formed and brought forth as by mothers in labor by those who are more perfect, until they are born and reborn unto the greatness and beauty of virtue. And when by their progress these too have become the Church, they co-operate in their turn in the birth and rearing of other children, bringing to term in the receptive soul as in a mother's womb, the spotless desire of the Word.

9. So we must also consider the case of the glorious Paul. When he was not as yet perfect in Christ,[43] he was first born and nursed: Ananias preached the Gospel to him and made a new being of him in Baptism, as history tells us in the Acts.[44] When he had grown to manhood and was remade and fully developed in spiritual perfection, he had been made into a helpmate and a bride of the Word. Then, receiving the seed of life and conceiving, he who had before been called a child now became Church and Mother, himself bearing in travail those who believed in the Lord through him until Christ was likewise formed and born in them. *My little children*, he says, *of whom I am in labor again until Christ be formed in you.*[45] And again: *For in Christ Jesus, by the gospel, I have begotten you.*[46]

It has thus been established that the meaning of the story of Adam and Eve is to be referred to the Church and to Christ. This is in truth the great, the transcendent *mystery,*[47] of which, because I am so weak and dull-witted I am unable to speak as its dignity and grandeur deserves. Still, I shall make the effort. I must then continue this discussion and speak to you of what remains to be considered.

10. Surely Paul, in exhorting all men to holiness and self-control, has thus directed the passage on the first man and Eve, in its second interpretation, to Christ and the Church in a way that should silence the ignorant by depriving them of all subterfuges. For licentious men, impelled by the unbridled impulses of their own passions, dare to force the meaning of the Scriptures against the orthodox sense, holding up as a defence of their own incontinence the texts—*God said: Increase and multiply,* and *Therefore a man shall leave father and mother . . .;*[48] and they are not only not ashamed to attack the Spirit, they even fan and enkindle their smouldering evil[49] passions by provocation, as though they had been born for this precise purpose.

Hence Paul very sharply annihilates their artificial pretexts and disingenuous follies, and in developing an instruction on how husbands should act towards their wives, shows them that their model should be the way Christ acted towards the Church, who *delivered Himself up for it that He might sanctify and cleanse it by the laver of water in the word.*[50] He then had recourse to Genesis, recalling what was said of the first man and explaining it as also having a bearing on the subject which he had proposed for himself, but in such a way as to give no grounds for the misinterpretation of these passages by those who advocate sexual pleasure under the pretext of procreating children.

11. Now consider, my dear virgins, how Paul, in his

desire to have all the faithful practice chastity so far as possible,[51] endeavors to emphasize the dignity of chastity by many arguments. So, for example, when he says: *Concerning the things whereof you wrote to me: It is good for a man not to touch a woman*,[52] in proposing and prescribing it without qualification he already shows quite clearly that *it is good not to touch a woman*. But then, realizing the weakness and the passion for intercourse of those who are less continent, he gave permission to those who could not control the flesh to enjoy their own spouses for fear that they would sin shamefully and give themselves up to fornication.[53] And after giving this permission, he immediately added these words, *lest Satan tempt you for your incontinency*,[54] that is to say: 'If you whom this concerns cannot remain completely continent because of the incontinence and softness of your bodies, I am permitting you rather to enjoy your own wives, and that for fear that if you professed to practice chastity you would be continually tempted by the Evil One and would lust after other men's wives.'

12. Let us now look more closely into the actual text, seeing that the Apostle did not grant this concession to one and all without qualification, but first added the reason why he was brought to do so. Thus, after declaring that *It is good for a man not to touch a woman*, he immediately added: *But for fear of fornication, let every man have his own wife*—that is, because fornication is bound to follow if you do not have the courage to curb your concupiscence—*and let every woman have her own husband. Let the husband render the debt to his wife, and the wife also in like manner to the husband. The wife hath not power of her own body, but the husband. And in like manner the husband also hath not power of his own body, but the wife. Defraud not one another,*

except, perhaps, by consent, for a time, that you may give yourselves to prayer; and return together again, lest Satan tempt you for your incontinency. But I speak this by indulgence, not by commandment.[55] And this last, too, was said with careful deliberation. *By indulgence*, he said by way of distinction, to point out that he has given a counsel, and *not by commandment*, because whereas with regard to continence and the matter of not touching a woman he is using a command, he is merely giving permission with regard to those who, as I have said, are unable to chastise their passion.[56]

So much, then, for his regulations with regard to those men and women who are with one spouse and whose marriage is continuing. But next we must again scrutinize closely the Apostle's message for whatever inspired word it may contain with regard to men who have already lost their wives and women who have lost their husbands. *But I say to the unmarried and to the widows: It is good for them if they so continue, even as I. But if they do not contain themselves, let them marry. For it is better to marry than to be burnt.*[57] Here again he consistently gives his preference to chastity. For holding himself up as the greatest example, he challenged his hearers to emulation in this state of life, teaching that it is better for one who had been married to one spouse to remain single, just as he himself did.[58]

If, however, anyone should find this difficult by reason of his surging carnal passion, Paul would allow one in such a condition to contract a second marriage *by indulgence*; he does not declare that a second marriage is a good thing in itself, but merely states that it is his opinion that it is *better than to be burnt*. A good parallel would be if someone were to offer food to another who was dangerously ill on the fast day before Easter, and urged him because of his infirmity to taste of what was brought, saying: 'My good friend, it would indeed be very fine for you bravely to persevere like ourselves and share our privations,[59] forbidden as it is even to think of food today. But since you are bedridden and weakened by illness and cannot bear it, therefore we grant you this indulgence, and counsel you to partake of food; otherwise, because of your disease you may be completely unable to withstand your desire for food and thus perish.' This is the tone in which the Apostle is speaking here: he says first that he would prefer that everyone would be healthy and self-controlled as he is, whereas afterwards, for those who are weighted down with the disease of the passions, he allowed a second marriage in his desire to prevent them from being completely ruined by fornication, provoked to promiscuity by the pricking of their generative parts. For he judges that a second marriage is far better than 'burning' and impurity.[60]

13. I have now said quite enough on the subject of continence and marriage, human intercourse and abstinence, and on which of these offers the greatest advantage for the practice of holiness. Now it remains to speak of virginity and whether anything has ever been laid down concerning it. Surely we ought to discuss this point too.

We read as follows: *Now concerning virgins, I have no commandment of the Lord; but I give counsel, as having obtained mercy of the Lord, to be faithful. I think therefore that this is good for the present necessity, that it is good for a man so to be. Art thou bound to a wife? Seek not to be loosed. Art thou loosed from a wife? Seek not a wife. But if thou take a wife, thou hast not sinned. And if a virgin marry, she hath not sinned. Nevertheless such shall have tribulation of the flesh. But I spare you.*[61]

Paul is on the point of counselling a man who so wishes to give his virgin daughter in marriage, and here he has introduced the subject of virginity with extreme caution, that nothing pertaining to sanctification may be forced or compulsory, but in accordance with the soul's free choice,[62] for this is what is acceptable to God. Yet he does not wish this matter of giving one's daughter in marriage to be proposed as though it were the Lord's will and authority. And so, after saying that *if a virgin marry, she hath not sinned*, he presently modifies his position with some caution, stressing the fact that he is here counselling according to human and not divine permission.[63] At any rate, immediately after the text, *if a virgin marry, she hath not sinned*, he adds: *nevertheless such shall have tribulation of the flesh. But I spare you.* What he means is: 'Speaking to those of you who are concerned, I am giving you this permission in order to spare you, seeing that this is what you have chosen to think, lest I give the impression of urging you to this against your will or of compelling anyone by force. Nonetheless, even though you become impatient with the burden of chastity and change to marriage, I think that it will be advantageous for you to control your carnal inclinations and not to abuse your vessels for uncleanness just because you are married.'[64]

Then he adds: *This therefore I say, brethren: the time is short; it remaineth that they also who have wives be as if they had none.*[65] Then dwelling once more on the point and challenging them to the same contest, he confirms his message, giving strong support to the state of virginity. Indeed, expressly adding the following to what he had already said, he exclaims: *But I would have you to be without solicitude. He that is without a wife is solicitous for the things that belong to the Lord, how he may please God. But he that is with a wife is solicitous for the things of the world, how he may please his wife. And the wife and the virgin are divided. The unmarried woman thinketh on the things of the Lord, that she may be holy in body and in spirit. But she that is married thinketh on the things of the world, how she may please her husband.*[66] Now everyone will undoubtedly agree that to be concerned for *the things of the Lord* and to please Him is much more important than being concerned for the things of this world and pleasing one's wife. Who is so foolish and blind as not to perceive that in this text Paul's praise is preponderantly on the side of chastity? *For this,* he says, *I speak for your own profit, not to cast a snare on you, but for that which is decent.*[67]

14. In addition to what has been said, consider too how he recommends the practice of virginity as a gift of God. Hence if any have embraced it from a motive of vanity without being continent, Paul would reject them, suggesting that they get married; otherwise, when the body's vigor rouses them to the heat of passion, they may be provoked into defiling their souls.

Let us then consider the doctrine he hands down. *But if any man think that he seemeth dishonored,* he says, *with regard to his virgin, for that she is above the age, and it must so be: let him do what he will; he sinneth not, if she marry.*[68] Here he points out in simple language the advantage of marriage over dishonor for those who, although they may have chosen chastity, subsequently become wearied of it and find it too difficult; and though out of human respect they may boast in speech that they are persevering, the fact is that they are unable to go on with it. But he who with perfect freedom and determination decides to keep his flesh *virgin, with no necessity*[69]—that is, the passion that excites the loins to intercourse; for there are naturally differences between one body and another—such a one as this, who wrestles and struggles and sincerely abides by his resolution and valiantly tries to keep it to the end, Paul bids him to preserve it and to persevere, assigning the highest place to virginity. Anyone who is unable to do this and marries lawfully and does not live in secret corruption, does well, he says; but he who has the zeal to preserve his flesh a virgin and can do so, does better.

But we have said enough on this point. Let anyone who will pick up the Epistle to the Corinthians and examine all the texts in detail and then compare them with what I have said, and see if there is not a perfect harmony and correspondence. Such then, my dear Arete, is my contribution, to the best of my ability, on the subject of chastity.

[Interlude I]

Eubulion. My dear Gregorion, Thalia said a good deal, although after measuring and crossing an enormous sea of words, she scarcely got to the point at issue.

Gregorion. I quite agree. But come, let us try to recall and consider the rest of the banquet in order, repeating it as faithfully as we can, while I still feel I have the sound of it ringing in my ears. Otherwise it may all fly away and disappear:

> For easily erased is news that is fresh
> From the memory of the aged.[70]

Eubulion. All right, go on then. It is for that purpose we have come, to have the pleasure of listening to these discourses.

Gregorion. Well then, after Thalia's ship, as you put it,

had come to land, after an unruffled voyage, Theopatra—so she said—picked up the discourse in order and spoke as follows.

LOGOS 4: THEOPATRA

1. My dear virgins, if the art of eloquence ever followed on the same road and always trod on the same path, I could not avoid boring you with arguments which have already been brought forward. But if there exist innumerable verbal tactics and thrusts—for God inspires us *at sundry times and in divers manners*[1]—does one have the choice of hiding one's face and being afraid? No, anyone who has the gift of expression, would surely be blameworthy if he did not use it to enhance what is beautiful with grateful speech. Wherefore let us too sing the praises of the most brilliant and glorious star of all Christ's charisms, virginity. For this path of the Spirit is a most broad and generous one. I must consider therefore how I should begin to present a discourse which may be suitable and a fitting contribution to the subject we are discussing.

2. Now I think I perceive quite clearly that of all the means offered to men to guide us to eternal life, nothing is superior to chastity in its power to restore[2] mankind to Paradise, reconcile them with God and transform them into a state of incorruptibility. I shall attempt to show you why I hold this view on these matters, that when you have clearly perceived the power of this charism we have been speaking of, you may realize what a great source of good it has become to us.

In days of old, then, after man was exiled from his home because of the Fall, the waters of corruption poured forth in a flood tide; rushing along with violent waves, it carried away in confusion whatever came in contact with it from without and overwhelmed and engulfed the souls of men. And these souls were constantly at its mercy, dumbly and stupidly borne along: they were unable to steer their vessels aright because they had nothing secure to fasten on to. The senses of the soul[3]—as we are told by those who are learned in these matters—are overwhelmed by the passions which rush upon them from without, and subjected to the attacks of the flood of folly which dashes in on them, they become darkened and immediately force off course the entire[4] ship which by nature had been so easy to steer.[5]

And so God took pity on us in our plight, incapable as we were either of standing or of rising again, and sent down from heaven that excellent and most glorious auxiliary, chastity, that we might bind our bodies to it, like vessels, and moor them in calm beyond corruption, as the Holy Spirit also tells us. For this is what is said in Psalm 136, in which a hymn of thanksgiving is joyously raised to God by those souls who have been seized and caught up to live with Christ in heaven, and not dragged down by the floods of matter and the body.[6]

Thus too it has been said that the Pharaoh of Egypt was a type of the devil, in that he cruelly ordered the males to be cast into the Nile[7] and permitted the females to live. So too, the devil, ruling over the great Egypt of the world *from Adam unto Moses,*[8] made an effort to carry off and destroy the male and rational offspring of the soul in the flood of the passions, while he takes delight in seeing the carnal and sensual offspring increase and multiply.

3. But not to stray from our subject, let us take in our hands and explain that Psalm which the pure and unblemished sing to God, saying: *Upon the rivers of Babylon,*

there we sat and wept, when we remembered Sion; on the willows in the midst thereof we hung up our instruments.[9]

By 'instruments' in their lamentation they obviously mean their bodies, which they have hung up on the branches of chastity, fastening them to the wood to keep them from ever being pulled down again and swept away by the flood of incontinence. 'Babylon,' which means confusion or disturbance, refers to this wave-buffeted life, in the midst of which we sit so long as we are in this world, while the waters dash about us and the streams of wickedness keep constantly rushing in on us. And therefore we are terrified and cry and call upon God with tears to prevent our instruments from slipping, from being torn from the tree of chastity by the waves of pleasure. As for the willow tree, you know that sacred Scripture everywhere uses it as a symbol of chastity, because if you drink its flower steeped in water it extinguishes whatever arouses carnal desires and passions within us, even to the point of making a person utterly sterile and rendering ineffectual all efforts at procreation. Even Homer refers to this, and for this reason calls willows fruit-destroying.[10] So too in Isaias, the just are said to *spring up as willows beside the running waters.*[11] Then truly does the tiny slip of chastity grow to a great and glorious height when the just man, to whose care and keeping it has been entrusted, waters it with the most gentle streams of Christ, sprinkling it with wisdom. For as this tree is naturally made to bud and bear green leaves by watering, so too it is the nature of chastity to flower and come to maturity, luxuriant with spiritual doctrine,[12] so that anyone may hang his instrument upon it.

4. Now if 'the rivers of Babylon,' as the scholars tell us, represent the floods of passion which confuse and

disturb the soul, then the willows must stand for chastity, on which we may draw up and hang our 'instruments' of generation which weigh down and burden the mind, so as to prevent them from being carried along the channels of incontinence and, like worms, come in contact with purulence and putrefaction. For God has given us virginity as a most useful and helpful possession for our integrity,[13] sending it as an ally to those, as the Psalmist teaches, who strive and long for Sion, that is, for that shining charity and the commandment which enjoins it on us;[14] for Sion really means 'ordinance of the watch-tower.'[15]

Let us then briefly resume here the rest of the Psalm. Why is it that the souls declare that they had been requested by their captors to *sing the song of the Lord in a strange land*?[16] Surely they are teaching us that the Gospel is a holy song, a song of mystery, which only sinners and adulterers sing to the Evil One. For these abandon the commandments, doing the will of the *spirits of wickedness*,[17] and cast *that which is holy to dogs* and *pearls before swine*.[18] They are like those of whom the prophet speaks in wrath: *And they read the Law without*.[19] Now manifestly it was not because the Jews went out of their homes or outside the gates of Jerusalem to read the Law that the prophet sternly rebukes them and cries out that they are liable to condemnation; rather because, while breaking the commandments and committing sacrilege against God, they were only pretending to read the commandments, as though they were pious; whereas actually they had not received them into their souls as something to be preserved by faith, but rather rejected them and *in their works denied* them.[20] Thus it is that they *sing the song of the Lord in a strange land*, dragging the Law into the mire by their interpretation of it, looking forward to a sensual kingdom in this 'strange land' which divine Wisdom tells us *shall pass away*,[21] and putting all their hopes in it; while here those who are trying to ensnare them lie in ambush to entice and deceive them with the bait of pleasure.

5. Now those who sing the Gospel to the foolish are indeed like those who *sing the song of the Lord in a strange land*, of which Christ is not the husbandman. But those who have put on and shone in the immaculate and bright and pure and reverent and precious beauty that is chastity, these are found to be sterile and unproductive of seething and painful passions; these do not *sing the song in a strange land*. For they are not borne thither by their expectations, nor do they cleave to the lusts of their mortal bodies, or basely despise the meaning of the commandments. Rather, well and nobly, with lofty sentiments do they contemplate the promises that are above, thirsting after heaven as their natural abode. And so, God, pleased with their dispositions, promises with an oath that He will bestow upon them special honors, setting and establishing them as 'the beginning of His joy.' For He says: *If I forget thee, O Jerusalem, let my right hand be forgotten. Let my tongue cleave to my jaws, if I do not remember thee, if I make not Jerusalem the beginning of my joy.*[22] By 'Jerusalem,' as I have said, he means those immaculate and untouched souls who have austerely drained the pure draught of chastity with unsullied lips.[23] These are *espoused to one husband*, to be *presented as a chaste virgin to Christ*[24] in heaven, *winning the reward of undefiled conflicts.*[25]

So too the prophet Isaias utters the command: *Be enlightened, be enlightened, O Jerusalem, for thy light is come, and the glory of the Lord is risen upon thee.*[26] Now it is clear to all that these promises will be fulfilled after the resurrection. For the Holy Spirit's revelation here does not concern the well-known city of Judaea,[27] but rather that heavenly city, the Jerusalem of the blessed, which they say is the community of those souls whom God unequivocally promises to place in the front rank, in *the beginning of His joy* in the new dispensation. He will bring them to dwell in the pure habitation of innermost light, clad in the snow-white garment of virginity, because they remembered not to remove their wedding garment, that is, not to relax their minds with straying[28] thoughts.

6. So too Jeremias' words about *the bride* who is not *to forget her ornament or a virgin her breastband*[29] surely teach us not to give up or to loosen the bond of chastity through wiles and distractions. For the breast is reasonably taken to mean the mind and heart. Hence the 'breastband,' the girdle which binds and girds up the purpose of the soul towards chastity, is the love of God. And this love, my fair virgins, I pray that Jesus our Captain and Shepherd, our Prince and Bridegroom, may grant us to preserve sealed and unbroken to the end. As a safeguard for mankind, it would not be easy to find a better one than this, or a possession more acceptable and pleasing to God than this. Hence I say that we should all honor chastity and practice it, and sing its praises before all else.

Let these first fruits of my discourse, too, Arete, be an offering to you, partly for our entertainment, but also to serve a serious purpose.

Arete, she said, replied: Thank you for your gift then. And now let Thallusa speak after you. I must have a discourse from every one of you.

Logos 5: THALLUSA

1. Thallusa, then, she said, paused a little and, having collected her thoughts for a moment,[1] spoke as follows:

I beg you, Arete, to assist me in my thoughts, that what I have to say may be worthy of you and of our audience. For I have become fully convinced, from what I have observed from Holy Scripture, that the greatest and most illustrious offering and gift is the prize of chastity, and that there exists no other comparable in value with it that man can offer to God. For although many men have accomplished many fine things according to their vows under the Law, only those were said to fulfill a great vow who offered themselves to God by a deliberate resolve. Thus the text says: *And the Lord spoke to Moses, saying: Speak to the children of Israel, and thou shalt say to them: When a man, or woman, shall make a great vow to consecrate and sanctify himself to the Lord. . . .*[2] One man may make a vow to dedicate gold and silver utensils for the temple; another, to offer a tithe of his produce; another, of his property; another, the finest of his flocks; another, his substance. And yet no one can be said 'to make a great vow to the Lord' save him who consecrates himself entirely to God.

2. Now, my dear virgins, I must try to explain to you by true reasoning the spiritual meaning of the Scripture. The person who only partially controls and restrains himself, and is partially distracted and commits sin, he is not wholly consecrated to God. The perfect man must offer up all, both of his body and of his soul, that he may be complete and not deficient.

This is of course the reason why God commands Abraham: *Take me a heifer of three years old, and a she-goat of three years, and a ram of three years, a turtle-dove also, and a pigeon.*[3] This has an auspicious meaning, for in giving this command, He also has our subject in view: 'Offer them to me and keep them unyoked and unharmed: your soul like a heifer, and your flesh and your mind as well. The flesh is like a goat that wanders on lofty heights and crags; the mind is like a ram that must not skip away and slip and fall from the truth. In this way, Abraham, you will be perfect and irreproachable, when you have brought and offered to me your soul, your senses, and your mind.'[4]

To these He refers symbolically as the heifer, the goat, and the ram *of three years*, as though they suggested the perfect knowledge of the Trinity. Possibly, too, He is giving us a symbolic picture of the three stages of our span of life, the earliest, the middle, and the last, seeing that He wishes men, so far as possible, to live their lives chastely, offering them up to Him in childhood, in adulthood, and in old age.

This too is Our Lord Jesus Christ's command in the Gospel where He bids us: *Let your lamps be not extinguished and your loins not loosed.* Wherefore *you yourselves should be like to men who wait for their lord when he shall return from the wedding, that when he cometh and knocketh, they may open to him immediately. Blessed* are ye, for he will *make* ye *sit down to meat and passing will minister unto* ye. *And if he shall come in the second watch, or in the third watch, blessed* are ye.[5]

Now reflect, my dear virgins, that in setting forth the three night watches—the evening watch, the second, and the third—and His three comings, He meant to symbolize the three ages of our life, childhood, adulthood, and old age. Thus even if He should come and remove us from the world while we are still in the first age, that is, while we are still children, He wished to find us prepared and pure, in the pursuit of no wicked thing; and so likewise with the second and the third watch. For the evening watch is the time of man's youth and prime, when his reason[6] is beginning to be disturbed and clouded by the changes of life, while his flesh is already developing towards puberty and is inclined towards the passions. The second watch is the period when, having advanced *unto a perfect man*, the mind begins to acquire a firmness and stability against mental confusion and self-conceit. And the third watch is when most of the phantasms of our desires grow dim, since the flesh is beginning to wither and decline into old age.

3. And so we ought to light the unquenchable lamp of faith in our hearts, gird up our loins with purity, and watch and wait for the Lord, that if He should decide to take anyone of us in the first stage of life, or in the second, or in the third, He may come and find us all ready, doing His will, that thus He may make us recline in the bosom of Abraham, Isaac, and Jacob.

It is good for a man, says Jeremias, *when he hath borne the yoke in his youth*;[7] and his *soul* shall not *depart from the Lord.*[8] It is indeed a good thing to submit one's neck sincerely to the divine guidance right from childhood and to persevere into old age without seeking to shake off that Horseman who rides us with pure mind, whilst the Evil One is ever trying to drag down our minds to what is base. For who is there who does not receive through eyes, ears, taste, smell, and touch, delights and pleasures, when he would no longer bear chastity, his driver, that holds back her steed from sin with bloody bit? Some may favor this, and others that, and praise it accordingly, but in our opinion, whosoever strives to keep his flesh undefiled from childhood by the practice of virginity is the one who offers himself perfectly to God. For virginity, to those who practice it, quickly brings a great and most desirable realization of their hopes, in that it causes the soul-destroying lusts and passions to wither away.

But now let me explain how we consecrate ourselves to the Lord.

4. The ordinance in Numbers, *to make a great vow*,[10] brings out a point which I shall explain more at length when I try to show that chastity is the greatest of all vows. For it is clear that I have then completely consecrated myself to God when I struggle to preserve my flesh not only untouched by actual intercourse, but unsullied also by any other offense.

Now *the unmarried woman*, it is said, *thinketh on the things of the Lord, how she may please the Lord*,[11] not only that the glory she wins for her virtue may not be deficient in any part, but also that by offering her limbs to the Lord she may be sanctified in both, in the words of the Apostle, *both in body and in spirit*. Now I must explain what it means to offer oneself totally to the Lord. It is when I open my mouth only for some things and close it for others, as, for instance, when I open it to explain the Scriptures or to praise Him with all honor and true faith so far as it is in my power; and when I close it by putting a door and a guard against foolish speech, then is my mouth pure and an offering to the Lord. *My tongue is become a pen*,[12] Wisdom's instrument; for the Word, the Lord, the swift Scribe of the ages uses it to write in the clearest of letters from the power and depths of the Scriptures, shedding light on *the law of the spirit*;[13] quickly and speedily does He alone write, fulfilling the will of the Father as He hears the words, *Take away the spoils with speed, quickly take the prey.*[14] *My tongue is His pen*; for like a lovely pen is it consecrated and offered to Him, to write things more beautiful than the compositions of poets and rhetoricians who support merely mortal doctrines.

My eyes, too, are pure and an offering to the Lord, when I accustom my sight not to lust after bodily beauty or to take pleasure in seeing impure things, but rather to look at the *things that are above.*[15] I offer up my hearing, too, to the Lord, when I close my ears to slander and blasphemous speech, and open them to the word of God, walking among the wise. When I restrain my hands from ignoble trade and barter, from avarice, from unchaste acts, then my hands too are sacred to God. When I keep my feet from walking on perverted paths, then have I also offered up my feet; and then I do not stray to the law courts and to revels where malefactors are born,[16] but I walk in the way of the upright fulfillment of the commandments. If I sanctify my heart as well and consecrate all its thoughts to the Lord, what more is left? I have no evil in my thoughts, I meditate on no worldly thing, conceit and anger have no place with me. Day and night I meditate[17] on the law of the Lord. This is what it means 'to consecrate and sanctify oneself' and 'to make a great vow.'

5. I shall try now, my dear virgins, to speak to you of the various precepts which follow from what we have said; for these too are bound up with your obligations, being laws and directives concerning chastity which tell us the things the virgin should abstain from and how she is to make progress.

Thus it is written: *And the Lord spoke to Moses, saying: Speak to the children of Israel, and thou shalt say to them: When a man or woman shall make a great vow to consecrate themselves to the Lord, they shall abstain from strong drink and wine and they shall not drink vinegar of wine, or vinegar of strong drink, or whatever is made of the grape; nor shall they eat fresh grapes or dried grapes, all the days of their vow.*[18] This means that anyone who has pledged and consecrated himself to the Lord is not to partake of the fruits of the plant of evil, because of its natural propensity to produce drunkenness and intoxication. Now we perceive from the Scriptures that there are two kinds of vines which are separately developed and with no similarity to each other: the one produces justice and immortality, the other, madness and folly.[19] In the case of the one, the vine of gladness and sobriety, its doctrines like so many branches are gaily hung with clusters of grace distilling love: this vine is Our Lord Jesus who expressly says to His apostles, *I am the true vine, you the branches; and my Father is the husbandman.*[20]

But the wild and death-bringing vine is the devil, who distills madness, poison, and wrath, as Moses teaches us when he says of him: *Their vine is of the vine of Sodom, and their vine-branch of Gomorrha. Their grapes are grapes of gall, their cluster is one of bitterness. Their wine is the rage of dragons and the incurable rage of asps.*[21] The inhabitants of Sodom, gathering their vintage from these vines, were provoked to an unnatural and fruitless passion for men.[22] It was from the same source that men in the days of Noe got drunk, and then, slipping into unbelief, were overwhelmed and drowned by the Flood. Of this Cain drank when he stained his hands red with hatred of his brother, to become the first man to defile the earth with the blood of his own kin. It is this which intoxicates the heathen and whets their passions to murder one another in battle. For actually it is not so much the wine that arouses a man or makes him lose control of himself as it is anger stemming from rivalry. A man does not become so drunk and insane from wine as he does from grief, as he does from love or from incontinence.[23]

It is of this wine that the virgin is commanded not to taste: she is to remain sober and not asleep in the cares of this life, and with the Word[24] she may kindle her lamp of the light of justice with a brilliant glow. *Take heed*, says the Lord, *lest your hearts be overcharged with surfeiting and drunkenness and the cares of this life, and that day come upon you as a snare.*[25]

6. Further, the virgin is forbidden to touch in any way whatsoever not only the things that are made from this vine, but also whatever resembles or is similar to them. Now there is that artificial and spurious wine called *sekar*,[26] sometimes prepared from the fruit of the date palm or from other fruit trees. This drink upsets a man's reason in the same way wine does, only much more so. As a matter of fact, experts refer to all non-vinous drinks that produce drunkenness and intoxication in the soul as 'strong wine.' While guarding herself against those things which are intrinsically sinful, the virgin must not on the other hand be defiled by such things as resemble or are equivalent to the same; for in that case, while conquering the one, she would be overwhelmed by the other. Such would be the case if she pampered her body with the textures of clothing, or with gold and precious stones and luxury and all other bodily finery—things which of themselves intoxicate the soul. Wherefore she is bidden not to lose control of herself and give herself to feminine weaknesses and silliness and wasting time and fatuous conversation, things which confuse and muddle the mind. So too we are told elsewhere: 'You shall not eat of the hyena or of anything like it, nor of the weasel or of anything like it.'[27] For this

is the quick and direct way to heaven, not merely to surmount those obstacles which unseat a man distracted by pleasure and passion, but also all things which resemble them.

What is more, it has been a tradition that the community of those who are chaste is God's unbloody altar: so great and glorious a thing is virginity.[28] And therefore it should be kept absolutely pure and undefiled, removed from contact with the impurities of the flesh; it should be set up within, *before the testimony*, gilded with divine wisdom in the Holy of Holies, sending forth to the Lord the sweet odor of love.

Indeed He says: After the altar of bronze for the holocausts and the offerings *thou shalt make* another *altar of setim-wood . . . and thou shalt overlay* it *with gold . . . and thou shalt set it over against the veil that is over the ark of the testimony, before the propitiatory*, that is, *over the testimonies, wherein I shall make myself known to thee. And Aaron shall burn sweet-smelling incense upon it in the morning. When he shall dress the lamps, he shall burn an everlasting incense before the Lord throughout your generations. He shall not offer upon it incense of another composition, nor oblation nor victim; and he shall not offer a libation.*[29]

7. If, according to the Apostle, *the Law is spiritual* and contains within itself the images *of the good things to come*, then let us remove *the veil* of the letter which is spread over it and contemplate its true meaning stripped bare.[30] The Jews were commanded to adorn their Tabernacle as an imitation of the Church, that though the things of sense they might be able to prefigure the image of things divine. For the exemplar which was shown forth on the mountain and on which Moses gazed when he constructed the Tabernacle,[31] was in a way an accurate picture of the

dwelling in heaven, to which indeed we pay homage insofar as it far surpasses the types in clarity, and yet is far fainter than the reality. The fact is that the unmingled truth has not yet come to men as it is in itself, for here we would be unable to contemplate its pure incorruptibility, just as we cannot endure the rays of the sun with unshielded eyes. The Jews announced what was a shadow of an image, at a third remove from reality,[32] whereas we ourselves clearly behold the image of the heavenly dispensation. But the reality itself will be accurately revealed after the resurrection when we shall see the holy Tabernacle, the heavenly city, *whose builder and maker is God,*[33] *face to face*, and not *in a dark manner* and only *in part.*[34]

8. Just as the Jews foretold our present dispensation, so too we foreshadow the celestial: the Tabernacle was a symbol of the Church, as the Church is a symbol of heaven. And since this is so, and the Tabernacle, as I have said, is taken as a type of the Church, the altars too must represent something within the Church. Thus the brazen altar is to be compared with the enclosure and assembly of holy widows; for they indeed are a living altar of God, and to this we bring calves and tithes and free-will offerings as a sacrifice unto the Lord.[35] And so the golden altar within the Holy of Holies that is placed *before the testimony*, on which it is forbidden to offer sacrifices and libation, should be applied to those who live in the state of chastity and have fortified their bodies with unalloyed gold, uncorrupted[36] by intercourse.

Now people commonly speak in praise of gold for two reasons: first, because it does not rust, and secondly, because its color seems in a way to resemble the rays of the sun. And thus it is a very appropriate symbol of virginity, which does not admit any stain or spot, but is ever brilliant with the light of the Word. For this reason it stands farther within the Holy of Holies, and before the veil, sending up prayers like incense to the Lord, with undefiled hands, acceptable for *an odor of sweetness.*[37] So too did John teach us when he said that the incense in the *vials* of the *twenty-four elders* were *the prayers of the saints.*[38]

This, Arete, is my own contribution on the subject of chastity, offered on the spur of the moment to the best of my ability.

LOGOS 6: AGATHE

1. When Thallusa had done speaking, Theopatra said that Arete touched Agathe with her staff, and that when she felt it, she immediately arose and replied as follows.

If you will accompany me, Arete, with great confidence in my ability to persuade and to continue this excellent discussion, I shall try to make my own contribution to the subject; but this will be in accordance with my own talents, not to be compared with what has already been said. For I should scarcely be able to compete in philosophical discourse with what has already been elaborated with such variety and brilliance. Indeed, I should think myself deserving of the reproach of foolishness were I so rash as to seek to emulate my superiors in wisdom. If then you will bear with whatever words come to me, I shall try to speak, with nothing lacking in good will; and on this note let me begin.

All of us, my dear maidens, come into this world with an extraordinary beauty which has a relationship and kinship with wisdom. And then it is that men's souls most clearly resemble Him who begot and formed them, when they continue to reflect the pure image of His likeness and the lineaments of that vision which He saw when He fashioned them and gave them an imperishable and immortal form.[1]

For the unbegotten and incorporeal beauty, that knows neither beginning nor decay, but is unchangeable and ageless and without need, He who abides in Himself and is Light itself in secret and unapproachable places,[2] embracing all things in the orbit of His power, creating and arranging them—He it was who made the soul in the image of His likeness.[3] This is why it is endowed with reason and immortality; for, fashioned, as I have said, in the image of the Only-Begotten, it has an unsurpassed loveliness. It is for just this reason that *the spirits of wickedness*[4] become enamored of it and lie in wait for it: they would force it to defile that godlike and lovely image which it possesses. Thus too the prophet Jeremias tells us, in reproaching Jerusalem: *Thou hadst a harlot's forehead, thou wouldst not blush* before thy lovers,[5] where he is speaking of Jerusalem as having submitted herself to the enemy forces for her profanation. Her 'lovers,' understand, are the devil and his angels, who scheme to dirty and defile, by their sinful contact, the spiritual and translucent beauty of our minds, and lust to commit adultery with every soul that is espoused to the Lord.

2. If anyone, therefore, will keep this beauty spotless and intact and just as it was when the Creator Artist Himself fashioned it according to type, in imitation of that eternal and intelligible nature of which man is the image and expression, then, becoming like some beautiful sacred statue transported from this world to the city of the blessed in the heavens, he will dwell there as within a temple.[6] Now this beauty of ours is then best preserved intact when, shielded by virginity, it is not blackened by the

heat of corruption from without, but, remaining within itself, it adorns itself with justice and is led as a bride to the Son of God. And this indeed is His own teaching, when He inculcates the duty of kindling the unquenchable light of chastity in one's own flesh as in so many lamps.[7] For the number of the ten virgins stands for the number of souls who believe in Jesus, the number '10' symbolizing the only direct road to heaven.[8] Five of them were prudent and wise, and five were stupid and foolish: they did not have the foresight to fill their vessels with oil, thus remaining empty of justice. And so by the foolish ones He symbolizes those who make strenuous efforts to reach the confines of virginity and do everything properly and prudently in their striving to bring this love to fruition, and they solemnly profess that this is their purpose; yet they become careless and are overcome by the vicissitudes of the world; they are like those artists who paint with shadows, portraying a mere image of virtue instead of the truth itself.[9]

3. Certainly, when it is said that *the kingdom of heaven is like to ten virgins who took their lamps and went out to meet the bridegroom*, the meaning is that all of them entered upon the same path of life, for this is signified by the letter 'I.'[10] They went forth all[11] equally pledged to the same life, and this is why they are said to be ten, for they chose, as I have said, the same purpose. But they did not all go forth to meet the bridegroom in the same way: some had provided themselves with abundant fuel, enough even for the repeated replenishing of their oil lamps; the others had been careless, thinking only for the present. And so they are divided equally, five and five: that is to say, the first group kept their five senses, which are generally called the portals of wisdom, virginally pure of

sin; the second group, on the contrary, mingling their senses with wickedness, dishonored them with innumerable sins. They practiced their abstinence and sobriety by keeping away from justice, and only reaped a greater harvest of transgressions; and hence, of course, it happened that they were locked out and excluded from the divine precincts. For whether we act virtuously or commit sin, it is through these our senses that our deeds, both good and evil, are strengthened.[12]

Thallusa has said that there is a chastity of the eyes, ears, tongue, and so on of the other senses. So too, in this case, the five wise virgins refer to the one who keeps undefiled the fidelity of the five pathways of virtue—sight, taste, smell, touch, and hearing—because she has preserved intact for Christ the five perceptions of her senses, like a lamp causing holiness to shine forth from every one of them. Indeed, our body is truly, as it were, a lamp with five lights, which the soul carries as a torch to meet Christ her Bridegroom on the day of the resurrection, thus manifesting her faith, which leaps up brightly through her every sense. This too He Himself taught us, saying, *I am come to cast fire on the earth, and what will I but that it be kindled?*[13] By 'the earth' He means our bodies,[14] in which He wanted to see enkindled the swift and fiery operation of His doctrine. For the oil represents wisdom and righteousness: when the soul rains and pours this generously upon the body, the inextinguishable light of virtue flares up high, making its good works *shine before men* so as *to glorify* our *Father who is in heaven.*[15]

4. This was the oil they offered in Leviticus, *fine . . . oil of olives, pure, beaten to burn in the lamp, without the veil . . . before the Lord.*[16] But it was for a very short time that they were ordered to tend their flame, *from evening until morning.*

Their light does indeed resemble the prophetic word, which shines in encouragement to continence, a light which is tended by the faith and works of the people; and the temple stands for *the lot of their inheritance*,[17] since a lamp can shine in one building only. This lamp, then, was to be kept burning until day: *they shall burn it*, it says, *until morning*—that is, until the coming of Christ; for when *the Sun* of chastity and *of justice*[18] had risen, there was no need of a lamp.

So long as that people stored up fuel for their lamp, supplying the oil by their deeds, the lamp of continence did not go out on them, but ever shone and gave light in *the lot of their inheritance*. But when their oil ran out because of their turning from faith to incontinence, the lamp was completely extinguished, so that the virgins have to kindle their lamps once again by passing on the light from one to another, bringing the fire of incorruption to the world from above.[19]

In our day too, then, we must abundantly supply the pure oil of wisdom and good works, an oil strained of every form of corruptibility: we do not want our lamps to go out in the same way *while the Bridegroom tarries*. The time of tarrying is, of course, the period before Christ's final coming,[20] and the drowsiness and sleep of the ten virgins is their departure from this life. Midnight stands for the reign of the Antichrist, when the destroying angel will pass over the houses.[21] And the cry that was raised, *Behold, the bridegroom cometh, go ye forth to meet him*,[22] is *the voice* that will come from heaven, and the *trumpet* call, when all the saints with their risen bodies *shall be taken up* and walk upon *the clouds to meet the Lord*.[23] For it is to be noticed that the Word says that after the cry all the virgins got up, meaning that after the voice is heard from heaven the dead will rise again. And this, too, Paul teaches us somewhere when he says: *The Lord Himself shall come down from heaven with commandment, with the voice of an arch-angel, and with the trumpet of God: and the dead who are in Christ shall rise first*—that is, the bodies which died when they were put off like garments by their souls: *then we who are alive shall be taken up together with them*—referring to our souls.[24] 'We who are alive' clearly refers to our souls, which, having resumed their bodies, will go forth *with them to meet* Him *in the clouds*, with lamps trimmed,[25] trimmed indeed not with any alien or worldly ornament, but with the adornment of prudence and temperance, like stars reflecting a full glow of heavenly splendor.

5. These, my fair maidens, are the secret rites of our mysteries,[26] the mystical rites of initiation into virginity; these are *the rewards of undefiled conflicts*[27] of chastity. I am espoused to the Word, and as my dowry I receive the eternal wealth and crown of incorruptibility from my Father, and *I walk in triumph crowned forever*[28] with the bright unfading flowers of wisdom. I am in the choral band in heaven with Christ my Rewarder, around the King who always was and ever shall be. I am the lamp-bearer of unapproachable lights,[29] and I sing the *new song* in the company of the archangels, announcing the Church's new grace. For the Scriptures proclaim that the band of virgins ever follows the Lord and forms His train wherever He may be. This too is the meaning of John's symbolism when he speaks of *the hundred forty-four thousand.*[30]

Go then, virgin band of the new dispensation, go fill your vessels with justice. For it is time now to rise and meet the Bridegroom. Go, and with light hearts turn from the charms and spells of this life, which confuse and bewitch the soul; for you will receive what was promised

—I swear it by Him who has shown us the path of life.[31]
I offer you, Arete, this garland which I have adorned and plaited from the meadows of the Prophets.

LOGOS 7: PROCILLA

After Agathe too had thus finished her excellent discourse, and had been applauded for speaking equally well,[1] she told us, Arete next requested Procilla to speak.

1. Procilla then arose, and going to a spot in front of the entrance, spoke as follows: After such discourses, dear Arete, I must not be remiss, but place unqualified trust in *the manifold wisdom of God*,[2] which has the power to give to whomsoever it wills in rich abundance. Experienced sailors tell us that, although it is the same wind that blows on all who sail the sea, yet different men have different ways of managing their course, and they do not all strive to reach the same harbor. For some the wind is fair, striking astern; for others it blows across their course, and yet both easily accomplish their course. Well, then, in the same way *the spirit of understanding, holy, one*,[3] blowing gently from our Father's treasure rooms above, will give us all a sharp, fair wind of knowledge, and this should suffice us to steer the course of our speech without difficulty. And now it is time for me to begin.

The only true and impressive method of eulogy, my dear maidens, is that in which the one who pronounces it brings forward a witness who is superior to the praises of the person being eulogized.[4] For then one can learn for certain that the words of commendation are not uttered merely to curry favor, nor are they forced, nor are they simply an expression of common rumor, but are in accordance with truth and judgment without any flattery. And thus the Apostles and the prophets,[5] who instructed us at great length about the Son of God existing before the ages and predicated divinity of Him[6] in a sense above all other men, in order to praise Him did not refer this praise to any angelic message, but rather to Him who is the authority and power upon which all things depend. For it was fitting that He who is greater than all others after the Father should have as His witness the Father, who alone is greater than He.[7]

Similarly, in praise of chastity I shall not refer to the opinion of men, but to Him who has made it wholly His own and in whose keeping we are, showing that He is a creditable witness as the husbandman of chastity and the lover of its beauty. And this is something that anyone who so wishes can see clearly in the Canticle of Canticles, where Christ Himself, in praising those who are firmly established in the state of virginity, says: *As the lily among thorns, so is my neighbor among the daughters,*[8] comparing the gift of chastity to a lily because of its purity, its fragrance, its sweetness and its charm. For chastity is a spring flower, ever putting forth in delicate white petals the blossom of incorruptibility. Hence He is not ashamed to admit that He is indeed in love with its ripe beauty: *Thou hast wounded my heart, my sister, my spouse,* He goes on to say, *thou hast wounded my heart with one of thy eyes, with one chain of thy neck. . . . Thy breasts are more beautiful than wine, and the smell of thy garments above all aromatical spices. Thy lips, my spouse, are as a dropping honeycomb, honey and milk are under thy tongue; and the smell of thy garments, as the smell of frankincense. A garden enclosed art thou, my sister, my spouse, a fountain sealed up.*[9]

Such are the praises that Christ sings of those who have achieved the perfection of virginity, comprising them all under the title of His spouse. For the spouse must be betrothed to the bridegroom and call herself by his name, and till then she must remain pure and undefiled, like a *sealed garden* in which all the spices of heaven's fragrance grow, that Christ alone may come and pluck them as they blossom and grow with incorporeal seed. For the Word is in love with none of the things of the flesh—such as, for example, hands or face or feet—for He cannot by nature admit anything corruptible. But He takes delight in regarding only spiritual and immaterial beauty, without touching the beauty of the body.

2. Now consider, dear virgins, that in saying to the spouse in His keeping, *Thou hast wounded us with one of thy eyes*, He is referring to the clear-sighted eye of reason, with which, when the inner man has wiped it clean, he can get a sharper vision of the truth.[10] For I think that it is obvious to everyone that there are two powers of sight, one of the body and one of the soul. Now it is not the eye of the body but only the eye of the understanding for which the Word declares His love when He says: *Thou hast wounded us with one of thy eyes, with one chain of thy neck*. And this means: By the lovely glance of thy mind, my dear, thou hast winged my heart to love, as thou dost radiate from within the brilliant adornment of chastity. Now the chains of the neck are necklaces,[11] which are composed of various precious stones. Those souls who are absorbed in their bodies[12] put around the outer neck of the flesh this visible ornament in order to beguile those who look at them. But those who live chastely, on the contrary, put on their jewelry interiorly, genuine ornaments made of precious and brightly colored stones, of freedom, generosity, wisdom, and love; and they have little thought for the temporal ornaments of this life, for

these like leaves are green for a season and then wither away with the changes of the body.[13]

Indeed in man there is a twofold ornament, but the Lord accepts only the interior, the immortal one, when He says that His heart has been wounded by 'one chain' of His bride's neck. Thus He means that He has, as it were, been seized with desire for the radiance of the interior man, resplendent with modesty, and it is to this, no doubt, that the Psalmist testifies: *All the glory of the king's daughter is within.*[14]

3. But let no one think that only we who are virgins will be led on to attain the promises, and that all the rest of the faithful are lost. For thus he would not understand that there will be tribes and families and orders, *according to the rule of faith* in each.[15]

And Paul, too, teaches us this when he says: *One is the glory of the sun, another the glory of the moon, and another the glory of the stars. For star differeth from star in glory. So also is the resurrection of the dead.*[16] And the Lord does not promise to give the same rewards to everyone. Some He says He will number in *the kingdom of heaven*, others that *they shall possess the land*, others that they *shall see* the Father.[17] So too in this case He reveals that the order and holy choir of virgins will be the first to follow in His train as it were into a bridal chamber, into the repose of the new ages. For they were martyrs, not by enduring brief corporal pains for a space of time, but because they had the courage all their lives not to shrink from the truly Olympic contest of chastity. And by resisting the fierce torments of pleasure and fear and grief and other evils[18] that come from men's wickedness, they carry off the first prize before all the rest, being ranked higher in the land of promise.

Surely only these souls does the Word call His true and chosen bride, referring to the others as concubines, maidens and daughters, when He says: *There are threescore queens and fourscore concubines and young maidens without number. One is my dove, my perfect one; she is the only one of her mother, the chosen of her that bore her. The daughters saw her and will declare her blessed; the queens and concubines praise her.*[19] For the Church obviously has many daughters, but one alone is most precious and honored above all others in her eyes, namely the order of virgins.

4. Now someone may have a difficulty about these matters, seeing that the main points have not been fully explained, and she may wish to have a fuller perception of their spiritual significance, with regard to who the queens and the concubines and the virgins are. I shall say that these may refer to all those who have been outstanding in righteousness from the beginning throughout the course of history: those, for example, who lived before the Deluge, those who lived after the Deluge, and those who have lived since the time of Christ. The bride, of course, is the Church. The queens are all those royal souls who lived before the Deluge and were pleasing to God, that is, those who lived in the days of Abel and Seth and Henoch. And the concubines are those who came after the Deluge and lived in the days of the prophets: for before the Church was espoused to the Lord, He lived with them as concubines, as it were, and sowed the seeds of truth in a rich and pure philosophy, that by conceiving faith they might bring forth to Him the spirit of salvation.[20] Such indeed is the fruit that is brought forth by those souls who are wed to Christ, fruit that has an everlasting beauty. Look, if you will, at the writings of Moses or David or Solomon or Isaias or the later prophets, my

dear maidens, and you will see the progeny they left behind them for the salvation of men's lives after their communion with the Son of God. Thus it is with special meaning that the Word spoke of the souls of the prophets[21] as concubines; for these He did not espouse openly, as He did indeed the Church, for whom He sacrificed the fatted calf.[22]

5. Now an additional point to be considered, that nothing of importance may escape us, is just why we are told that there are sixty queens, eighty concubines, and so many virgins that they cannot be counted, and only one bride.

First, let us discuss the sixty. I think by the sixty queens He referred to all those who pleased God from the first man down to Noe, because the creation of the world in six days was still recent for them, and hence they had no further need of laws and commandments for their salvation.[23] Thus they recalled that God fashioned His creation in six days; also what had happened in Paradise: how man, though commanded not to touch the Tree of Knowledge, ran his ship aground, being lured off his course by the Sophist of Evil. This was the reason therefore why He designated, symbolically, as sixty queens all those souls in order who loved God right from the beginning of the world; for they were almost the offspring, as it were, of the first age, and neighbors to the great six days of creation, having, as I have said, been born immediately afterward.

Great honor was theirs, living as they did with the angels, often seeing God with their eyes and not merely in dreams. Look at the familiarity with God that was enjoyed by Seth, Abel, Enos, Henoch, Methuselah, and Noe, those first lovers of virtue, the first of *the firstborn* sons *who are written in the heavens,*[24] having been deemed worthy of the Kingdom, the first fruits, as it were, of what was planted unto salvation, growing like early-ripening fruit unto God.[25]

So much then for this group. Next we must consider the concubines.

6. To those who lived after the Deluge the knowledge of God was now more remote, and so they needed, especially as idolatry was creeping in, further instructions as a help to ward off evil. Hence God, to prevent the human race from being completely destroyed through forgetfulness of the good, bade His own Son[26] to reveal to the prophets a knowledge of His future coming into the world in the flesh, when the knowledge and joy of the spiritual Eighth Day should be proclaimed, bringing about the remission of sins and the resurrection of the body; and that thus would be effected the circumcision of man's passions and his corruptibility. And hence He referred to the list of the prophets from the days of Abraham as eighty concubines, because of the dignity of the circumcision—and this comprises the number eight—on which, again, the Law depends.[27] They were the first, before the marriage of the Word with His bride the Church, to receive the divine seed and to proclaim the Circumcision of the spiritual Eighth Day.

And again, in referring to maidens of an incalculable number, He designates the entire multitude of those who, though inferior to the higher group, yet practiced justice and fought nobly and youthfully against sin.

7. But of all these neither the queens nor the maidens nor the concubines are to be compared with the Church. For she is considered to be perfect and excellent beyond all of these, formed and composed of all the Apostles:

she is the bride that surpasses all others in the perfection of her beauty and her virginity. Hence is she blessed and extolled by all the others, because she saw and heard abundantly what all the others had desired to see, even for a little, but saw not, and to hear, but heard not. As the Lord said to His disciples: *Blessed are your eyes that see the things which you see. For I say to you that many prophets . . . have desired to see the things that you see and have not seen them, and to hear the things that you hear and have not heard them.*[28]

Surely then this is the reason why the prophets bless and admire the Church: the things which they did not have the good fortune to see and hear, these the Church was judged worthy to participate in: *there are threescore queens and fourscore concubines and young maidens without number. One is my dove, my perfect one.*[29]

8. Taking it in another sense, however, one might say that the bride is the undefiled flesh of the Lord,[30] for the sake of which He left His heavenly Father and came down to earth, to which He was united, and upon which, becoming incarnate, He descended. Hence by a metaphor He calls it His dove, because the dove is a tame and domestic creature, easily adapted to live with human beings. Indeed, it alone, so to speak, was found pure and without spot, surpassing all others in the beauty and adornment of justice, so much so that not even those who in the past were most eminently pleasing to God could approach it in a comparison of virtue. And therefore was this flesh deemed worthy to share in the kingdom of the Only-Begotten, being espoused and united to Him.

And so it is in the forty-fourth Psalm the queen who, taking precedence over many, takes her place *on the right hand* of God, who is clad in the golden raiment of virtue, whose beauty the King desired, is, as I have said, that blessed and immaculate flesh which the Word brought to heaven and placed *on the right hand* of the Father, ornate *in a golden gown*,[31] that is, with the pursuits of immortality, which he called by way of allegory, *golden borders*.[32] For here is a garment skillfully embroidered and woven of all kinds of virtuous acts, such as chastity, prudence, faith, love, patience, and all other good qualities; and these, by hiding the shame of the flesh,[33] clothe man in a raiment of gold.

9. Now we must consider what the Spirit further teaches us in the remainder of the Psalm, following the enthronement of the humanity[34] which the Word assumed *on the right hand* of the Almighty. He says: *After her shall virgins be brought to the king, her neighbors shall be brought to thee. They shall be brought with gladness and rejoicing, they shall be brought into the temple of the king*.[35] Here it is quite plain that the Spirit praises virginity, in promising that the virgins will come to the Almighty in the second place after the bride, as I have explained, *with gladness and rejoicing*, guarded and escorted by angels. For so lovely, indeed, and thrice desirable is the glory of virginity that the choir and order of virgins is conducted directly following the Queen herself, whom the Lord has brought to sinless perfection and has presented to the Father, because they have won as their lot a place next to the bride.

There, Arete, let these words be inscribed in the record[36] as my efforts on behalf of chastity.

LOGOS 8: THECLA

When Procilla had finished speaking, Thecla said: Now it is my turn to enter the contest, and I am happy that I am to have as my companion wisdom in speech; for I feel that I am like a cithara inwardly attuned and prepared to speak with care and with grace and dignity.

Arete. I am very happy, Thecla, to accept your spontaneous offering, and I feel confident that you will give us a suitable discourse to the best of your ability. We know that you are second to none in your grasp of philosophy and universal culture,[1] and I need hardly mention that you were instructed in divine and evangelical doctrine by Paul himself.

1. Let us then begin our discourse ⟨, said Thecla,[2]⟩ with the name *parthenia*, and let us discuss the reason why this most sublime and blessed way of life has been so called, what is its nature and power, and finally what sort of fruit it brings forth. For almost all men are in danger of being ignorant of chastity and its superiority over all the other advantages of virtue to which we devote ourselves for the purification and perfection of the soul.

Now the word *parthenia*, merely by changing one letter, becomes *partheia*,[3] and this is significant of the fact that virginity alone makes divine those who possess her and have been initiated into her pure mysteries.[4] Greater good than this it is impossible to find, dwelling apart from either pleasure or pain: and the wings of the soul, impregnated with it, truly become firmer and lighter, accustomed daily to fly from the interests of men.[5]

Learned men[6] have told us that our life is a festival and that we have come into the theater to put on the drama of truth, that is, of justice, with the devil and his demons plotting and striving against us. Hence we must keep looking upwards, and, soaring on high, fly from the charm of their beautiful voices and from their forms,[7] which are colored over on the outside with an appearance of continence, even more than we would from Homer's Sirens. Thus many who enter on our way of life, become weighted down and bemused by the pleasures of error and lose their wings; for the sinews which support the substance of the wings of continence and keep them soaring when they tend to droop towards the corruption of the body, have become instead soft and flabby.

And so, Arete, whether you have been so named because ⟨you are pleasing[8]⟩ or because you lift the soul and make it rise towards heaven, ever moving within the purest minds, come, give me your support in my discourse, which you yourself directed me to speak.

2. Those who thus lose their wings and fall into pleasure will have no end of grief and pain, until, because of the yearning of their passions, they fulfill their irresistible longing for incontinence, and thus they will remain outside of the mysteries, uninitiated into the drama of truth,[9] madly indulging the wild pleasures of love instead of living a chaste and temperate life as procreators of children. But those who are nimble and light of wing, soaring up into the supramundane regions above this life,[10] see from afar things that no mortal has gazed upon, the very meadows of immortality bearing a profusion of flowers of incredible loveliness. And there they are ever and always contemplating the sights of that place. And hence they care nothing for the things which the world thinks good—riches and fame and family trees and marriage ties—and there is nothing they esteem higher than the things they see above.

So too, if they should wish their bodies to be condemned and punished by fire or the beasts,[11] they find it easy to despise physical pain, because of their transports of love for the things of that world. Thus they seem to be living in the world and yet not living in it, and to be already enjoying the company of those who are in heaven in their thoughts and their intense longing.

Now it is not right that the wings of chastity should be dragged down to earth by their own nature; rather, they should soar aloft into the pure ether[12] and to the life that is close to the angels.[13] Hence those who have loyally and faithfully lived as virgins for Christ, after their call and departure from this life, carry off, before all the others, the prizes of their contest, crowned by Him with the blossoms of immortality. For as soon as their souls have left the world, we are taught that angels meet the virgins and in solemn silence[14] escort them to the meadows we spoke of, which they had longed to enter before, picturing them in their imaginations from afar,[15] while, even though they still dwelt in their bodies, they had images of things divine.[16]

3. And when they arrive there, they behold things of marvelously glorious and blessed beauty, and such as are difficult to describe to men. There[17] is Justice itself, and Love itself, and Truth and Prudence and all the other flowers and plants of Wisdom in like splendor, of which we in this world see merely ghost-like shadows as in a dream, when we think we see them come into being from the actions of men; because in this world[18] there is no clear image of them, but only faint copies, and even these copies we often perceive only obscurely as we try to represent them to ourselves. Thus no one has ever seen with his own eyes the form and beauty and grandeur of Justice or of Understanding or of Peace as they are in themselves. But in that world they can be seen clearly and perfectly as they are in actual reality.[19] Yes, there is a tree of essential Continence there, one of Love, and one of

Understanding, just as truly as there are fruit trees in this world, such as the grape, the pomegranate, and the apple. And thus their fruits, too, are visible and edible, and those who pluck them will not waste away and die, but will grow into immortality and divinity.[20] Indeed, in the same way he from whom all of us descend, before his fall and blindness, being in Paradise, enjoyed its fruits, God ordaining that man was to work and guard the trees of Wisdom. For such were the fruits which even the first Adam was entrusted to cultivate.

So too Jeremias realized that these things exist in a special way in a place far removed from our world, in the text where, pitying those who have lost the eternal blessings, he says: *Learn where is wisdom, where is strength, where is understanding, that thou mayst know also where is length of days and life, where is the light of the eyes, and peace. Who hath found out her place or who hath gone in to their treasuries?*[21] Now the meaning of this is that the virgins enter into these treasuries and pluck the fruit of the virtues, while a magnificent array of lights bathes them in the glow that God pours down on them like water, making the world beyond bright with mystical illuminations. And they join their voices harmoniously in praise of God; and over them is shed a pure atmosphere, not oppressed by the sun.[22]

4. Thereafter, my dear virgins, daughters of immaculate continence, our efforts now should be directed to the abundant life of the kingdom of heaven. Entertain generously the same desire for the glory of chastity as those before you, despising this life. For chastity contributes not a little towards the ready attainment of incorruptibility: it makes the flesh buoyant, raising it up and drying out its moisture and overcoming its sodden weight

with a more powerful counter-attraction. Let not any uncleanness, which you may hear, weigh you down towards earth; let no grief divest you of your joy, melting away your hopes for a better life. But you must ceaselessly shrug off the sorrows that come upon you, not troubling your reason with lamentation. Let faith extend its conquest everywhere, and let its light dispel the specters of the Evil One that crowd around the heart.

Just as when the brilliant moon fills the heaven with its light and all the air begins to glow, and all of a sudden malevolent clouds, rushing in from somewhere in the west, overshadow its brilliance for a time but cannot quite destroy it, for they are soon dispelled by a blast of wind, so too, my dear maidens, shining in the world by your chastity, though you may be troubled by afflictions and sorrows,[23] you must not grow weary and abandon your hopes. For the clouds sent by the Evil One will be blown away by the Spirit, if only, like your mother, the virgin who brought forth a man child in heaven, you will not be afraid of the Serpent that watches and lies in wait to assault you. It is of her that I shall proceed to speak more clearly, as best I can. For it is now time.

In the course of the Apocalypse John tells us: *And a great sign appeared in the heaven: a woman clothed with the sun, and the moon under her feet, and on her head a crown of twelve stars; and being with child, she cried travailing in birth, and was in pain to be delivered. And there was seen another sign in heaven: and behold a great red dragon, having seven heads and ten horns, and on his heads seven diadems; and his tail drew the third part of the stars of heaven, and cast them to the earth. And the dragon stood before the woman who was ready to be delivered, that when she should be delivered, he might devour her son. And she brought forth a man child, who was to rule all nations with an iron rod; and her son was taken up to God, and to His throne. And the woman fled into the wilderness, where she had a place prepared by God, that there they should feed her a thousand two hundred sixty days.*[24]

So much then, briefly, for the account of the Woman and the Dragon. To find the interpretation of the passage and to explain it to you is beyond my powers. But nonetheless I must make the attempt, relying on Him who has bidden us to search the Scriptures.[25] If then you are pleased with what I have been saying, it will not be difficult to begin. You will, at any rate, pardon me if I am unable to do justice to the precise meaning of the sacred text.

5. The Woman who *appeared in heaven clothed with the sun* and crowned with *twelve stars* and with the moon as her footstool, *travailing in birth* and *in pain to be delivered,* this, my dear virgins is properly and in the exact sense of the term our Mother, a power in herself distinct from her children, whom the prophets have, according to the aspect of their message, sometimes called Jerusalem, sometimes the Bride, sometimes Mount Sion, and sometimes the Temple and God's Tabernacle. She is the force mentioned by the prophet, whom the Spirit urges to be enlightened, crying out to her: *Be enlightened, O Jerusalem, for thy light is come, and the glory of the Lord is risen upon thee. Behold darkness and storm clouds shall cover the earth, they shall cover the people: but the Lord shall appear upon thee, and the Lord's glory shall be seen upon thee. And kings shall walk in thy light, and nations in thy brightness. Lift up thy eyes round about, and see thy children gathered together. All thy sons have come from afar, and thy daughters shall rise up at thy side.*[26] It is the Church whose children by baptism[27] will swiftly come running to her from all sides after

the resurrection.[28] She it is who rejoices to receive the light which knows no evening, clothed as she is in the brightness of the Word as with a robe. Surely, having light for her garment,[29] what was there more precious or more honorable for her to be clothed in as befitted a queen, to be led as a bride to the Lord, and thus to be called on by the Spirit?[30]

Continuing therefore, I beg you to consider this great Woman as representing virgins prepared for marriage, as she gleams in pure and wholly unsullied and abiding beauty, emulating the brilliance of the lights. For her robe, she is clothed in pure light; instead of jewels, her head is adorned with shining stars. For this light is for her what clothing is for us. And she uses the stars as we do gold and brilliant gems; but her stars are not like those visible to us on earth,[31] but finer and brighter ones, such that our own are merely their copies and representations.

6. And her standing on the moon, I think, refers by way of allegory to the faith of those who have been purified from corruption by baptism; for moonlight is rather like lukewarm water, and all moist substance depends upon the moon. Thus the Church stands upon our faith and our adoption—signified here by the moon—*until the fullness of the Gentiles shall come in*,[32] laboring and bringing forth natural men as spiritual men,[33] and under this aspect is she indeed their mother. For just as a woman receives the unformed seed of her husband and after a period of time brings forth a perfect human being, so too the Church, one might say, constantly conceiving those who take refuge in the Word,[34] and shaping them according to the likeness and form of Christ, after a certain time makes them citizens of that blessed age. Hence it is necessary that she should stand upon the laver[35] as the mother of those

who are washed. So too, the function she exercises over the laver is called the moon because those who are thus reborn and renewed shine with a new glow,[36] that is, with a new light; and hence too they are designated by the expression 'the newly enlightened,' and she continues to reveal to them the spiritual full moon in her periodic representation of His Passion,[37] until the full glow and light of the great day shall appear.

7. But someone might take objection to what I have said—there is no objection to speaking openly[38]—and ask: And how can this exegesis, my dear virgins, express the true meaning of the Scriptural text, when the Apocalypse explicitly states that the Church brings forth *a man child*, whereas you have taken it as referring to those who have been cleansed, and that the term of her labor is fulfilled in the baptized?

To this I shall reply: My dear fault-finder, you yourself cannot prove that Christ Himself is the one that is brought forth. Remember that the mystery of the Incarnation of the Word was fulfilled long before the Apocalypse, whereas John's prophetic message has to do with the present and the future.[39] And Christ, who was conceived long before, was not the child who *was taken up* to the throne of God for fear lest he be injured by the Serpent; rather He descended from the throne of His Father and was begotten precisely that He might stay and check the Dragon's assault on the flesh.[40] Hence you too must admit that it is the Church that is in labor, and it is those who are washed in baptism who are brought forth. And the Spirit tells us this too somewhere in Isaias: *Before she was in labor and before her time came to be delivered, she escaped and brought forth a man child. Who hath heard such a thing? And who hath seen the like to this? Has the earth been in labor in one day, and has even a nation brought forth at once, because Sion hath been in labor and brought forth a man child?*[41]

From whom then did she not fly except, of course, the Dragon, in order that she, the spiritual Sion, might bring forth her *man child*, that is, a people that would return from its feminine passions and immorality to the unity of the Lord, and would be made strong in spiritual endeavor?

8. Now let us consider the matter from the beginning, until, explaining what has been said, we come in due course to the end. And so, consider whether you think the doctrine is being explained to your satisfaction.

Now I think that the Church is here said to bring forth *a man child* simply because the enlightened spiritually receive the features and image and manliness of Christ; the likeness of the Word is stamped on them and is begotten within them by perfect knowledge and faith, and thus Christ is spiritually begotten in each one. And so it is that the Church is with child and labors until Christ is formed and born within us,[42] so that each of the saints by sharing in Christ is born again as Christ. This is the meaning of a passage of Scripture that says: *Touch ye not my anointed; and do no evil to my prophets*:[43] those who are baptized in Christ become, as it were, other Christs by a communication of the Spirit, and here it is the Church that effects this transformation into a clear image of the Word. And Paul confirms this doctrine, clearly teaching it where he says: *For this cause I bow my knees to God and the Father, of whom all paternity in heaven and the earth is named, that He would grant you, according to the riches of His goodness, to be strengthened by His Spirit with might unto the inward man, that Christ may dwell by faith in your hearts.*[44] Thus the word of truth must be stamped and imprinted on the souls of those who are born again.

9. And in especial agreement and accordance with what has been said would appear to be the words which were pronounced from above by the Father Himself to Christ when He came for the hallowing of water in the river Jordan: *Thou art my son, this day have I begotten thee.*[45] Now it should be noted that He was declared to be His Son unconditionally and without regard to time. For He says, *Thou art my son*, and not 'Thou hast become,' emphasizing the fact that He had not recently attained to Sonship, and that having had a previous existence He would not ever after terminate it, but simply that, having been begotten before, He is and always will be the same. By the expression, *This day have I begotten thee*, He means that though His Son had already existed before in the heavens before the ages, He desired that He should also be begotten for the world, that is, what was previously unknown should be made manifest.[46]

Christ, of course, has not yet been born in those souls who have not as yet perceived the manifold wisdom of God; that is to say, He has not yet become known, He has not yet been revealed, has not yet appeared to them. If, however, these too should perceive the mystery of grace, Christ will also be begotten in them by wisdom and understanding as soon as they are converted and believe. And thus it is that the Church is said ever to be forming and bringing forth *a man child*, the Word, in those who are sanctified.

So much then for the travail of the Woman, explained to the best of my ability. I must now change to the subject of the Dragon and the other matters. Let us again try to explain them, my dear virgins, however we can, without flinching before the tremendous obscurities of Scripture. And if some difficulty should occur in our discussion, I shall on my part try to assist you as though to cross a river.

10. The *great red dragon*, cunning, wily, with *seven heads*, and horned, that drags down *the third part of the stars*,[47] and lies in wait to devour the child of the Woman in labor, is the devil who lies in ambush to abuse the mind of the illumined faithful that is Christ's possession, and to destroy the clear image and representation of the Word that has been begotten in them. But he misses and loses his prey, for the reborn are snatched up on high to the throne of God: that is, the minds of those who have been renewed are raised up to the divine throne and to the irrefragable foundation of truth, being taught to try to see and to picture to themselves the things of that world,[48] and not to be tricked by the Dragon who tries to prevail over them. For he is not permitted to destroy those who look upwards and are turned towards heaven.

The stars which he touches with the tip of his tail and draws down to earth are the seditious groups of heresies. For the dark, faint and low-circling stars are to be explained as the assemblages of the heretics. They too, of course, profess to be proficient in heavenly things and to believe in Christ, to have the abode of their soul in the heavens and to draw near to the stars as *children of light*. But they are swept down and driven away by the Dragon's coils, because they did not abide within the triangular forms of religion and were mistaken with regard to its orthodox practice. Thus, too, are they called a *third part of the stars*, because they have gone astray with respect to one of the numbers of the Trinity:[49] as, for example, with regard to the Father, a man like Sabellius, who claimed that it was the Almighty Father Himself who suffered; with regard to the Son, such as Artemas and those who claimed that He was manifested in appearance only; and with regard to the Spirit, such as the Ebionites, who contend that the prophets spoke only by their own power. Indeed, there is Marcion, Valentinus, Elchasai and his disciples, and the rest, whom it is best not even to mention.

11. Now, as we have shown, the Woman who has brought forth and continues to bring forth *a male child*, the Word, in the hearts of the faithful, and who went forth into the desert undefiled and unharmed by the wrath of the Beast, is our Mother the Church. And *the wilderness* into which she comes, and where she is nourished for *a thousand two hundred sixty days*, is a wilderness truly bare of evil, unfruitful and sterile in what is corruptible, difficult of access and hard for the majority to pass through. But it is fruitful and abounding in pasture, blossoming and easy of approach to the holy, full of wisdom and flowering with life. And this is none other than the lovely place of Virtue, full of fair trees and gentle zephyrs, where the south wind rises and the north wind blows and the *aromatical spices flow*.[50] Here all is drenched with ambrosial dew and garlanded with the unfading blossoms of eternal life, and it is for this that we are now gathering flowers and weaving a brilliant chaplet of sea-purple for our Queen with chaste fingers: for the bride of the Word is being adorned with the fruits of Virtue.

And the *thousand two hundred sixty days* we sojourn here,[51] my dear maidens, signify the direct, clear and perfect knowledge of the Father, Son, and Spirit, in which as she grows, our Mother rejoices and exults during this time until the restoration[52] of the new ages, when, entering into the heavenly assemblage, she will contemplate Being, now no longer through abstract knowledge, but with clear intuition, entering in with Christ.

For the thousand, consisting of 100×10, contains the full and perfect number, and is a symbol of the Father

Himself, who by His own power has created and rules over all things. 200 consists of two perfect numbers added together and so is a symbol of the Holy Spirit inasmuch as He produces our knowledge of the Father and the Son. And the number 60 is 10×6 and is thus a symbol of Christ, because the number 6, if we proceed from 1, is composed of its own proper parts, so that nothing in it is excessive or deficient.[53] Thus it is complete when it is resolved into its components, such that when 6 is divided into equal parts by equal parts, it must result in the same number again from its divided segments. For first, if it is divided by 2 it makes 3; then divided by 3, it makes 2; and again, divided by 6 it makes 1, and is again completed in itself. For when it is divided into 2×3, and 3×2, and 6×1, when 3 and 2 and 1 are added, they make up 6 again. Now a thing is necessarily perfect when it needs nothing further for its completion beyond itself and never has anything left over.

Of the other numbers, some are over-perfect, as, for example, the number 12: one half of 12 is 6, one third is 4, one fourth is 3, one sixth is 2, and one twelfth is 1. The numbers into which it can be divided, when added together, are more than twelve: it does not preserve itself equal to the sum of its parts as the number 6 does. Other numbers are less than perfect, as, for example, the number 8: one half of 8 is 4, one fourth is 2, and one eighth is 1. These quotients when added up give only 7, one less than the complete integer: it is not completely harmonious with itself as 6 is.

And thus it is that the number 6 has taken on a relationship with the Son of God, who came into this world from *the fullness of the Godhead*. For, having *emptied Himself* and *taking the form of a slave*,[54] He was restored once again to the fullness of His perfection and dignity. For having been made smaller in Himself and divided into His parts, from His smallness and His parts He was restored again to His former fullness and grandeur without ever losing anything of His perfection.

So too it is clear that the entire creation of the world was achieved out of the harmony of the number 6: for *in six days the Lord made heaven and earth and all the things that are in them,*[55] since the creative power of the Word contains the number 6 insofar as it produces bodies.[56] For just as bodies have length, width, and breadth, so too the number 6 is made up of triangles. But I have not sufficient time at the moment to discuss these points in precise detail; we must not neglect our main topic with a consideration of what is secondary.

12. The Church, then, comes to this spot which is a wilderness and, as we have said before, is barren of evil, and she receives nourishment; borne on the heaven-traversing wings of virginity, which the Word has called the pinions of a mighty eagle,[57] she has crushed the Serpent and driven away the storm clouds from the full light of the moon which is hers. It was for this that all of our discourses up till now have been held, in order to teach you, my fair virgins, to imitate your Mother as best you can, and not to be disturbed by the pains, afflictions, and reverses of life, that thus you may enter joyously with her into the bridal chamber, holding your lamps lighted.

Do not then lose heart at *the deceits* and the slanders of the Beast, but equip yourselves sturdily for battle, arming yourselves with *the helmet* of salvation, your *breastplate* and your greaves.[58] For if you attack with great advantage and with stout heart you will cause him untold consternation; and when he sees you arrayed in battle against him by Him who is his superior, he will certainly not stand his ground. Straightway will the hydra-headed, many-faced Beast retreat and let you carry off the prize for the seven contests.

> Lion in front, serpent behind, in the midst chimaera,
> Belching forth dread might of flaming fire.
> And He slew it, relying on His Father's omens,
> Christ the King. Many indeed had it destroyed, nor could
> any endure
> The deadly foam that spilled from its jaws,[59]

had not Christ weakened and crushed it, making it completely impotent and contemptible in our eyes.

13. With sober and virile heart, then, take up your arms against the swollen Beast; do not on any account yield your ground, and do not be terrified by his fury. Endless glory will be yours if you defeat him and carry off his *seven diadems*, for this is the prize of our contest as our teacher Paul tells us.[60] The virgin who first overcomes the devil and destroys his *seven heads*, wins *seven diadems* of virtue, after engaging in the seven great contests of chastity.[61] One of the Dragon's heads is luxury and incontinence; whoever crushes it wins the diadem of temperance. Another head is weakness and cowardice; whoever tramples on this wins the diadem of martyrdom. Another is folly and disbelief, and so on through all the other fruits of wickedness. Whosoever overcomes and destroys these will carry off the respective rewards, and in this way the Dragon's power is uprooted in various ways.

And further, the *ten horns* and the goads which he is said to have on his heads, my fair maidens, represent the ten opposites of the Ten Commandments, by which he has been wont to gore and throw the souls of the many, by planning and scheming the opposite of the Commandment,

Thou shalt love the Lord thy God,[62] and so on with the other precepts. Take for instance, the sharp and fiery horn of fornication by which he throws the incontinent; consider adultery, lying, avarice, theft, and all the others which are akin and related to these, which naturally flourish on those death-dealing heads. But if, with the help of Christ, you tear them out by the roots, you will receive the divine heads, adorned with the diadems taken from the Dragon.

Now it is possible for us to determine beforehand and to prefer what is better instead of what is earthly, since we have received minds that are independent of all compulsion in the choice of whatever we, as our own masters, think best: we are not slaves to Fate or to the whims of Fortune.[63] ★ ★ ★ . . . So that each one of us might not be merely human, but might become good and blessed by following the human example of Christ and by modelling oneself on Him and living in imitation of Him. . . .

For of all the evils that have been implanted among the many, the worst is the attribution of the cause of sin to the motions of the stars, and the doctrine that our lives are controlled by the necessities of Fate, as is taught by the astronomers[64] with all their false pretension. And these rely not on true knowledge but on surmise—that is, something between truth and falsehood—and have wandered far from a vision of things as they really are.

And so, Arete, now that I have completed the discourse which you, my Lady, assigned to me, if you will give me leave to continue, I shall try with your favor and assistance, against those who angrily dispute our statement that man has free will, to explain carefully that

> By their own wickedness they suffer misery beyond what is fated,[65]

since they choose the pleasant instead of the expedient.[66]

Arete. You have my permission and my support. For your discourse will be perfectly adorned if you include this discussion as well.

14. *Thecla.* To resume then, let us first discuss these matters so far as we can, and expose the witchcraft whereby they boast that they alone have understood the structure of the heavens according to the hypotheses of the Chaldaeans.[67]

Thus they teach that the curved shape of the universe is like the circling of a well-wrought sphere with the earth as its center point. And since the shape of the earth is spherical and distances to all parts are equal if similarly measured, the earth itself, on their view, is necessarily the sphere's center, and, being the oldest part, is the point about which all the heavens revolve. For if a circumference arises from a central point, being thus considered a circle—and without a center a circle can neither be drawn nor exist—it follows, they say, that the earth and the chaos and the deep that was on it must have come into existence before everything else. Actually it is these wretched fools who have slipped into a chaos and a deep of error, because *when they knew God, they have not glorified him as God, or given thanks; but became vain in their thoughts, and their foolish heart was darkened,*[68] and this despite the fact that their own philosophers have said that nothing on earth was older or nobler than the Olympian gods.

Wherefore those who have come to know Christ truly do not constantly remain children,[69] like the Greeks who hid the truth in myth and fiction rather than treat it in a systematic way, and ascribed men's fortunes to the heavenly beings.[70] Nor are they at all ashamed to describe the revolving vault of the world in terms of geometric theorems and figures, explaining that the heavens are adorned with the shapes of birds and animals that live in water and on land, and that the configurations of the stars arose from the fortunes of the men of old, so that, according to them, the movements of the planets depend upon the bodies of such creatures.[71] Thus they say that the stars spin around the substance of the twelve figures of the Zodiac, being drawn by the force of the zodiacal circle, such that they are able to see what is happening to many in accordance with the conjunctions of these bodies, their approaches to each other and their separations, their rising and their setting.

Now since all the heavens, as they hold, are spherical in shape with the earth at the center, since all lines drawn straight to the earth from the periphery of the sphere are equal to one another, it follows that the heavens are controlled by the circles which constitute the sphere.[72] Of these the most important is thought to be the meridian; next comes the horizon which cuts the meridian into equal sections; then, thirdly, the equinoctial which cuts across these. On both sides of the equinoctial are the two tropics, the summer tropic and the winter tropic, the one to the north and the other to the south. Next, down through these runs the axis, as it is called, about which are the Bears on one side and the Antarctic region on the other, beyond each of the tropics. The Bears, revolving about themselves and weighing down the axis which intersects the heavenly poles, cause the movement of the entire universe, with their heads opposite each other's loins and without ever coming in contact with the horizon, while the Zodiac intersects all the other circles, revolving at an oblique angle.

Now according to them the Zodiac is made up of a number of figures which are called the Twelve Signs of the Zodiac, going from Aries to Pisces, and their constitution, they claim, was due to mythological events. Thus they hold that Aries was the ram that carried Phrixus and Helle, the daughter of Athamas, to Scythia;[73] that Taurus was in honor of Zeus who, in the shape of a bull, carried Europa over to Crete; and that the so-called circle of the Milky Way, which extends from the constellation of Pisces to Aries, had originally poured from Hera's breasts at the command of Zeus in order to nurse Heracles. Thus, on their account of it, there would as yet have been no horoscopes before the days of Europa, Phrixus, or the Dioscuri, or before the origin of the other signs of the Zodiac which were established from men and from animals, and hence our forefathers lived without such things. Let us, then, as we thus meditate upon the truth, try, like physicians, to prevent the disease from ever getting stronger, and by taking the edge off it to extinguish it with the healing medicine of reasoning.

15. You evil men, if it were better for men to be born under a horoscope than not, how do you explain the fact that there were no horoscopes from the beginning of man's existence? And if these were present, what need was there for the constellations which originated only later, as Leo, Cancer, Gemini, Virgo, Taurus, Libra, Scorpio, Aries, Sagittarius, Pisces, Capricorn, Aquarius, Perseus, Cassiopeia, Cepheus, Pegasus, Hydra, Corvus, Crater, Lyra, Draco,[74] and all the others, from whose dispositions you represent to the masses that you have arrived at your mathematical—or, rather, anathematical—predictions? Now, then, in the days of our ancestors either there were horoscopes, and in that case the entire present system is absurd; or there were not, and then God must have changed the entire system and course of life for the better,

and our ancestors must have been worse off than we. But surely our ancestors were better off than we: that is why theirs has been called the Golden Age.[75] It follows therefore that there are no horoscopes.

If the sun accomplishes the changes of the world and the cycle of the seasons only by driving across these heavenly circles and by annually passing through the signs of the Zodiac, how was it possible for the men who were born before these signs were established, and before the heavens were adorned with them, to have persevered in existence? For then summer, autumn, winter and spring would not have been divided, the seasons through which our bodies grow and are made strong. And yet they did persevere, and they lived longer and were stronger than men of today: in those days, too, God directed the seasons in the same way. And therefore the heavens are not made of such embroidered figures.

If the sun and the moon and the other stars which were created to divide and watch over the units of time,[76] and were made for the adornment of the heavens as well as for the changes of the seasons, are really divine and superior to men, then they must of necessity lead a better, a happy and peaceful life, and one far superior in justice and virtue to ours, following a well-ordered and happy motion.[77] If, on the other hand, they actually plot and execute the calamities and evil deeds of men, being concerned with the licentiousness and the changes and vagaries of life, then they are more miserable than men, since while they gaze upon the earth and upon men's lawless deeds that bring only death, they themselves fare no better—if, indeed, our lives depend upon their influence and their motion.[78]

16. No act can occur without a desire, and no desire

without a need. But what is divine has no needs. Hence it can have no experience of evil.[79] Further, if the stars have by nature been made closer to God and are superior even to the best of men in virtue, then the stars must be without experience of evil and without needs.

To put it another way: all who believe that the sun, the moon, and the stars are divine and are far removed from evil or from earthly actions, will agree that they are not susceptible of pleasure and pain. For such shameful desires would not be suitable to celestial beings. If then by nature they have no needs, and are removed from such things, then how could they contrive in men the very things which they themselves do not desire and from which they dwell apart?

Those who lay down the definition that man has no free will but is governed by the ineluctable necessities and the unwritten decrees of Fate, commit impiety against God Himself, since they declare that He is the source and cause of man's sins. For if He harmoniously directs the entire circular motion of the stars with ineffable and inscrutable wisdom, and if, on the other hand, the stars produce the qualities of vice and virtue[80] in life, dragging men to these things by the chains of necessity, then they declare that God is the cause and source of all evil. But God is not the cause of harm to anyone. Hence there are no horoscopes.

Anyone even of meager intelligence would admit that the divine is just, good, wise, true, beneficent, not responsible for evil, free from passion, and so forth. And if the just are superior to the unjust, and if wrongdoing is abominable to the good, then God being just must rejoice in righteousness, and wrongdoing must be hateful to Him, since it is the enemy and the contradiction of righteousness. Hence God is not the cause of wrongdoing.[81]

If what is beneficial is good, and temperance is beneficial to one's life, and to one's household and one's friends, then temperance is a good. Further, if temperance is a good in itself and intemperance is the contradictory of temperance, it follows, since the contradictory of good is evil, that intemperance is an evil. And if intemperance is intrinsically evil, and if theft, adultery, wrath, and murder arise from intemperance, then the intemperate life must be intrinsically evil. But the divine has no part in passion. Therefore destiny does not exist.[82]

If the temperate are superior to the intemperate, and if they find intemperance disgusting, and if God rejoices in temperance, having no experience of passion, then it follows that intemperance must be abominable to Him. And the fact that an act performed out of temperance, as a virtue, is superior to one performed out of intemperance, as a vice, may be seen in the case of kings, of officials, military commanders, women and children, private citizens, masters and servants, paedagogues and schoolmasters. For each of these is beneficial to himself as well as the community when he is temperate, and harmful alike to himself and to the community when he is intemperate.

Again, if there is any difference between the manly and the effeminate, between the temperate and the intemperate, and if the state of those who have manliness and temperance is better and their opposite is worse, and if those who belong to this superior state are closer to God and are His friends, and those of the opposite state are distant from Him and are His enemies, then it follows that those who talk in terms of Fate assert that righteousness and wrongdoing are the same, so too effeminacy and manliness, temperance and intemperance—and this is impossible.

For so long as good is the contradictory of evil, and wrongdoing is evil, and its opposite is righteousness, and righteousness is good, and so long as good is inimical to evil just as evil is dissimilar to good, then righteousness and wrongdoing must be distinct.[83] And thus God is not the cause of wickedness, nor does He rejoice in it, seeing that He, as reason itself shows, is all good. And if there are wicked men, they are wicked not because of any destiny but because of the craving of their hearts;

> By their own wickedness they suffer misery beyond what is fated.[84]

Let us suppose that destiny makes a person kill someone and to bloody his hands with murder. Yet the law forbids this, since it punishes malefactors and so by its threats restrains the decrees of destiny, as for example, injustice, adultery, theft, poisoning. Hence the law is in opposition to destiny. For the law forbids the things which destiny determines; and destiny compels men to do the things which the law forbids. Thus the law is at war with destiny. And if this is so, then legislators cannot be legislators in accordance with destiny; for those who pass decrees contradictory to destiny tend to destroy destiny. Now either destiny exists, and then there should not be any laws, or laws exist and they are not in accord with destiny. But nothing can exist or be done apart from destiny: they claim that no one may move even a finger without destiny.[85]

Hence it follows that Minos and Rhadamanthys and Draco and Lycurgus and Solon and Zaleucus[86] became legislators and made their laws in accordance with destiny when they prohibited adultery, murder, assault, robbery,[87] theft—suggesting that these crimes do not exist or take place according to destiny. For if they did exist according to destiny, then the laws were not in accord with destiny. For destiny could not be destroyed by itself by attempting to cancel itself through conflict with itself—in this case, by making laws, on the one hand, which prohibit murder and adultery, and by prosecuting and punishing the wicked, and, on the other, by actually causing murder and adultery. But this is impossible. For nothing is alien or repugnant to itself, nothing at variance with itself and self-destructive. Hence destiny does not exist.

If everything whatsoever occurs according to destiny, and nothing is contrary to destiny, then the law itself must exist according to destiny. But the law destroys destiny, teaching that virtue can be learned and is acquired by effort, and that vice is to be avoided and arises from lack of discipline. Hence destiny does not exist.

If destiny is responsible for the injustices committed by men against one another, what need is there of laws? But if their purpose is to check the wrongdoer—seeing that God takes care of those who are wronged—it would be better for Him, in accordance with destiny, not to create wicked men, rather than, after creating them, to try to correct them by means of law. But God is good and wise and He acts for the best. Hence destiny does not exist.

Indeed, the cause of sin is either education and habit, or the soul's passions and the body's desires. But whichever of these is the cause, God is not responsible.[88]

If it is better to be just than to be unjust, how is it that a man is not made so directly from birth? And if later he is disciplined by the law and by doctrine in order to make him better, he is disciplined as one who is free and not by nature evil. If the wicked are wicked because of their destiny by the decrees of Providence, then they are not to be held culpable and deserving of the legal penalties, seeing that they are living according to their proper natures and it is impossible to change them.

To put it another way: if the good are praised because they live in accordance with their proper natures, and if the lives of the good are ultimately attributed to destiny, then surely the wicked are not to be blamed either, by any fair-minded judge, for living according to their proper natures. And to state the matter clearly, a man who lives in accordance with his nature does not commit sin; for he has not made himself what he is, but Fate has; and he lives according to its motion, led on by inescapable necessity. Then no one would be bad. But the wicked do exist,[89] and vice is hated and censured by God, as reason has shown, virtue is loved and praised, and God has established a law to punish the wicked. Fate then does not exist.

17. But I need not prolong my discourse further by dwelling so long on refutation. I have sufficiently set forth the essential points to persuade and convince you of what is expedient, and I have exposed briefly, but in a way that should be clear to everyone, the internal contradictions in their deceptive doctrine, so that even a child could by now see clearly and perceive their error; for good and evil are within our power and are not determined by the stars. For we have two motions within us, the desire of the body and that of the soul, and they are distinct from each other. Hence too they have received two different names, virtue and vice. And we of course, should be led on by the most glorious and golden persuasion of virtue, choosing what is best rather than what is base.

But that will be enough on these points, and I must bring my discourse to a close. For after these discussions on chastity I am really ashamed and embarrassed to introduce the view of astronomers or foolish pedants who waste their lives in false speculation, living with nothing but the figments of their minds.

I offer you, my lady Arete, these gifts of mine woven as they are from God's own words.

[Interlude II]

Eubulion. How truly magnificent and in the spirit of a contest was Thecla's discourse, Gregorion!

Gregorion. What then would you have said had you listened to her in person as she spoke so gracefully with fluent tongue, with great charm and acclaim? All of us who paid attention to her marvelled at the way her beauty seemed to flower in speech, how intelligently and truly vividly she developed her points, her face growing red with a modest blush. She is a woman wholly fair in body as well as in soul.

Eubulion. You are right, Gregorion, and none of this is false. I was aware of her wisdom from other noble deeds of hers and from all the excellent things she said in proof of her overmastering love of Christ. And so outstanding did she frequently show herself as she engaged in those first great contests of the martyrs, possessing a zeal equal to her generosity, and a physical strength equal to the maturity of her counsels.

Gregorion. You too are quite right! But we must not waste time. We shall often have occasion to discuss these matters again in future. But now I should first give you an account of the discourses of the other virgins in order, as I promised, and especially of Tusiane and Domnina, for these still remain.

LOGOS 9: TUSIANE

Now when Thecla had finished her discourse, Theopatra said that Arete directed Tusiane to speak. And Tusiane, smiling, came before her and said: Arete, dearest source of pride to those who love virginity, I too beg you to stand by and help me so that I will not be at a loss for words; so much has already been said and so variously treated. So too, I ask you to excuse me from any exordia or introductions; otherwise I shall be using up too much time in trying to arrange something suitable for them and so lose sight of the subject under discussion. For virginity is a subject so worthy, so glorious, and so magnificent.

Now God in instructing the true Israelites to observe the true Feast of Tabernacles in Leviticus,[1] tells them how to celebrate it with due honor, saying that each should adorn his tabernacle above all with chastity. And I shall give you the very words of Scripture, from which it will be clear to everyone and beyond all doubt how acceptable and how very dear is this precept of chastity: *And on the fifteenth day of the seventh month, when you shall have gathered in all the fruits of the land, you shall celebrate a feast to the Lord seven days; and on the eighth shall be a sabbath, that is, a day of rest. And you shall take to you on the first day fair fruit of trees, and branches of palm trees, and boughs of thick trees, and willows and branches of the chaste-tree of the brook, to rejoice before the Lord your God, seven days in the year. It shall be an everlasting ordinance in your generations. In the seventh month shall you celebrate this feast. You shall dwell in tabernacles seven days: everyone that is of the race of Israel, shall dwell in tabernacles, that your posterity may know, that I made the children of Israel to dwell in tabernacles, when I brought you out of the land of Egypt. I am the Lord your God.*[2]

The Jews, who hover about the bare letter of the Scriptures like so-called butterflies[3] about the leaves of vegetables instead of the flowers and fruit as the bee does, understand these words and ordinances to refer to the sort of tabernacles which they build. It is as though God took pleasure in such ephemeral structures as they erect from the branches of trees and decorate, ignorant of the wealth *of the good things to come.*[4] Such structures are as air and ghostly shadows, which foretell the resurrection and the building of our tabernacle once it has collapsed on earth.[5] And recovering it once again in all its immortality, in the Seventh Millennium we shall celebrate the great Feast of the true Tabernacle in that new creation where there will be no pain,[6] when all the fruits of the earth will have been harvested, and men will no longer beget or be begotten, and God will rest from the work of His creation.

For God made heaven and earth and completed the entire universe in six days: *And on the seventh day He rested from the works which He had done. And he blessed the seventh day and sanctified it.*[7] Thus under a figure we are bidden to celebrate a feast in honor of the Lord *in the seventh month* when all the fruits of the earth have been gathered in, that is, when this world shall come to an end at the time of the Seventh Millennium, when God will really have finished the world and will rejoice in us.[8]

For even now He is still creating by His omnipotent will and inscrutable power: the earth still yields its fruit, the waters still gather together into their receptacles, light is still being divided from the darkness, the number of men is still growing through creation, the sun still rises to rule over the day and the moon over the night, and four-footed creatures and beasts and creeping things are still being brought forth by the earth, as are winged things and fish by the watery element.[9] But when the days shall be accomplished and God shall cease to work in this creation of His in that Seventh Month, the great day of the resurrection, then will our Feast of Tabernacles be celebrated to the Lord.[10] The things mentioned in Leviticus are merely types and figures of this Feast, and it is under this aspect that we must explore them if we would understand their essential truth. As Scripture tells us, *A wise man shall hear this and shall be wiser, he shall also understand a parable and the interpretation, the words of the wise also and their mysterious sayings.*[11]

Hence the Jews have reason to be ashamed at not having grasped the profound meaning of the Scriptures, thinking that the Law and the Prophets expressed nothing but external things. For their hearts were fixed on worldly things, and they preferred external wealth to the wealth of the soul.[12]

Now the texts of Scripture differ, inasmuch as some present us with a type of what is past and others with a type of what is to come. Yet these miserable people, turning away, celebrate types of the future as though they were types of things already past. An instance of this is the slaying of the lamb: they think that the mystery of the lamb is merely a memorial of the deliverance of their forefathers out of Egypt, at the time the Lord struck the first-born of the Egyptians, and they themselves were saved by painting the door-posts of their homes crimson with blood. They have not yet realized that this was also a figure foretelling the slaughter of Christ: for when the world comes to an end in fire, and the first-born sons of Satan are destroyed, those who have been confirmed and sealed with His blood[13] will be delivered from His wrath, and His avenging angels will respect the seal impressed on them with His blood.

2. Let this then stand as an instance to prove that the Jews, by misinterpreting things present as types of things that are already past, have foundered their hopes *of the good things to come*, unwilling as they are that their types should foreshadow images, and that these images should represent the truth.[14] For the Law is a shadow and type of the image, that is to say, of the Gospel; and the image, the Gospel, represents the truth which will be fulfilled at the Second Coming of Christ. Thus the ancients and the Law foretold and prophesied to us the features of the Church, and the Church foretells those of the new order. And we, who have accepted the Christ who said *I am the Truth*, are aware that the shadows and types have come to an end, and we press on towards the truth, proclaiming it in vivid images. For as yet *we know in part*, and, as it were, *through a glass*, for *that which is perfect* is not yet come to us, the kingdom of heaven and the resurrection, when *that which is in part shall be done away*.[15]

Then will all our tabernacles be established, when our bodies rise again, their bones once more fixed and compacted with flesh. Then shall we celebrate to the Lord the day of joy in a pure manner,[16] receiving now eternal tabernacles, never more to die or to be dissolved into the earth of the grave.

For our tabernacle of old had been firmly made; but it tottered and fell by the Fall. And God put an end to sin by man's death, lest man become a sinner for all eternity, and, since sin would be living in him, be under eternal condemnation. And this is the reason why man, though he was not made mortal and corruptible, dies and his soul is separated from his body, in order that his transgression might be destroyed by death, being unable to live after he was dead.[17] Thus with sin dead and destroyed, I can rise again in immortality and sing a hymn of praise to God who saves His children from death by means of death; and in accordance with the Law I celebrate the Feast in His honor, adorning the tabernacle of my flesh with good works, just as the prudent virgins there[18] with their five-flamed lamps.

3. When I am judged on that first day of the risen life, I shall bring what is required if I am adorned with virtue's fruits, if I am shaded by the branches of chastity. For realize that the resurrection is the building of that tabernacle, and realize that the things required for the construction of the tabernacle are the works of justice. And so I shall take what is required on *the first day*, the day, that is, on which I am judged, if I have adorned my tabernacle with the things that are commanded, and if within it are found those things which here on earth we are bidden to have and there to present them to God.

Let us consider then what follows in our text. *And you shall take to you on the first day fair fruit of trees, and boughs of thick trees, and willows and branches of the chaste-tree of the brook, to rejoice before the Lord your God.*[19]

The Jews, *uncircumcised in heart,*[20] believe that the most beautiful fruit of wood is that of the citron-tree because of its size, and they are not ashamed to say that God is honored by citron wood, He for whom *all the beasts* of the earth *are not sufficient for a burnt offering nor Libanus to burn.*[21] You stubbornhearted, if the citron appears so utterly beautiful, why is not the grape more beautiful, why not the pomegranate, why not the apple, or any of the other fruits which are much better than the citron? Actually Solomon in the Canticle of Canticles, though he mentions all the others as beautiful, omits the citron alone.

But these things seduce the unwary, who fail to realize that the *tree of life* which once grew in Paradise has now been made to bloom again for everyone by the Church, and it bears the fair and comely fruit of faith. And this is the fruit that we are to bring to the judgment seat of Christ on the first day of the Feast. And if we do not have it, we shall not be able to celebrate it together with God, we shall have no part, as John says, *in the first resurrection.*[22] And the tree is wisdom, the first-born of all things.[23] *She is a tree of life to them that lay hold on her,* says the prophet, *and she is a secure help to them that rest on her as on the Lord.*[24] The *tree which is planted near the running waters, which shall bring forth its fruit in due season,*[25] is none other than instruction and charity and understanding, such as is given *in due season* to those who come to the waters of Redemption.

He who does not believe in Christ and does not perceive that He is the first principle,[26] the *tree of life*, and is unable to show to God his tabernacle adorned with the loveliest of fruit, how will he be able to celebrate the Feast? How will he be able to rejoice?

Do you wish to know the *fair fruit of the tree*? Look at the words of the Lord Jesus Christ, and see how fair they are with a beauty that is *above the sons of men.*[27] The fair fruit that blossomed through Moses was the Law; and yet this was not so fair as the Gospel. For the Law was a kind of type and shadow *of the things to come*, but the Gospel is the *grace* of life and the *truth.*[28] Beautiful indeed was the fruit of the Prophets; but not so fair as the fruit of immortality harvested from the Gospel.

4. *And you shall take to you on the first day the fair fruit of the tree and the branches of palm trees.*[29] This refers to the ascetical practice[30] of the divine doctrines, by which, after sin is swept and cast out and passions are conquered, the soul is purified and adorned. For pure and adorned must they come to the Feast, and swept, as it were, by a broom,[31] with the habits and devoted practices of virtue. For it is only after the mind has been cleansed by laborious ascetical exercises from the different notions which obscure it, that it can look with sharp gaze upon the truth. Thus it was too that the widow in the Gospels found her mite only after she had swept her house and cast out the filth[32]—the passions which obscure and darken the soul, which grow strong in us through our carelessness and living in luxury.

Whoever, therefore, is eager to come to that Feast of Tabernacles and to be counted among the saints, must first obtain the fair fruit of faith; next, palm-branches, that is, the diligent practice of the Scriptures; and then, the thick and luxuriant branches of charity, which He bids us to take after the palm-branches. And most accurately does he refer to charity as thick branches, because it is compact and completely full of thick fruit, with nothing on it bare or empty, but utterly full, both in trunk and branches. For such is charity, being in no respect hollow or unfruitful. Indeed, *if I should sell my goods and give to the poor, and if I should deliver my body to be burnt, and if I have such faith so that I could remove mountains, and have not charity, I am nothing.*[33] Charity, then, is the thickest and most fruitful tree of all, filled and teeming with graces.

What next does He wish us to take? Willow branches,

it is said, and by willow branches He means justice; wherefore the prophet tells us that the just *shall spring up like grass in the midst of water and as willows beside the running water,*[34] blossoming by reason of the word. And after everything He bids them bring boughs of the chaste-tree to decorate their tabernacles, because it is by its very name the tree of chastity,[35] and with it all the afore-mentioned things are to be adorned.

Let the incontinent now be gone, and those who reject chastity for their passions. How can they come to the Feast with Christ if they have not decked their tabernacles with the branches of chastity? For that is a blessed and divinizing tree, which all of those who are hastening towards that wedding feast should use to bind and cover their loins. So then, my fair maidens, consider the Scriptures themselves and what they command, how the Word has taken chastity as the fulfillment of all the above-mentioned precepts, teaching us how fitting and thrice-desirable it will be for our resurrection, and how without it no one will attain the promised rewards.

This chastity we, who are devoted to virginity, cultivate to a special degree and offer it to the Lord. They also practice it who live chastely with their wives: they bring forth as it were little shoots around the trunk of the tree of chastity, blossoming with self-control, not coming high enough, as we do, to touch its mighty branches, but they too, nonetheless, produce shoots of chastity however small. Those, however, who, even though they are not committing fornication, are yet deluded into enjoying their sole and lawful spouses to excess,[36] how will they celebrate the Feast? How can they rejoice if they have not decorated their tabernacle, that is, their flesh, with the boughs of the chaste-tree, and have not listened to the saying, *That they also who have wives, be as if they had none?*[37]

5. Hence I say above all other things that those who are eager for the contest and who motivated by high principles, should without hesitation praise chastity and honor it as most beneficial and glorious.[38] For in the new creation, where pain will be unknown, whoever is found unadorned with the boughs of chastity will not find rest, since he has not fulfilled God's commandment according to the Law; nor shall he enter into the Promised Land, since he has not first celebrated the Feast of Tabernacles.

Only those then who have celebrated the Feast of Tabernacles will come to the Holy Land, advancing from their so-called tabernacles till they come to the Temple and to the City of God, progressing to a greater and more glorious happiness, as is established by the Jewish types. For just as the Israelites of those days first travelled from the border of Egypt and came to The Tabernacles,[39] and after departing from here again they came to the Promised Land, so it is with us. Setting out from here and making my way from the Egypt of this life, I come first to the resurrection, the true construction of the tabernacle; and there, setting up my tabernacle decorated with the fruit of virtue on the first day of the risen life, which is the Judgment, I shall celebrate with Christ the Millennium of Rest, the Seven Days as they are called, the true Sabbath Days. Then, once again, following Jesus, *that hath passed into the heavens,*[40] I shall arrive in heaven, just as the Jews after the rest of The Tabernacles came to the Promised Land. For I will not abide in The Tabernacles, that is, the tabernacle of my body will not remain the same, but after the Millennium it will be changed from its human appearance and corruption to angelic grandeur and beauty. And then, my dear virgins, after the Feast of the resurrection has been celebrated, we shall pass from the wondrous place of the Tabernacle to the larger and better one, going up to the very *house of God* above the heavens, as the Psalmist tells us, *with the voice of joy and praise and the sound of one feasting.*[41]

This then, my lady Arete, is the robe I present you with, fashioned to the best of my ability.

[Interlude III]

Eubulion. I am greatly moved, Gregorion, to think of the embarrassment that Domnina must now have felt; her heart must have been in a state of trepidation and fear lest she be at a loss for words and not measure up to the discourses of the other virgins, for so much had already been said on the topic with the approach to it always different. Come, complete your story and tell me whether she showed that she was troubled. I am surprised that she found anything to say at all, being the last in turn to speak.

Gregorion. Indeed, Theopatra told me that she was disturbed and very much so, but she was not at a loss for words. After Tusiane had stopped, Arete looked at Domnina and said: Now come up here too, my daughter, and give your discourse; we shall thus bring our banquet to a perfect close.

Logos 10: Domnina

Domnina then blushed a deep crimson and became short of breath;[1] but she arose and turned to pray and invoke Wisdom to stand by her and assist her. After she had prayed, said Theopatra, she promptly found courage, and a divine self-confidence, as it were, possessed her, and she spoke as follows:

Dear Arete, I too shall omit the usual long-winded preliminaries; I want to go directly to our subject to the best of my ability; otherwise, if I linger over accidentals, I shall be giving more time to them than to the core of my subject. For I think that it is the first law of prudence not to make long roundabout speeches merely to please the ear before coming to the point,[2] but to begin at once directly with the question at issue. And so I shall begin now: it is time.

My fair virgins, nothing can so help a person towards virtue as chastity. For chastity alone causes the soul to be guided in the noblest and best possible way and to be washed clean of the stains and impurities of the world. Indeed, ever since Christ taught us to practice it and revealed to us its unsurpassable beauty, the reign of the Evil One has been destroyed, whereas before he had continually been capturing and enslaving mankind; so that none of the men of old were fully pleasing to the Lord, but all were overwhelmed by error, for the Law was not at all adequate to free mankind from corruption, until virginity, succeeding the Law, held men in thrall to the commands of Christ.[3] For surely, if the justice of the Law had been sufficient for salvation, they would not have fallen so often into war and murder, lust and idolatry. As it was, they were in those days often confused by many great catastrophes. But from the moment when Christ became man and armed the flesh with the ornament of virginity, the cruel despot that rules incontinence was overpowered; and peace and faith reign, and men are not so much given to idol worship as they were of old.

2. But I do not wish to give some the impression, my

dear maidens, of being sophistical, of drawing these conclusions from mere probabilities[4] and so to be merely babbling; and in proof of what I say I shall bring forward a document of the Old Testament, a prophecy from Judges, in which the reign of chastity was already clearly foretold. It says: *The trees went to anoint a king over them; and they said to the olive tree: Reign thou over us. And the olive tree said to them: I leave my fatness, which god and men have extolled, and go to rule over the trees? And all the trees said to the fig tree: Come thou and reign over us. And the fig tree said to them: I leave my sweetness and my delicious fruit and go to rule over the trees? And the trees said to the vine: Reign over us. And the vine said to them: I forsake my wine that cheereth man, and go to rule over the trees? And the trees said to the bramble: Come, reign over us. And the bramble said to the trees: If indeed you anoint me to be king over you, come, trust my shelter; if not, let fire come out from the bramble and devour the cedars of Libanus.*[5]

Now it is clear that this was not meant of actual trees that grow out of the earth. For inanimate trees would hardly assemble to elect a king: they are fixed to the ground by their roots. The story then surely refers to those souls who, before the Incarnation of Christ, having grown all to wood by their sins, approach God and beseech Him to accept their tears and to allow His pity and mercy to reign over them. And this Scripture symbolizes under the figure of the olive tree, since oil is beneficial to men's bodies, easing their fatigue and pain as well as giving light; for the light of a lamp always grows brighter when you pour oil on it.[6] So too the mercies of God surely dissolve death and sin, are a help to mankind, and nourish the light of the heart.

Consider too how all the commandments that were

given from the time of the first man in succession until Christ set forth in the Scriptual text; the devil, however, has deceived the human race with fictions made in imitation of them. Thus Scripture likens the fig tree to the commandment given to man in Paradise, for after he had been deceived he covered his nakedness with fig leaves.[7] It makes the vine stand for the precept given to Noe at the time of the Deluge, because he was mocked when overcome with wine.[8] The olive tree represents the commandment given to Moses in the desert, because the charism of prophecy—the holy oil—failed their inheritance when they sinned against the Law.[9] Lastly, the bramble refers to the commandment given to the Apostles for the salvation of the world;[10] for it was through them that we were instructed in chastity, and of this alone the devil has not been able to make a deceptive image.

For this reason, also, four Gospels have been handed down, because God has four times evangelized and instructed mankind with four laws, and the occasions of these are clearly suggested by the different types of fruit. Thus the fig tree by its sweetness and beauty represents the pleasure man enjoyed in Paradise before the Fall. Indeed, not infrequently does the Holy Spirit use the fruit of the fig tree as a symbol of what is more perfect, as we shall afterwards show. Next the vine, because of the gaiety that is the result of wine and the joy of those who are rescued from wrath and from the Flood, intimates their transformation from fear and anxiety to joy. The olive, because of its fruit of oil, reveals the divine compassion after the Deluge, when God bore patiently with men's turning aside to impiety, so that He gave them the Law and manifested Himself to a few and fed with oil the flame of virtue that was by now all but extinguished.

3. Now the bramble bush represents chastity. For the bramble is the same as the chaste-tree, only some call it bramble, others the chaste-tree.[11] Perhaps precisely because of this plant's kinship with virginity is it called by these two names: the bramble because of its firm and sturdy attitude towards pleasure, and the chaste-tree because of its persistent chastity.

Thus we are told that when Elias fled from the face of Jezebel,[12] he first came under a bramble bush,[13] and there, after his prayer was heard, took strength and nourishment; because for those who run away from lust and pleasure (that is, the woman), the tree of chastity blossoms as a refuge and a shelter, ruling over men ever since the coming of Christ the Archvirgin. For where all those early laws of the days of Adam, Noe, and Moses had not been competent[14] to save mankind, the law of the Gospel alone has saved all.

And therefore is it said that the fig tree did not rule—the trees being understood as mankind, the fig tree the precept: hence after the Fall man wished to be ruled by virtue again and not to be exiled from the delights of immortality in Paradise. But, having sinned, he was rejected and cast far out, as being no longer capable of being governed by immortality.

And the first message to him after the Fall came through Noe, and by it he might have been saved from sin if he had paid attention to it. It promised joy and a cessation of his evils, if only he would practice it according to his powers, just as the vine promises to produce wine to those who will work and cultivate it. But this precept did not govern man either, for however zealously it was preached by Noe, men would not obey it. When, however, they were being engulfed and drowned by the waters, then they began to repent and to promise that they would obey the commandments.

And now they are scorned as subjects to be ruled over, that is, they are scornfully refused the assistance of the commandment; and this is the reply of the Spirit, chiding them for deserting those whom God had ordered to help them (O stubborn men!), to rescue them and make them glad, men such as Noe and those with him: Am I to come and assist you who have been so unfruitful in prudence and not unlike dry wood, you who would not believe me before when I preached flight from the things of the present?

4. And so, when those men had thus been rejected by divine providence, and the human race had once again given itself over to error, God at the time of Moses again sent them a law to govern them and to recall them to the path of righteousness. But this too they put far from their minds, and turned to idol worship. And so God gave them up to mutual slaughter, to exile and captivity; the law itself renounced its attempt to save them; and men, after being constrained by their calamities, cried aloud to God and once again promised they would obey the commandments, until God took pity on man the fourth time and sent chastity to govern him, and this Scripture consequently called the bramble.

For this bramble not only destroys sinful pleasures, it further issues a warning: that unless they give her unquestioning obedience and approach her in all sincerity, she will consume all with fire; for there will be no further law or doctrine hereafter, but only the Judgment and fire.[15] This was the reason that men from that time forward began to lead virtuous lives, to believe firmly in God and to break with the devil. Such was the great benefit and assistance that chastity brought to men. For her precept was the only one which the devil was unable to counterfeit for the deception of mankind, as he had been able to do in the case of the other ones.

5. Now the fig tree, as I have said, because of the sweetness and beauty of its fruit, has been taken as a type of the delights of Paradise; the devil, however, led man astray and took him captive by means of his imitations of it, persuading him to cover the nakedness of his body with fig leaves, that is, with sensual pleasure from the friction they would cause. Again, those who were saved from the Deluge by the wine of spiritual joy he made fun of, getting them drunk with a drink that resembled the other, stripping man naked of his virtue. But what I am saying will become clearer as I go on.

The power that is set against us always tries to imitate the outward forms of virtue and righteousness, not to encourage their practice, in truth, but for the purpose of hypocritical deceit.[16] He is outwardly made up with the artifices of immortality, that he may entice to death those who are trying to escape death. Thus he would like to be taken for a fig tree or a vine and bring forth sweetness and joy, transforming himself into *an angel of light*,[17] beguiling many with a façade of piety.

Thus in Scripture we find two sorts of fig trees and vines: *figs that are good, very good, and the bad figs, very bad*;[18] and *wine that may cheer the heart of men*,[19] as well as a wine that *is the wrath of dragons and the wrath of asps, which is uncurable.*[20] But ever since chastity established her reign over men, the error was exposed and crushed, and Christ the Archvirgin put it to flight. But now that chastity has gained control over mankind, the true olive and the true fig and the true vine bring forth their fruit, as also the prophet Joel teaches us, saying: *Be of good courage, O land, be glad and rejoice, for the Lord hath done great things. Be of good courage, ye beasts of the plain, for the plains of the wilderness have flowered, for the tree hath brought forth its fruit, the vine and the fig tree have yielded their strength. And you, O children of Sion, rejoice, and be joyful in the Lord your God, because He hath given you food unto justice.*[21] Here he calls the ancient laws the vine and the fig, trees that bore fruit unto justice for the children of the spiritual Sion. These bore fruit after the Incarnation of the Word, when chastity began to reign over us; formerly they had withheld and closed their buds by reason of sin and constant error. The true vine and the true fig tree were not yet able to afford us the nourishment that would give us life; whereas the false fig tree blossomed with all kinds of flowers to deceive men. But when the Lord dried up those false and spurious trees, saying to the bitter fig tree, *May no fruit grow on thee henceforward for ever,*[22] then those that were true fruit-bearing trees flourished and blossomed with *food unto justice.*[23]

Moreover, in many instances in Scripture the vine refers to the Lord Himself and the fig tree to the Holy Spirit; for the Lord gladdens men's hearts, and the Spirit heals them. Thus Ezechias was first ordered to make a poultice with *a lump of figs,*[24] that is, with the fruit of the Spirit, that he might be healed by love according to the Apostle who says: *The fruit of the Spirit is, charity, joy, peace, patience, benignity, faith, modesty, continency.*[25] This fruit the prophet calls figs because of their sweetness. And Micheas says: *And every man shall sit under his vine and under his fig tree, and there shall be none to make them afraid.*[26] For it is clear that all those who take refuge and who rest under the Spirit and in the shelter of the Word need not be afraid or terrified at him who troubles the heart.[27]

6. Again, Zacharias shows how the olive tree symbolizes the Mosaic Law when he says: *And the angel that spoke in me came again; and he waked me, as a man that is wakened out of his sleep. And he said to me: What seest thou? And I said: I have looked, and behold a candlestick all of gold, and its lamp upon the top of it; . . . and two olive trees . . ., one upon the right side of the lamp, and one upon the left side thereof.*[28] And a little farther on, the prophet enquires, *What are the two olive trees upon the right side of the candlestick, and upon the left side,* and *the two olive branches that are in the hands of the two funnels?*[29] And the angel answered and said: *These are the two sons of fatness who stand before the Lord of the whole earth,*[30] by which is meant the two first-born powers who stand as bodyguard[31] to the Lord, who in His dwelling supply the wick with God's spiritual oil through *the two olive branches,*[32] that man may have the light of divine knowledge. And *the two branches of the two olive trees* are the Law and the Prophets, made to blossom by Christ and the Holy Spirit, and mentioned as placed round the wick of inheritance: for we were unable to bear all the weight and fruit of these plants before chastity came to rule and govern the world. In former times we cultivated merely *the two branches,* as it were, of the Law and the Prophets, and these not to any great extent, because we let them slip again and again.[33]

Indeed, who was ever able to grasp Christ or His Spirit perfectly without first purifying himself? Chastity is the exercise which from childhood prepares the soul for glory by making it attractive and lovable, and with ease brings this adornment for her to the next world untried. It holds up great expectations as the reward for small toil and renders our bodies immortal. It is only fitting then that all should gladly praise and esteem chastity above all other things; some, because by practicing virginity they have been espoused to the Word; others, because by chastity they have been emancipated from that condemnation, *Earth thou art, and unto earth thou shalt return.*[34]

Here then, Arete, is my discourse on the virtue of chastity to the best of my ability. And if it seems but meager or mediocre, my Lady, I beg you to accept it from me in good part, seeing that I was the last to be chosen to speak.

[Logos 11: The Discourse of Arete[1]]

But of course, said Arete—so Theopatra told me—I accept your discourse, and, in fact, I commend everyone of you. And if you, Domnina, had not spoken so lucidly, but had merely picked up the discussion and proceeded with earnestness, you would have done excellently. As it was, you prepared for the audience no mere entertainment but a document[2] for their sobriety and self-improvement. For whosoever teaches me that chastity should, of all the ways of life, be preferred and embraced above all others, gives the right counsel; for many think they honor and cultivate this virtue, but few, if I may say so, actually do so. For if a person endeavors to restrain his body from the pleasures of carnal love without controlling himself in other respects, he does not honor chastity; indeed, he rather dishonors it to no small degree by base desires, substituting one pleasure for another.

Again, even though a person may persevere in resisting the desires of the senses, if he should take excessive pride in this very ability to control the impulses of the flesh, considering them all as utterly insignificant, he does not honor chastity. Rather does he dishonor it by his arrogance and pride, purifying *the outside of the dish*[3] and the platter, that is, the flesh, the body, while doing harm to his heart by his domineering conceit. So too the person who prides himself on material wealth, makes no effort to honor chastity. In fact, such a one would dishonor it most of all, since he puts it below insignificant profit, when nothing is comparable to it of all the valuable things in life; *for all gold in comparison to it is as a little sand.*[4]

Neither does he who loves himself excessively, and strives always to look to his own private good regardless of his neighbor, do honor to chastity; indeed, he even dishonors it. For he is far from the number of those who worthily cultivate this virtue, since he does violence to the love and generosity and sympathy which are its fruit.

No, it is not proper to practice chastity and virginity and then become defiled and incontinent by evil deeds; or to profess purity and self-control and then become polluted by sin; or to say that we are not concerned with the things of this world, and then to try to possess them and make ourselves anxious over them. Rather, all our members must be preserved intact and untouched by corruption, not only the actual organs of generation but all others which stimulate them. Thus it would be ridiculous to keep one's generative organs pure, but not one's tongue; or to keep one's tongue pure, but not one's sight, one's ears or hands; or to keep all these pure, but not one's heart, allowing it to consort with anger and conceit.[5]

It is most imperative then that anyone who intends to avoid sin in the practice of chastity must keep all his members and senses pure and sealed—just as pilots caulk a ship's timbers—to prevent sin from getting an opening and pouring in. For great falls necessarily attend great enterprises; and evil is more opposed to the essential good[6] than it is to that which is not good.

And so, many who thought that chastity consisted rather in the repression of sexual desires to the neglect of other impulses, have failed in it and have brought reproach upon those who tried to pursue it as they should.[7] But such reproaches you have refuted, being exemplary in all things and practicing virginity as you do in deed as well as in word.

So much then for the description of what the ideal virgin should be. And now, after hearing you compete so efficiently in this contest of words, I declare and crown all of you as winners; but to Thecla I must give a larger and thicker chaplet, for she has been your leader and has shone more magnificently than the rest.

When she had finished, Theopatra said, she bade everyone to rise from table and, standing underneath the chaste-tree, to sing a becoming hymn of thanksgiving to the Lord; and she asked Thecla to begin and lead the way. And when they stood up, she said that Thecla took her position in the midst of the virgins, with Arete on her right. She then began to sing beautifully; and the other maidens stood around her in a circle, thus forming a choir, and joined her in the refrain.[8]

[THECLA'S HYMN[1]]

(*Refrain:*) Chastely I live for Thee,
And holding[2] my lighted lamps,
My Spouse, I go forth to meet Thee.

1. From on high, there has come, O virgins, the sound of the cry that wakes the dead,[3] bidding us to go to meet the Bridegroom in the east[4] with all speed in white robes

and with our lamps. Awake, before the King enters within the gates!

> Chastely I live for Thee,
> And holding my lighted lamps,
> My Spouse, I go forth to meet Thee.

2. Flying from the riches of mortals that brings only wealth of sorrow, from love, from the delights and pleasures of this life,[5] I desire to be sheltered in Thy life-giving arms and to gaze forever on Thy beauty, Blessed One.

> Chastely I live for Thee,
> And holding my lighted lamps,
> My Spouse, I go forth to meet Thee.

3. For Thee, my King, have I refused a mortal marriage and a home rich in gold, and I have come to Thee in immaculate robes that I may enter with Thee Thy blessed bridal chamber.

> Chastely I live for Thee,
> And holding my lighted lamps,
> My Spouse, I go forth to meet Thee.

4. I have escaped the Dragon's countless betwitching wiles, O Blessed One. Awaiting Thy coming from heaven, I have braved fire and flame and the ravenous assaults of wild beasts.[6]

> Chastely I live for Thee,
> And holding my lighted lamps,
> My Spouse, I go forth to meet Thee.

5. Longing for Thy grace, O Word, I think not of my native city;[7] I think not of the dances of maidens of my

own age, the merry life[8] with mother and family. Thou, O Christ, art all these things to me!

Chastely I live for Thee,
And holding my lighted lamps,
My Spouse, I go forth to meet Thee.

6. Provider of life, O Christ, hail, Light that knowest no evening![9] Receive my cry: the choir of virgins calls upon Thee, perfect Flower, Love, Joy, Prudence, Wisdom, Word!

Chastely I live for Thee,
And holding my lighted lamps,
My Spouse, I go forth to meet Thee.

7. O Queen arrayed in beauty, receive us too with open doors[10] within the bridal bower, O Bride of unsullied body, gloriously triumphant, breathing loveliness! At Christ's side we stand in robes like thine,[11] singing, O youthful maiden of thy blessed nuptials.

Chastely I live for Thee,
And holding my lighted lamps,
My Spouse, I go forth to meet Thee.

8. Now outside the bridal doors are maidens weeping bitterly with deep sobs, and pitiful are their cries. The light of their lamps has gone out, and they have come too late to see the chamber of joy.

Chastely I live for Thee,
And holding my lighted lamps,
My Spouse, I go forth to meet Thee.

9. For, unhappy maidens, they have turned aside from the path of holiness and have neglected to take more oil

for life's contingencies. Carrying lamps whose bright flame is dead, they groan inwardly in spirit.

> Chastely I live for Thee,
> And holding my lighted lamps,
> My Spouse, I go forth to meet Thee.

10. Full bowls of sweet nectar stand by. Let us drink![12] It is a heavenly draught, O virgins, which the Groom has set before all those worthy to be invited to the marriage.

> Chastely I live for Thee,
> And holding my lighted lamps,
> My Spouse, I go forth to meet Thee.

11. Clearly did Abel foreshadow Thy death, O Blessed One, as bleeding he looked to heaven and said: O Word I beseech Thee, receive me cruelly slain by my brother;[13]

> Chastely I live for Thee,
> And holding my lighted lamps,
> My Spouse, I go forth to meet Thee.

12. Thy valiant servant Joseph, O Word, did carry off the greatest prize of chastity,[14] when a woman burning with desire sought to draw him by force to an unlawful bed. But he paid no heed and fled naked, crying aloud:

> Chastely I live for Thee,
> And holding my lighted lamps,
> My Spouse, I go forth to meet Thee.

13. Jephte offered to God in sacrifice his daughter, a maid that knew not man, freshly slain like a lamb before the altar.[15] And she, nobly fulfilling a type of Thy Body, Blessed One, bravely cried out:

Chastely I live for Thee,
And holding my lighted lamps,
My Spouse, I go forth to meet Thee.

14. Bold Judith with a well-planned ruse enticed the general of the enemy hosts with her beauty—nor were her body's members defiled—and then cut off his head.[16] And this was her victory cry:

Chastely I live for Thee,
And holding my lighted lamps,
My Spouse, I go forth to meet Thee.

15. The two judges were inflamed with desire when they saw the texture[17] of Susanna's fair form. Said they: We have come, dear lady, desirous of secret intercourse with you. But she with timorous cry, said:

Chastely I live for Thee,
And holding my lighted lamps,
My Spouse, I go forth to meet Thee.

16. Far better would it be for me to die than to betray my marriage bed for you, women-mad men,[18] and suffer God's eternal justice in fiery penalties.[19] Save me, O Christ, from these men!

Chastely I live for Thee,
And holding my lighted lamps,
My Spouse, I go forth to meet Thee.

17. Thy forerunner, who bathed multitudes of men in the purifying streams, was unjustly led to slaughter by a wicked man because of his chastity.[20] And as he dampened the dust with his own life's blood, he cried out to Thee, O Blessed One:

Chastely I live for Thee,
And holding my lighted lamps,
My Spouse, I go forth to meet Thee.

18. Even the Virgin who gave Thee life, Grace undefiled, who bore Thee her Child without stain in her virgin womb, was thought[21] to have betrayed her bed. And she, with child, O Blessed One, did say:

Chastely I live for Thee,
And holding my lighted lamps,
My Spouse, I go forth to meet Thee.

19. Eager to see Thy wedding day, Blessed One, all the angels whom Thou their Ruler didst summon, are present with costly gifts, O Word, vested in spotless robes.

Chastely I live for Thee,
And holding my lighted lamps,
My Spouse, I go forth to meet Thee.

20. Unsullied maid, God's blessed Bride, we thy bridesmaids hymn thy praise, O Church of body snow-white, dark-tressed, chaste, spotless, lovely!

Chastely I live for Thee,
And holding my lighted lamps,
My Spouse, I go forth to meet Thee.

21. Fled is corruption and the tear-flooded pains of disease. Death is made captive, all folly is crushed, heart-melting grief is dead. Of a sudden the lamp of God's joy has shone again on mortals.

Chastely I live for Thee,
And holding my lighted lamps,
My Spouse, I go forth to meet Thee.

22. Paradise is no longer bereft of men. Once again, by God's decree as before, he lives in it who was cast out because of the Serpent's scheming wiles.[22] Now he is incorruptible, blessed, free from fear.

> Chastely I live for Thee,
> And holding my lighted lamps,
> My Spouse, I go forth to meet Thee.

23. Chanting the new strain,[23] our virgin choir escorts thee, our Queen, to heaven, bathed in light.[24] And garlanded with white lily cups, we bear in our hands light-bearing flames.

> Chastely I live for Thee,
> And holding my lighted lamps,
> My Spouse, I go forth to meet Thee.

24. O Blessed One, who dwellest in heaven's pure seat from all eternity, and dost govern all with everlasting sway, behold, we are come! Receive us too, O Father, with Thy Servant,[25] within the Gates of Life.

> Chastely I live for Thee,
> And holding my lighted lamps,
> My Spouse, I go forth to meet Thee.

EPILOGUE

Eubulion. Thecla has deservedly won the first prize, Gregorion.

Gregorion. She has indeed.

Eub. And tell me, what of our Termessian friend?[1] Was she not listening from the outside? I should be surprised if she sat idle when she heard about this banquet and did not immediately run to listen to our discussions, like a bird in search of food.

Greg. No; the report is that she was with Methodius when he was questioning Arete about this matter. It is indeed a good and blessed thing to have a guide and teacher like Arete.[2]

Eub. Well, now, Gregorion, whom are we to call the better, those who are superior to concupiscence without experiencing it, or those who have concupiscence and yet practice virginity?

Greg. ⟨Those, I should think, who practice virginity without experiencing concupiscence,⟩[3] because with both mind and senses undefiled they are completely uncorrupted, without sin of any sort.

Eub. By chastity, Gregorion, that was excellently and intelligently answered! But I am not being unpleasant, am I, if I dispute your words? It is merely to obtain further information, that no one may refute me hereafter.[4]

Greg. Why, dispute as much as you like, Eubulion. I shall be able to show to your satisfaction that a person who has no desire is better than one who has. And no one will be able to refute you.

Eub. My goodness! I like to hear you answer with such confidence and to see how rich you are in wisdom.

Greg. If I may say so, Eubulion, you do chatter.

Eub. How so?

Greg. Because you talk this way just to tease me rather than to tell me the truth.

Eub. You must not say that, my dear. Really, I have great admiration for your intelligence and your reputation. But I said what I did because you not only claim to understand something which many philosophers frequently dispute among themselves; but you even boast that you can explain it to others.

Greg. Well, tell me then: Do you really find it difficult to believe that those who have no concupiscence are wholly superior to those who do and still practice virginity? Or are you simply joking with me?

Eub. How could I be merely teasing you when I say that I do not know? But come, tell me, my lady philosopher, how are those who are chaste without concupiscence superior to those who practice virginity and yet experience concupiscence?

Greg. First of all, because such persons keep the soul itself pure; the Holy Spirit ever dwells within it, and it is never disturbed or dragged down by impure thoughts or imaginings which could sully the soul if it reflected on them. Souls that have no concupiscence are inaccessible to lust in every way, in body and in mind, and live in tranquil freedom from passion. Those, however, who are deceived in their faculty of sight by images from without, and receive like a flood the onset of desire in their hearts, are nonetheless often soiled, even though they may think they fight and struggle against their lust, since they are conquered in mind.

Eub. Are we then to call pure those souls who lead lives of calm, unruffled by concupiscence?

Greg. Indeed we are. For these are the ones whom the Lord calls divine[5] in the Beatitudes, declaring plainly that those who trust in Him without question *shall see God*; for they introduce nothing into their souls which might darken or disturb the eye of the soul in its divine contemplation. And they not only keep, as I said, their flesh pure of carnal knowledge, dwelling as they do beyond the reach of worldly desires, but in addition they make their hearts inaccessible to all impure thoughts; and it is especially here that the Holy Spirit takes up His abode as in a sanctuary.

Eub. Now just a moment, and answer this question—I think that we can thus proceed on a straighter path in our endeavor to discover what is truly the best: is there anyone you would call a good pilot?

Greg. Yes, indeed.

Eub. Is it the one who saves his ship in great and overpowering squalls or when he is on calm and quiet seas?

Greg. The one who is in great and overpowering squalls.

Eub. Should we not then say that, in like manner, the soul which does not give up though overwhelmed by the towering waves of the passions, but steers its ship, the body, courageously into the harbor of self-control—shall we not say that such a soul is better and more trustworthy than one that sails on calm seas?

Greg. Yes, we shall.

Eub. To be prepared against the attacks and blasts of the Evil Spirit, and not to yield or to be overcome, while refusing all things for Christ,[6] and to struggle valiantly against pleasure—certainly this deserves a greater meed of praise than he wins who lives a life of virginity in unruffled ease.

Greg. Yes, so it would seem.

Eub. And do you not think that the Lord, too, makes it clear that a life of chastity with conflict is superior to the life of virginity without concupiscence?

Greg. Where does He say this?

Eub. In the passage where He compares the wise man to a house built on good foundations, saying that he is unshakable because he cannot be thrown down by rains, floods, or winds.[7] Here, I think, He compares the passions to storms, and by the rocks He means the immovable and unshaken attitude of the soul with regard to chastity.

Greg. I think you are right.

Eub. Now take the doctor. Do you not consider that doctor to be the best who has cured many patients and has already been put to the test in serious diseases?

Greg. Yes, I do.

Eub. And would you not consider that doctor to be completely unacceptable who as yet has had no practice to his credit and has never had to care for the sick at all?

Greg. I would.

Eub. Now consider the soul that has to put up with a very moist[8] body and calms with the medicines of sobriety the diseases that arise from the passions; should we not say that it is superior in the healing art to the soul that has been assigned to control a body that is healthy and free from passion?

Greg. Yes, indeed.

Eub. And how is it in wrestling? Who is the better wrestler, the man who has to face strong and powerful opponents and constantly wrestles with them without being thrown, or the man who has had no opponents?

Greg. Obviously the one who has opponents.

Eub. And in wrestling would not an athlete who has opponents be the more acceptable?

Greg. Obviously.

Eub. Therefore does it not necessarily follow that every soul that struggles against the assaults of concupiscence without being dragged down, and instead fights and resists them—is not such a soul obviously stronger than the soul that has no passions?

Greg. It is.

Eub. And further, do you not think, Gregorion, that

there seems to be greater fortitude in this vigorous attitude towards the attacks of base desires?

Greg. There does indeed.

Eub. And is not this fortitude the very driving force of virtue?

Greg. Of course.

Eub. Well, then, if the force of virtue is perseverance, then the soul that is violently disturbed, and yet perseveres against its passions, does it not seem stronger than that which is not so disturbed?

Greg. Yes.

Eub. And if it is stronger, is it not superior?

Greg. Yes, it is.

Eub. It is clear then, from what has been agreed, that the soul which has concupiscence and yet controls itself is superior to the one that controls itself and has no concupiscence.[9]

Greg. Yes, that is true, and I should like to discuss this further with you. So, if you like, I shall come back tomorrow and listen again to these matters. But now, as you see, it is already time to go and to give attention to the outer man.[10]

NOTES

LIST OF ABBREVIATIONS

ACW	Ancient Christian Writers (Westminster, Md.—London 1946–)
ASS	Acta Sanctorum (Antwerp and Brussels 1643–)
Bardenhewer	O. Bardenhewer, *Geschichte der altkirchlichen Literatur*, 5 vols., 4 in 2 ed. (Freiburg i. Br. 1913–32)
Bo	G. N. Bonwetsch, *Methodius*: GCS 27 (1927)
CSEL	Corpus scriptorum ecclesiasticorum latinorum (Vienna 1866–)
DB	Dictionnaire de la Bible (Paris 1895–)
DHGE	Dictionnaire d'histoire et de géographie ecclésiastique (Paris 1912–)
DS	Dictionnaire de spiritualité, d'ascétique et de mystique (Paris 1937–)
DTC	Dictionnaire de théologie catholique (Paris 1903–)
EC	Enciclopedia cattolica italiana (Vatican City 1946–57)
GCS	Die griechischen christlichen Schriftsteller der ersten drei Jahrhunderte (Leipzig—Berlin 1901–)
Krumbacher	K. Krumbacher, *Geschichte der byzantinischen Litteratur von Justinian bis zum Ende des oströmischen Reiches* (527–1453) 2 ed. by A. Ehrhard—H. Gelzer (Munich 1897)
LSJ	H. G. Liddell—R. Scott, A Greek-English Lexicon, rev. by H. S. Jones (Oxford 1940)
LTK	Lexikon für Theologie und Kirche (2 ed. Freiburg i. Br. 1930–38)
LXX	A. Rahlfs, *Septuaginta*, 2 vols. (4 ed. Stuttgart 1950)
MT	R. Kittel—P. Kahle, *Biblica Hebraica* (9 ed. Stuttgart 1954)
NP	*Liber psalmorum cum canticis Breviarii romani nova e textibus primigeniis interpretatio latina cum notis criticis et exegeticis cura professorum Pontificii Instituti Biblici edita* (New York 1945)
NT	E. Nestle, *Novum Testamentum graece et latine* (16 ed. [21 Greek ed.] Stuttgart 1954)
PG	J. P. Migne, Patrologia graeca (Paris 1857–66)
PL	J. P. Migne, Patrologia latina (Paris 1844–55)

PO	Patrologia orientalis (Paris 1903–)
Quasten	J. Quasten, *Patrology* 1–2 (Utrecht—Antwerp—Westminster, Md. 1950–53)
RAC	Reallexikon für Antike und Christentum (Stuttgart 1950–)
RE	A. Pauly—G. Wissowa—W. Kroll, etc., Real-Encyclopädie der classischen Altertumswissenschaft (Stuttgart 1893–)
SC	Sources chrétiennes (Paris 1941–)
SCA	Studies in Christian Antiquity (Washington 1941–)
SEG	Supplementum epigraphicum graecum (Leiden 1923–)
Sophocles	E. A. Sophocles, Greek Lexicon of the Roman and Byzantine Periods (Boston 1870)
ThQ	*Theologische Quartalschrift* (1819–)
TWNT	G. Kittel, Theologisches Lexikon zum Neuen Testament (Stuttgart 1933–)

SELECT BIBLIOGRAPHY

A. *Texts*

G. N. Bonwetsch, *Methodius*, GCS 27 (1917).

A. Vaillant, *Le De autexusio*, PO 22 fasc. 5 (1930) 631 ff.

B. *Other Works and Studies*

E. Amann, 'Méthode,' DTC 10 (1929) 1606–1614.

B. Altaner, *Patrologie* (2 ed. Freiburg i. Br. 1950) 179 f.

T. Badurina, *Doctrina S. Methodii de Olympio de peccato originali et de eius effectibus* (Rome 1942).

O. Bardenhewer 2.334–351.

—— 'Methodius,' Kirchenlexikon 8 (1893) 1440–1442.

E. Beck, 'Metodio,' EC 8 (1952) 888–890.

G. N. Bonwetsch, *Die Theologie des Methodius von Olympus* (Abh. kön. Ges. der Wiss. Gött., phil.-hist. Kl., n. F. 7.1, Berlin 1903).

—— 'Methodius,' *Schaff-Herzog Enc. of Religious Knowledge* 7 (1910) 556 f.

H. Delehaye, P. Peeters, and others, ASS: Propylaeum Dec. (1940) 404 (Sept. 18, no. 2).

F. Diekamp, 'Über den Bischofssitz des hl. Methodius,' ThQ 109 (1928) 285–308.

J. Farges, *Les idées morales et religieuses de Méthode d'Olympe* (Paris 1929).

—— *Méthode d'Olympe. Du libre arbitre* (Paris 1929).

—— *Méthode d'Olympe. Le banquet des dix vierges* (Paris 1932).

G. Fritschel, *Methodius von Olympus und seine Philosophie* (diss. Leipzig 1879).

A. Harnack, *Geschichte der altchristlichen Litteratur bis Eusebius* 1.1 (Leipzig 1893) 468–469; 2.2 (1904) 147–149.

P. Heseler, 'Zum Symposium des Methodius I,' *Byz.-neugr. Jahrb.* 6 (1928) 95–118; 'Zum Symposium des Methodius. II,' *ibid.* 10 (1933) 325–340.

H. Jordan, *Geschichte der altchristlichen Literatur* (Leipzig 1911) 41, 248 f., 299.

G. Lazzati, 'La tecnica dialogica nel Simposio di Metodio d'Olimpo,' *Studi Ubaldi* (Pubbl. della Univ. cattolica 16, Milan 1937) 117–124.

M. Margheritis, 'L'influenza di Platone sul pensiero e sull' arte di S. Metodio d'Olimpo,' *Studi Ubaldi* 401–412.

G. Mercati, 'Emendazione a Metodio d'Olimpo,' *Didaskaleion* (1927) fasc. 2. 25–29.

M. Niccioli, 'Metodio,' *Encic. italiana* 23 (1934) 93.

Sr. R. Nugent, *Portrait of the Consecrated Woman in Greek Christian Literature of the First Four Centuries* (Catholic University Patristic Studies 64, Washington 1941).

J. Quasten 2.129–137; see also the French transl. with latest literature added: *Initiation aux Pères de l'Eglise* 2 (1957) 154–163.

K. Quensell, *Die wahre kirchliche Stellung und Tätigkeit des fälschlich so gennanten Bischofs Methodius von Olympus* (typescr. diss. Heidelberg 1953).

J. Stiltinck, ASS Sept. 5 (1866) 768 ff. (*die* 18 *Sept.*).

M. Viller—K. Rahner, *Aszese und Mystik in der Väterzeit* (Freiburg i. Br. 1939) 41–59.

INTRODUCTION

[1] *Haer.* 64.63 (GCS 2.500); elsewhere Epiphanius calls him the 'Blessed presbyter'; see Bo x f. for the texts. Both the names Methodius (='the wily') and Eubulius (='good counsellor') may well have been soubriquets which had become *cognomina*; Methodius' *praenomen* and *gentilicium* are unknown.

[2] First, in his conception of chastity (celibacy) as the focal point of all asceticism: see A. Harnack, *Lehrbuch der Dogmengeschichte* (5th ed. Tübingen 1931–1932) 1.790 f.; *Dogmengeschichte* (6th ed. Tübingen 1922) 170 f. Secondly, in his use of nuptial imagery in order to illustrate the relationship between Christ and the virgin, adapted particularly from the Canticle and the epithalamian Psalm 44 (Hebr. 45): on these literary motifs, see in general R. Nugent, *Portrait of the Consecrated Woman in Greek Christian Literature of the First Four Centuries* (CUPS 64, Washington 1941) Index *s.v.* 'Methodius.' It is this application of the Canticle (and related texts) to virginity that marks Methodius' advance on Origen; in Origen, the 'mystical marriage' was between the Church (or the Church in microcosm, the faithful soul) and the Logos: see R. P. Lawson, ACW 26.10–16; also J. Quasten, *Patrology* 2.98–101, with the bibliography there cited. In a general history of the exegesis of the Canticle, however, Methodius would be considered Origenistic although he does not seem to have studied the actual language or literary form as closely as Origen. For an account of the classical interpretations of the Canticle from patristic times down to the present, see especially H. H. Rowley, 'The Interpretation of the Song of Songs,' in *The Servant of the Lord and Other Essays on the Old Testament* (London 1954) 187–234; cf. also R. H. Pfeiffer, *Introduction to the Old Testament* (London 1953) 708–716, and W. Baumgartner in *The Old Testament and Modern Study: A Generation of Discovery and Research. Essays by Members of the Society for Old Testament Study* edited by H. H. Rowley (Oxford 1951) 230–235.

Methodius' influence in the West, whether direct or indirect, is best illustrated by Ambrose's constant use of marriage symbolism in his treatises on virginity (*De virginitate, Exhortatio ad virgines, De virginibus*). For Methodius' influence in the East, see E. Buonaiuti, 'The Ethics and Eschatology of Methodius of Olympus,' HTR 15 (1921) 255–266.

[3] *C. Ruf.* 1.11 (PL 23.423C): 'Eusebius . . . in sexto libro Ἀπολογίας

Origenis hoc idem objicit Methodio episcopo et martyri . . . et dicit: "Quomodo ausus est Methodius nunc contra Origenem scribere, qui haec et haec de Origenis locutus est dogmatibus?"' This *Apologia on Behalf of Origen* was first undertaken by Pamphilus (who died a martyr in 309/10) in five books, and to this Eusebius is said to have added a sixth (Photius, *Bibl.* cod. 118). See Quasten 2.145 f.; E. Peterson, 'Panfilo,' EC 9 (1952) 676 f.

[4] Cf. *De praep. evang.* 7.22 (GCS 8.405 ff.). For other possible references to this Maximus, see G. Salmon, 'Maximus (24),' *Dict. Christ. Biog.* 3 (1882) 884 f.; there is, however, no foundation for Salmon's suggestion that Methodius plagiarized the text.

[5] See Bo ix for the relevant texts.

[6] See n. 3 above, and Bo xi for the other texts.

[7] *Acta concil. oecum.* 1.3 (Berlin 1922) 297: 'In the West indeed Damascus, Innocent, Ambrose, and others; in Hellas and Illyricum, Methodius and other Fathers who were famous for their piety.' But even if we are to assume that John was accurate and not mistaken, 'Hellas' may perhaps represent in general the Greek-speaking world as opposed to the Latin; in any case, the reference is too vague and too late for any great weight to be laid on it.

[8] Porphyry of Tyre (232/3—ca. 305) published his fifteen-book attack on the Christians while he was still apparently in Sicily, not long after the year 268; but he did not publish the *Enneads* of his master Plotinus (d. 269/70) until 301: see R. Beutler, 'Porphyrius no. 21,' RE 22.1 (1953) 275–313.

[9] ASS Sept. 5 (1866) 768 ff. Stiltinck died in 1762, but his refreshingly skeptical attitude towards the pious exaggeration of hagiographical tradition made his article on Methodius still worthy of the 1866 volume of the *Acta Sanctorum.*

[10] See the articles on Chalcis in DHGE 12 (1953) 278 f., and RE 3.2 (1899) 2078 ff.

[11] 'Über den Bischofssitz des hl. Märtyrers und Kirchenvaters Methodius,' ThQ 109 (1928) 285–308. The evidence for the claims of the various cities to Methodius' bishopric may be summarized as follows:

(a) Patara in Lycia: so Leontius of Byzantium (6th cent.), *De sectis* 3.1 (PG 86.1213A), and the title of the *Symposium* as given by the MSS O and P as well as a MS of the *Sacra Parallela*; also the entry in Suidas (quoted earlier). Cf., however, Methodius, *De res.* 1.1.1 (Bo 219), where the scene is laid in Aglaophon's house at Patara, to which, says Methodius, 'I went with Proclus of Miletus.' See Diekamp, *art. cit.* 286.

(b) Side in Pamphylia: so the anonymous Catena which quotes Methodius' commentary on Job: Bo 511 (apparatus on frag. 1). See Diekamp, *ibid.* 287.

(c) Tyre in Phoenicia: so Jerome (*De vir. ill.* 83) and the derivative martyrologies, and the entry in Suidas. This is rejected by Diekamp (with Stiltinck and most scholars), chiefly on the ground that the series of bishops at Tyre, beginning with St. Tyrannion (about 310) is known, and it is difficult to imagine Methodius dying as bishop of Tyre about 311/12 without some other correcting references within the tradition. See T. Zahn, 'Uber den Bischofssitz des Methodius,' *Zeitschr. f. Kirchengeschichte* 8 (1886) 15–20. Zahn further suggested that Jerome may well have mistaken a source which gave Methodius as bishop of Phoenikous (=Olympus), and thought it referred to Phoenicia; W. M. Ramsay in *Class. Rev.* 7 (1893) 311 f. suggested a similar error. Harnack, however, in *Geschichte der altchristlichen Litteratur bis Eusebius* 2.2 (Leipzig 1904) 147 f., n. 3, suggested that Methodius may have been moved ('disloziert') from Olympus to Tyre during the persecution of Diocletian and died there. Finally, the tradition may have something to do with Methodius' opposition to Porphyry who came from Tyre, but there is too much uncertainty about the entire question to warrant any definite conclusion.

(d) Myra: the earliest reference is apparently Nicephorus of Constantinople, *Antirrhetica* (ca. 817); Diekamp (290 ff.) himself has found three other lemmata in late MSS, and suspects (rightly perhaps) that this attribution was due to a misunderstanding of the Greek suspension for the genitive μάρτυρος after Methodius' name.

(e) Olympus: so Jerome (*De vir. ill.* 83); Socrates, *Hist. Eccl.* 6.13; a scholion on Pseudo-Dionysius, *Eccles. hierarch.* 7.7 (PG 4.175B), attributed to Maximus Confessor; the Syriac floreligia which quote *De res.*; the proem of Zacharias Rhetor's *Syriac Church History* (cited by Diekamp 294). The reference to Mt. Olympus as 'a mountain in Lycia' in *De res.* 2.23.1 (Bo 377), if the text is right, might be taken as evidence for or against. Diekamp argues that no MS names Olympus as Methodius' see. But this is not a valid argument, for MSS also mention Patara, and Diekamp would not accept their testimony. See Diekamp 292 ff.

(f) Philippi in Macedonia: some of the old Slavonic MSS of the *De autexusio* and *De lepra* (Bo apparatus 145 and 451); some of the late MSS of florilegia which quote the *De res.*; two MSS which refer to 'Bishop of Philippi and Myra.' Now, though I should agree that it is difficult to explain the reference, as Bonwetsch does, as a mistake for Olympus, yet, can we, when all is said, lay greater weight on these florilegia and MSS rather than on other citations; and ought we accept Philippi in this case and reject Myra?

What finally convinces me that Diekamp's thesis is very far from being proven, is the great weight he lays (297 f.) on the passing reference of Bishop John of Antioch, in his letter to Proclus, quoted in n. 7 above. In the first place, John could have been as wrong as any of the others; secondly, accuracy here has nothing to do with the point of his argument in the passage; thirdly, his reference is not only to Methodius but to 'other Fathers,' and his intention is to distinguish the Latin-speaking and non-Latin world in general, not to give specific information on localities.

Lastly, to hold, as Diekamp does, that Philippi would fit in better with Jerome's reference to Chalcis as the place of martyrdom is an egregious example of the *circulus vitiosus*. For it presumes we know the Chalcis Jerome had in mind; and, worst of all, it presumes this detail of Jerome's account to be true, and that none of the other geographical places mentioned have any weight whatsoever. And this is enforced by the *ad hoc* assumption that Jerome would have been careful to ascertain the place of martyrdom. See Diekamp 295 ff.

The problem of Methodius' life has been the subject of a Heidelberg dissertation by a pupil of H. von Campenhausen: K. Quensell, *Die wahre kirchliche Stellung und Tätigkeit des fälschlich so gennanten Bischofs Methodius von Olympus* (Diss. Heidelberg 1953, in typescript), which I have been able to study in a microfilm copy; for a review, see *Theol. Literaturzeit.* (1954) 175 f. In addition to being dissatisfied with the evidence linking Methodius to several different sees, Quensell finds it strange that the earliest references to Methodius, in Eustathius of Antioch and Epiphanius, do not refer to his episcopacy. Quensell feels that the tradition which we find in Jerome and Socrates was gradually invented; he suggests therefore that Methodius was the 'last free teacher' of the patristic period and that he was the center of a theological school in Asia Minor. Without adducing any cogent proof, Quensell finds support for his suggestion in Methodius' freer handling of doctrine, especially by the use of the Platonic technique, than one would expect to find in a member of the hierarchy. In my own view, Methodius' teaching is far more dogmatic and less tentative than Quensell would seem to suggest, and not merely directed to a circle of virgins and ascetics. Quensell's thesis, however, is a fine presentation of a general doubt about Methodius' life and background, and although not convincingly supported it is a point of view which deserves serious consideration.

From the viewpoint of strict historical certitude, therefore, we must confess that there is very little we can assert about Methodius with complete confidence. That he flourished between the years 270 and 308 and wrote and worked in Asia Minor, especially in Lycia, is, as we have stated most likely; the tradition that he was a bishop who died perhaps by martyrdom some time after 308 cannot be fully supported from our conflicting evidence.

[12] This is the only way in which he could reconcile the various pieces of evidence dating from various periods from different parts of the world: ASS *loc. cit.* (n. 9 above) 768, 773. Modifying an earlier conclusion by his colleague G. Henschen (d. 1681) in ASS, June 5 (1867) 4 f., Stiltinck drew up a list of four possible Methodii:

(1) A bishop who died in the third century;
(2) A Methodius who was martyred in Greece;
(3) The author of the *Symposium*, who died in the last persecution—311/12 or even 320/23.
(4) A bishop of Patara who flourished somewhere between the fifth and seventh centuries.

There is no further evidence, so far as I know, since Stiltinck's death to force us to settle this question definitively; and the possibility of four (or more) Methodii, unlikely though it may seem, should perhaps be retained as a reasonable hypothesis. See also the notes of H. Delehaye, P. Peeters, and others, on the Roman martyrology for Sept. 18 (no. 2) in ASS *Propylaeum Dec.* (1940) 404, where a cautious but non-committal attitude is maintained.

[13] For the best discussions of the works, see Harnack, *Gesch. der altchr. Lit.* 1.468 ff.; Bardenhewer 2.339–350; A. Puech, *Histoire de la littérature grecque chrétienne depuis les origines jusqu' à la fin du IVe siecle* (Paris 1928) 2.513–534; Quasten, *Patrology* 2.130–137.

[14] No Slavonic version has yet turned up; J. B. Pitra, in *Analecta sacra spicilegio solesmiensi parata* 4 (1883) 438 f., first called attention to a tiny Syriac fragment, a translation of a few lines of *Symp.* 6.1 (Bo 64.14–20), which reflects an interesting but unacceptable textual variant: see Bo 64.15 f. (apparatus).

[15] *De autex.* 17.1 f. (Bo 189.9 ff.). For a good discussion, see A. Biamonti, 'L'etica di Metodio d'Olimpo,' *Riv. di studi filos. e relig.* 3 (1922) 272–298.

[16] PO, *loc. cit.* 653.

[17] Bardenhewer 2.347; cf. Bo xxxvii.

[18] PO, *loc. cit.* 652; cf. also Diekamp, ThQ, *loc. cit.* 307 f., who would date the *Symp.*, *De cib.*, and the first part of the *De res.* to Methodius' Lycian period, before he was made bishop of Philippi; the *De res.*

(part 2) and *De lepra* to Methodius' later, non-Lycian period. But, as we have suggested, there is no solid evidence that Methodius moved from Lycia to Macedonia.

[19] See n. 3 above.

[20] On the fragmentary and spurious works in the Methodian corpus, see Bardenhewer 2.348 ff.; Quasten, 2.137.

[21] See A. Siegmund, *Die Überlieferung der griechischen christlichen Literatur in der lateinischen Kirche bis zum zwölften Jahrhundert* (Munich 1949) 172, for the Latin MSS.

[22] ASS Sept. 5 (1866) 773.

[23] Thus we find a woman named Arete as a priestess of Demeter in Pamphylia in the time of Domitian, SEG 6.672; Thalia occurs on an inscription in Phrygia, SEG 6.206, and likewise Marcella, 6.203; Thecla occurs in Lycaonia, 6.291. A certain Domnina was venerated in Lycia as a martyr under Diocletian: see ASS, *Propylaeum Dec.* (1940) 450 (Oct. 12, no. 4). For Gregorion, Theophila, Theopatra, Agathe, as well as the previously mentioned names, see W. Pape, *Wörterbuch der griechischen Eigennamen* (2 vols., 3 ed. by G. E. Benseler 1884). Further, the three Roman names, Domnina, Marcella and Procilla, would seem to suggest the presence of Roman women in this predominantly Greek community of Lycia.

[24] Bonwetsch's index is a good guide to the variety of Methodius' reading. In order of frequency we have the Old Testament (especially Genesis, Psalms and Isaias), the New Testament (especially Matthew, 1 Corinthians and favorite references like Hebrews 10.1 which is used about ten times), then Plato (filling six columns in Bo), Origen, Irenaeus and Hippolytus. Of pagan Greek authors, besides Plato, there are references to Aristotle, a few from the *Iliad* and *Odyssey* (which could have been culled from an anthology), and a possible reference to Euripides, *Hippolytus* 73 ff. (Hippolytus' offering of a garland to Artemis, goddess of chastity) in *Symp.* 6.5 and 8.11. There are scattered and inaccurate references to some of the pre-Socratic philosophers, and a possible reminiscence of the second-century Greek novelist Chariton.

Methodius has more references to Plato than any other Greek Father: he seems to have been familiar with at least twenty-seven dialogues as well as the seventh epistle; but he does not distinguish authentic works from doubtful or spurious ones (e.g., *Alcibiades I, Axiochus, Epinomis, Eryxias, Hippias maior*). Those which are most used are (in order): *Symposium, Republic, Timaeus, Phaedo, Protagoras, Phaedrus.* Since the Platonic parallels are printed among the *testimonia* in Bo, I have not thought it necessary to quote them repeatedly, especially where the similarities would be primarily a question of the Greek words. In the *Symposium*, Methodius especially reflects the influence of the following places in the Platonic corpus:

Axiochus 371 C–D: man's liberation from the prison of this world to a realm of blessed peace: cf. *Symp.* prelude: Bo 6.2; 8.2: Bo 82.13.

Hipp. mai. 287 A, 'I wish to object that I may learn all the more strongly.' Cf. *Symp.* epilogue: Bo 137.19 ff., where Methodius has telescoped four of Plato's sentences, making them more obscure, and modifying the oath 'By Hera!' to 'By chastity!' This is typical of his stylistic borrowing; it is as if he kept his volumes of Plato, or perhaps his own collection of apt quotations, constantly at hand while writing.

Phaedr. 229 B ff.: the reference to the spring and the shade of the trees for the setting of the dialogue. Cf. *Symp.* prelude: Bo 6.4 and 10—246 A ff.: 'The Ride of the Gods' in Plato becomes the 'Ascent of the Soul' in Methodius. Cf. *Symp.* 1.1: Bo 7.18 ff.; 5.3: Bo 56.9; 8.2: Bo 82.9 ff. For further references, see Bo, Index.

Symposium (see the edition of Léon Robin, Paris 1929): there are very many parallels in Methodius, but usually of a superficial sort, having to do with the change of speakers, casual pleasantries, etc.: compare, e.g., Plato, *Symp.* 185 E. ff. ('since Pausanias did not finish the discussion,' etc.) with Methodius 2.1: Bo 15.3. Rarely does Methodius show that he has really grasped the profound message of Plato's dialogue, even though in several places, e.g. 6.1: Bo 64.7, he alludes to Plato's famous 'Ladder of Love' passage (Plato, *Symp.* 211 A).

Republic: there are a number of coincidences in Methodius, especially where he touches on his 'shadow-image-reality' theory of world history and God's revelation. Compare, e.g., *Rep.* 7.53 C with Methodius, *Symp.* 8.3: Bo 83.21. The Myth of the Craftsman's Cave in Methodius seems to have been inspired at least partially by Plato's Cave, but we need not remark on the superficiality of the resemblance. Finally, the Platonic theory of the '*coruptio optimi*' in *Rep.* 6.491 D is slightly irrelevant as it is used in *Symp.* 11: Bo 130.27.

Timaeus 29 A: on the way the Demiurge works with his eye fixed on Beauty. Cf. *Symp.* 6.1: Bo 64.12.

[25] In speaking of the duration of the Church on earth (the length of the sixth millennium, as symbolized by the Banquet of Arete),

Methodius never refers to the Church's difficulties with the State. Curiously enough, the two references to execution by fire and exposure to the beasts are both put into the mouth of Thecla (8.2: Bo 83.1; and 11: Bo 132.19 f.), apparently to lend verisimilitude to her discourse; but these would refer to the persecutions of the first century, at least insofar as Methodius knew of them from the legend of Thecla.

[26] The passages, for example, on procreation (2.12: Bo 16.12 ff.) and the like, may well have served an educative purpose in the case of some of the younger women for whom the book was intended.

[27] The virgins are bidden, for example, henceforth to 'consider and meditate on that angelic transformation of the body' (*Symp.* 2.7: Bo 25.14); they are not 'to relax their minds with frivolous thoughts' (4.5: Bo 51.23 f.); they must 'look upwards and, soaring on high, fly from' the flattery of evil spirits (8.1: Bo 81.14). The obvious content of these meditations must have been the Ascent of the Soul, the Craftsman's Cave, the Vision of the Father and the Heavenly Meadows.

[28] See the Index *s.vv.* For a discussion of the date and locality of Pseudo-Dionysius, see I. Hausherr, 'Le Pseudo-Denys est-il Pierre l'Ibérien?' *Orient. christ. period.* 19 (1953) 247 ff.

[29] For a comment, see Bonwetsch, *Die Theologie des Methodius von Olympus* (Abh. d. kön. Ges. d. Wiss. z. Göttingen, phil.-hist. Kl., n. F. 7.1, Berlin 1903) 92, who erroneously thought that Methodius held a hypostatic union between Adam and the Word; this is followed by Harnack, *Lehrbuch der Dogmengeschichte* (5th ed. Tübingen 1931–32) 1.785, and E. Mersch, *Le corps mystique du Christ* (Paris 1951) 1.343 ff., 389. See the difficult passage, *Symp.* 3.8, where Adam is said to be 'not merely a type, a likeness, or an image of the Only-Begotten, but he has himself become Wisdom and the Word,' with the notes below. J. Farges, *Les idées morales et religieuses de Méthode d'Olympe* (Paris 1929) 127, hit on the correct interpretation. Cf. also T. Badurina, *Doctrina S. Methodii de Olympio* [sic] *de peccato originali et de eius effectibus* (Rome 1942) 37; but Badurina falls into the fault of constantly minimizing Methodius' heterodox points of view and too often analyzes his teaching according to modern theological categories.

[30] See *Symp.* 3.8: Bo 35.13 ff., and for a parallel, see the Abbot Nilus *Ep.* 1.26 (PG 79.92).

[31] Cf. *Symp.* 3.1: Bo 34.21; *De autex.* 17.2: Bo 189.14. See also Farges, *Les idées morales et religieuses de Méthode* 98, 102 ff., 240 ff.; Bonwetsch, *Die Theologie des M.* 68 ff.; Badurina, *Doctrina S. Methodii* 25 ff.

[32] On the evil spirits' jealousy towards man, see *Symp.* 6.1: Bo 64.20 ff. Badurina, *op. cit.* 28 f., suggests that Methodius taught that the

evil spirits' jealousy was occasioned by man's power to embrace celibacy before the Fall.

[33] Cf. *Symp.* 9.2: Bo 116.13, and frequently in *De res.*, e.g., 1.32.7: Bo 269.12 ff. In the earlier literature, we find this idea most clearly reflected in Irenaeus, *Adv. haer.* 3.35.2 (Harvey).

[34] *Symp.* 3.6: Bo 33.6. Cf. Badurina, *op. cit.* 67; Farges, *op. cit.* 109 ff.

[35] *Symp.* 1.4: Bo 12.14 ff.

[36] *Symp.* 3.8: Bo 37.3 ff.

[37] *Symp.* 5.2: Bo 54.14; 8.10: Bo 93.2 ff.

[38] *Symp.* 1.1: Bo 8.13; cf. 4.3: Bo 49.10 ff.

[39] *Symp.* 8.8: Bo 90.7 ff., and *passim.*

[40] *Symp.* 3.4 and 6: Bo 30.22 ff. and 32.9 ff., provided these are not interpolated, for they are here closely linked with the use of the titles, 'eldest of the Aeons, first among archangels' (3.4: Bo 31.3), which savor of Gnosticism and Subordinationism. In his search for superlatives to describe the Word, Methodius did not perhaps realize how these logically contradicted his basic doctrine: cf. Harnack, *Lehrbuch der Dogmengeschichte* 1.784 n. 3. Bonwetsch (*Die Theologie des M.* 56 ff.) suggests an Origenist influence in Methodius' Christology; Bardenhewer (2.342), however, would defend Methodius on the grounds that dogmatic terminology was not fixed, and that this would naturally be reflected in the 'poetically daring, image-intoxicated style of the author.' Bardenhewer further suggests that such passages as these were perhaps the ones which gave Photius (*Bibl.* cod. 237) the idea that his copy of the *Symposium* had been interpolated by Arians. That the text has been edited, I feel convinced; but that the modifications were in a different direction, I shall try to show in the course of the Introduction.

[41] *Symp.* 3.4: Bo 31.3 ff.

[42] *Symp.* 7.8 f.: Bo 78 f. We have the various levels of meaning in this central typology of the *Symposium*: the bride of Christ is first of all His human flesh; then it is the Church, Mother and Virgin; then the perfect Christians who co-operate with her to convert the lukewarm; lastly, in a special way, the consecrated virgin.

[43] *Symp.* 6.5: Bo 69.15 ff., and see also *Thecla's Hymn.*

[44] *Symp.* 5.4, *passim.* Cf. *Christus Patiens* 557 (Brambs), where the Mother of Christ says to the Chorus: 'I am betrothed to God.'

[45] *Symp.* 3.12 with the relevant notes.

[46] *Symp.* 3.13: Bo 43.4 ff.; 9.4: Bo 119.22 ff.

[47] *Symp.* 9.4: Bo 119.8; 9.5: Bo 119.30.

[48] Methodius taught abstinence only from *sekar*, or strong alcoholic

drinks (5.6: Bo 60.7 ff.), as well as from excessive wine-drinking (5.5: Bo 58 f.). Authors have overlooked the fact that there is no trace of ascetical fasting in Methodius; the only reference to fasting is to the Good-Friday fast mentioned in passing in 3.12. For the rise of fasting as an ascetical practice, see J. Schümmer, *Die altchristliche Fastenpraxis, mit besonderer Berücksichtigung der Schriften Tertullians* (Liturgiegesch. Quellen u. Forsch. 27, Münster i. W. 1933); R. Arbesmann, 'Fasting and Prophecy in Pagan and Christian Antiquity,' *Traditio* 7 (1949/51) 1–71; H. Musurillo, 'The Problem of Ascetical Fasting in the Greek Patristic Writers,' *Traditio* 12 (1956) 1–64.

[49] Methodius seems not to forbid the use of jewelry and accessories, but simply counsels the consecrated woman to prefer spiritual ornamentation: 7.2, Bo 73.6 ff.

[50] *Symp.* 4.5: Bo 51.23 f.

[51] The word ἐκεῖ, so important in this connection, is omitted from Bonwetsch's index. It is first used in 8.3: Bo 84.5 (ἐκεῖ δὲ ἐν τῷ ὄντι), though throughout 8.2 we have several instances of ἐκεῖνα, 'the things of that world.' 'There' in 9.2: Bo 116.22 is difficult; and in 10.5: Bo 129.3 it implies little more than 'in heaven.' In the classical period we have a good many references to ἐκεῖ as a euphemism for 'in Hades:' see LSJ, *s. v.* Ἅιδης. There are two instances in Clement of Alexandria, cited by Stählin, *Registerband* (GCS 370), *Strom.* 6.6.46.3 (GCS 15.455.3) and 7.12.79.4 (17.56.25). 'There' in Methodius seems regularly to imply heaven as a place of Truth, derived from the vision of the divine essence and the essential virtues; the term has therefore an intellectual and philosophical connotation, and does not have the emotional, rhetorical overtones of 'bridal chamber,' 'the gates of Life,' in Methodius' terminology.

[52] 1.1: Bo 8.2 f. The implication throughout Methodius would seem to be that this 'stream' is essentially connected with the nature of the deity, with 'grace' as it is taken and 'drunk' by man, and with the incorruptibility of chastity as practiced by those who choose that way of life.

[53] 8.2: Bo 83.15 f. It is not, however, clear whether Methodius is referring to a true mystical experience or merely to an exercise of the imagination.

[54] 9.1: Bo 115.18. In this passage the 'seal' seems to refer to a mark on the elect, on all those who are to be saved, and hence not merely on those who are baptized. See the note *ad loc.*

[55] 9.5: Bo 120.20 f. But however this is interpreted, it is clear from *De res.* 3.2.4 f. (Bo 391) that Methodius is completely opposed to Origen's openly spiritualist point of view. For a discussion, see E.

Buonaiuti, 'The Ethics and Eschatology of Methodius of Olympus,' *Harv. Theol. Rev.* 14 (1921) 255–266; also A. Biamonti, 'L'escatologia di Metodio di Olimpo,' *Riv. di studi filos. e relig.* 3 (1922) 272–298; and H. Chadwick, 'Origen, Celsus and the Resurrection of the Body,' *Harv. Theol. Rev.* 48 (1948) 83–102.

[56] 8.11: Bo 94.5.

[57] 6.5: Bo 69.15. But this is overstressed by Harnack, *Lehrbuch der Dogmengeschichte* 1.786 n. 2 (for Methodius, so it is said, Christianity is a kind of *Mysterienkultus*).

[58] 'For our bodies are indeed a lamp, as it were'—6.3: Bo 67.11 f. For a similar idea, cf. Origen, *Comm. in Matt.* 25.1–5: ser. 63 f. (GCS 38.145–51), where the lamps represent the five senses and the oil, spiritual doctrine.

[59] For example, Harnack, *Lehrbuch der Dogmengeschichte* 1.791; A. Palmieri, 'Alexandrian Mysticism and the Mystics of Christian Virginity, Gregory of Nyssa and Methodius of Olympus,' *Amer. Cath. Quart Rev.* 41 (1916) 390–405; A. Puech, *Histoire de la littérature grecque chrétienne* 2.514 ff.; T. Badurina, *Doctrina S. Methodii* (see n. 29 above) *passim.*

[60] *Lehrbuch der Dogmengeschichte* 1.783–790. Harnack speaks of Methodius' 'speculative realism' (784) and his 'imaginative-realistic approach' (786), by which he means that Methodius combined the elements of monastic mysticism with the objectivity of ecclesiastical dogma (791). Or, again, Methodius 'combined a theoretical optimism with abnegation of the world in practice': *Dogmengeschichte* (6th ed., Tübingen 1922) 171. In Methodius we already have 'the ultimate stage of Greek theology': *Lehrbuch der Dogmengeschichte* 1.790 n. 1. But Harnack was too concerned with theological categories and generalizations to perceive fully the inconsistencies and insoluble difficulties in Methodius, both doctrinal and textual.

[61] J. C. Plumpe, *Mater Ecclesia. An Inquiry into the Concept of the Church as Mother in Early Christianity* (SCA 5, Washington 1943) ch. 7: 'ΜΗΤΗΡ ΕΚΚΛΗΣΙΑ in the Mysticism of St. Methodius of Philippi.' Cf. also Plumpe's note in J. J. Jepson, *Augustine. The Lord's Sermon on the Mount* 2.6.24 (ACW 5.199 f.), and E. Stauffer, *New Testament Theology* (tr. J. Marsh, London 1955) 155 f.

[62] See his summary in *Realenc. f. prot. Theol. u. Kirche* 13 (1903) 25 ff.

[63] See Bonwetsch, *Die Theologie des M.* 164 ff.; Farges, *Les idées morales et religieuses* 240 f.; Badurina, *Doctrina S. Methodii* 18 and *passim.* As Bonwetsch especially shows, Methodius is in basic agreement with Irenaeus in his doctrine of the fall of man and the Atonement; on Adam; on the providential purpose of the penalty of death after

the fall (cf. n. 33 above). On the typology of Adam's birth (from virgin earth) see J. P. Smith's version of Irenaeus' *Proof of the Apostolic Preaching* §32 (ACW 16.68); and on Moses' tabernacle as a pattern of heaven and a type of the Church, *ibid.* §§26 and 29 (64 f., 67). For the literature on Irenaeus, see Quasten 1.287 ff.

It is clear that the Christian community in which Methodius received his formation was deeply under the influence of Irenaeus, and, ultimately, of Pauline theology; but this solid pattern is curiously blended with Alexandrianism and with Methodius' personal mysticism. Cf. H. E. W. Turner, *The Patristic Doctrine of Redemption* (London 1952) 85–87. Despite the conflict between these two streams of thought, Methodius' mysticism can all but be summed up in the words Karl Barth has used of St. Paul: 'From Adam to Christ—this is God's way to men and among men,' *Der Römerbrief* (8 ed. Zürich 1947) 154.

[64] On Methodius' Origenism, see the discussions by Bonwetsch, *Die Theologie des M.* 168 ff., and especially Farges, *Les idées morales et religieuses* 188 ff. (on the use of Origen's nuptial imagery), and 224 f. (on allegorism). But anything like a debt to Origen should not, in my view, be overstressed. The judgment of A. Robertson, that Methodius' legacy was a modified Origenism, 'expurgated by the standard of the *regula fidei*,' is perhaps close to the truth (as quoted by B. J. Kidd, *A History of the Church to A.D. 461*, Oxford 1921, 1.427), Methodius seems undoubtedly to have come under the influence of Origenist or, perhaps more correctly, Alexandrian asceticism—on which see O. Chadwick, *John Cassian. A Study in Primitive Monasticism* (Cambridge 1950) 81 f., and my own study, 'The Problem of Ascetical Fasting in the Greek Patristic Writers,' *Traditio* 12 (1956), esp. 49–51 with the literature cited. Methodius' use of οἰκονομίαι μυστικαί, or mystical interpretations of the Scriptures, especially for ascetical exhortation, seems to derive from the Alexandrian tradition. Relevant passages in this connection are Origen, *In Cant. Cant.* hom. 1 (GCS 33.30.11 ff.=ACW 26.269, and *passim*), where Origen blends the imagery of the Canticle with that of the epithalamium, Psalm 44; and Origen, *Comm. in Lam.* 2.9 (GCS 6.257 no. 52), where he speaks of the 'disturbing floods' which crash against the gates of the senses, much as Methodius does in the *Symposium*; for an effective use of the same imagery, cf. *Christus Patiens* 624 ff. (Brambs). And yet, as I have suggested above, Methodius' imagery is not perhaps to be traced to a direct influence of Origenism, but to the general stream of Asiatic Greek theology, and to the general use of symbolism in the exposition of the faith to the catechumenate: cf. also H. Musurillo, 'History and Symbol: A study of Form in Early Christian Literature,' *Theological*

Studies 18 (1957) 357–386. For further details on Origen's theory of exegesis, see J. Daniélou, *Origène* (Paris 1948) 135–198, esp. 172 ff.; H. de Lubac, *Histoire et esprit: l'intelligence de l'Écriture d'après Origène* (Paris 1950); also R. P. C. Hanson, *Origen's Doctrine of Tradition* (London 1954) 101 ff.

[65] *Symp.* 2.4: Bo 20.2 ff.; 3.4: Bo 31.8; and cf. *De res.* 1.34.1 ff.: Bo 271 ff., where Methodius speaks of man as a bronze statue which God the Craftsman can melt down and recast anew. It is this image of bronze-casting, sometimes linked with the symbol of the Divine Potter, which is at the basis of Methodius' discussion of the Fall, the Atonement, and the Adam-Christ relationship. In thus combining Platonic with Old Testament imagery, Methodius emphasizes the mystery of the divine transcendence in the history of Redemption. Other important sequences of images in Methodius are: (1) the ancient marriage ceremony, with the *deductio* or marriage procession, the bride's apparel, the bridal chamber, the mystery of procreation; (2) the conquest of the passions is compared to piloting a ship against stormy seas; (3) the Platonic image of the rise of the chariot of the soul is used for man's contemplation of heavenly truths; (4) botanical imagery (trees, flowers, meadows, insects) used for various purposes; (5) water-imagery (of springs welling up), and milk-imagery (grace flowing from the bosom of the Church), symbolic of grace and immortality; (6) light-imagery, of the divinity and the atmosphere of heaven; (7) painting, with reference to the divine image in man; (8) medicine and anatomy, especially with reference to childbearing and the creation of the human soul; (9) imagery taken from Greek sports, especially chariot racing and wrestling. Although image-analysis should not be overestimated, it remains a most important source for our complete understanding of a patristic writer. In Methodius, for example, light, air, water, trees and flowers are symbolic of the peace and tranquillity of heaven and the supernatural life; athletics and ship-imagery refer to the journey and the struggle of life; symbols referring to women (as Mother Church, the milk of grace, the marriage procession, etc.) seem to suggest the love and security which we look for in the anxieties of the present life.

[66] All of *Discourse* 9 makes this clear; see also Farges, *Les idées morales et religieuses* 212 ff., 219 ff. Cf. n. 59 above. Methodius' chiliasm has been called 'spiritual' because it does not stress the material or temporal aspects of Christ's final reign on earth: see e.g., A. Piolanti, 'Millenarismo,' EC 8 (1952) 1008–1011. Indeed, it is difficult to form a concept of the doctrine. The 'millennia' (at least in the first six periods of the world) were not perhaps definite periods of time. On the

Seventh Day (or the seventh millennium) after the resurrection of the body, the material world would somehow be restored (*palingenesis*); all marriage would cease, and it would be a time of feasting with Christ in the Promised Land, a celebration of the true feast of Tabernacles. At the end of this Millennium of Rest, the bodies of the just would be changed to angelic form and beauty (9.5: Bo 120.20 f., and see n. 55 above). What was to happen to the wicked, those who are not 'sealed with Christ's blood' (cf. 9.1: Bo 115.18), Methodius does not explain. In *Symp.* 10.4: Bo 126.15 ff., however, he explains how God threatened men at the time of Moses with judgment and the eternal fire if they were not obedient (the passage is also quoted by Photius); and Susanna, in *Thecla's Hymn* §16: Bo 135.12 f., refers to the eternal, fiery penalties which awaited her had she consented to sin.

[67] F. J. Dölger, ΙΧΘΥΣ 1 (2nd ed. Münster i. W. 1928) 105; so, too, Plumpe, *Mater Ecclesia* 123. Cf. also F. Loofs, *Leitfaden zum Studium der Dogmengeschichte* (5th ed. by K. Aland, Halle 1950) 1.175–179.

[68] Peter Heseler, 'Zum Symposium des Methodius,' *Byzant.-neugr. Jahrb.* 6 (1928) 95–118 (=I), 10 (1933) 325–341 (=II).

[69] Thus it is difficult to quote anything outside of the ten central discourses, since the prelude, the interludes, Logos 11, *Thecla's Hymn*, and the epilogue are not subdivided in Bonwetsch; Bonwetsch's marginal numerals, taken from Allatius, are inconvenient, having no relationship to thought-divisions. The titles of each discourse are from the MSS—except for the 11th ('Arete') which, though omitted from the MSS, has been traditional with editors since Combefis.

[70] See E. Martini, *Catalogo di manoscritti greci esistenti nelle biblioteche italiane* (2 vols. in 3, Milan 1893–1902), 2.221. Here Heseler (I.108) shows that Bonwetsch (xviii) is wrong in claiming Allatius used B (Barb. 427); further Heseler (114 f.) proves conclusively that Allatius' MS, Vallicell. 119.2, is merely a copy of M and therefore useless.

[71] Heseler (I.110 ff.) proves conclusively that Possinus (or Valesius) used B (a copy of P), but made a mistake in referring to it as a 'codex Vaticanus.'

[72] *Art. cit.*, II.338 ff.

[73] See Heseler, *ibid.* 335 ff. On Andreas, Arethas and Oecumenius, see Krumbacher, 129 ff.; but the difficulty is cleared up by H. B. Swete, *The Apocalypse of St. John* (London 1911) cxcviii ff., who points out the dependence of Andreas on Oecumenius (who is not, however, useful for the text of Methodius), and of Arethas on Andreas, whereas the 'Oecumenius' printed by Cramer, *Catenae graecae patrum in N.T.* 8 (Oxford 1840) is nothing more than an abridged version of Andreas'

commentary. Thus it is called Pseudo-Oecumenius by Heseler (*art. cit.* II.336) and is still considered of value in restoring Methodius' text.

[74] A new Greek text, on which the present translation is based, is to appear in the series *Sources chrétiennes*. The Reverend Anselmo Albareda, O.S.B., of the Vatican Library, very kindly supplied me with an excellent microfilm of the important Vatican manuscript (O); Dr. Paul Maas of Oxford has shown himself most ready to help in the solution of difficult textual problems; a microfilm of M, the direct copy of O, was readily available from the Bibliothèque Nationale. I should also here mention my indebtedness to the Rev. Martin McCarthy, S.J. of the Vatican Observatory, who helped to solve some problems in connection with Methodius' astronomical knowledge; to Mr. William Hendricks, S.J., who did photographic work; and to Mr. John Grady of Columbia University whose help and advice were valuable in the final revision of the manuscript.

[75] And also omitted by Arethas and Pseudo-Oecumenius.

[76] In Fliche-Martin, *Histoire de l'Église* 2 (Paris 1948) 384 n. 5; see also Lebreton's review of Farges, *Les idées morales et religieuses* in *Rech. de sciences religieuses* (1930) 369 ff. The Christology of the passage stands in definite contrast with *Symp.* 3.4: Bo 31.3, where Christ is referred to as the eldest of the Aeons, and 10.6: Bo 128.24 ff., in which the Word and the Holy Spirit seemed to be referred to as the two first-born powers who stand as bodyguard to the Lord. But there is not sufficient evidence to decide that the 'orthodox' passages are interpolated, as against the possibility of later revision by the author himself.

[77] For an evaluation of the importance of the Chester Beatty papyrus in the problem of the Pauline text, see G. Zuntz, *The Text of the Epistles. A Disquisition on the Corpus Paulinum* (Schweich Lectures for 1946, London 1953).

[78] *Symp.* 3.1: Bo 27.4 f.

[79] *Symp.* 3.2: Bo 28 f.

[80] *Symp.* 9.1: Bo 113.23 ff.

[81] In the introduction to his masterly German translation, p. viii; Fendt sees the *Symposium* as a source of irritation to those who in Methodius' day attacked the notion of celibacy. But both Fendt and A. Puech (*Histoire de la littérature grecque chrétienne* 515) find in Methodius' elaboration on Plato a much more brilliant conception than I am prepared to admit. Closer to the truth, I feel, is G. Salmon, 'Methodius,' *Dict. of Christ. Biog.* 3 (1882) 910, when he says that Methodius 'caught very little of his [Plato's] style or spirit.'

[82] See 'History and Symbol,' *Theol. Studies* 18 (1957) 376–379.

TEXT

Prelude

[1] Gregorion is pictured as paying a visit to Eubulion—although the scene is not clear—and it is Gregorion who takes her leave at the close to go home, apparently, for dinner. It seems clear that Methodius here uses the form Eubulion to disguise his own part in the treatise (instead of the form Eubulius, as in the *De resurrectione*) and to indicate that the character is a woman; indeed, as Puech has pointed out, a male character would seem out of place in the discussion. Again, Methodius attempts in *Symp.* 11 (Bo 137.10) to distinguish himself from Eubulion; but the fact that all the MSS at times have adjectives or participles referring to Eubulion as though it were masculine, suggests that the author was not perhaps wholly successful in keeping up the illusion. But it would seem entirely unnecessary to change the name everywhere to Eubulius (and correct the agreement of adjectives) as Poussines, Jahn, and Bardenhewer would prefer.

The meeting of Eubulion and Gregorion—the request for information and the technique of the opening account (Gregorion tells the story in the first person but it is Theopatra whom she is quoting throughout)—is an obvious imitation of the opening of Plato's *Symposium* (172 A ff.). Methodius, however, is inconsistent: for here Gregorion was herself present at the banquet as cupbearer (the exact significance of this detail escapes us), and hence would not need to have received the story at second hand. Methodius had perhaps originally two alternative ways of starting the story and ended by incorporating both.

[2] Literally 'us'; though Eubulion uses this elsewhere, there is no indication that anyone else is present with her; hence this may represent either Methodius' prospective audience or, as I prefer, a simple use of the plural pronoun for the singular.

[3] This detail may have had some further meaning for Methodius' audience, seeing that it is unnecessary and inconsistent with Gregorion's own account. It may, however, merely mean that the character Gregorion stands for 'the Lady from Termessus' and that she had often acted as host for Methodius and his friends. Female cupbearers are apparently mentioned in Eccles. 2.8 (where the worldly rich man speaks of his pleasures).

[4] Adapted from Homer, *Il.* 4.3 f.; the original reads: 'And they

[the gods] drank to one another out of golden goblets, gazing upon the city of Troy.' For Methodius, the banquet of the virgins is symbolic of the Olympian bliss of the Millennium. This adaptation of the *Iliad* is an instance of the Christian technique of the spiritual interpretation of Homer: see H. Rahner, *Griechische Mythen in christlicher Deutung* (Zurich 1945) 353 ff.: 'Heiliger Homer.'

[5] After the Homeric quotation and the reference to wine pouring, Gregorion's remark hardly seems apropos; it would be more suitable if some further discussion had preceded, and thus I have marked a lacuna in the text.

[6] The description of Arete is reminiscent of the so-called *Choice of Heracles* by Prodicus of Ceos as paraphrased in Xenophon, *Mem.* 2.1.21 ff. There, as the young Heracles meditates on the two paths of life, two women 'of great stature' approach. The one, Arete, 'was lovely to look upon and of noble bearing; her body was adorned with purity, her eyes with modesty and her whole carriage with sobriety; and she was dressed in white.' The other, Eudaimonia, rushes up to him and tries to entice him with her charms: 'she was plump and soft and well-fed; her face was made up so that it was whiter and redder than it should be; and her bearing tended to exaggerate her height. Her eyes were fully opened, and her clothes such as to reveal her charms.' On the 'difficult parth to virtue,' see also Simonides, frag. 58 (Bergk); Hesiod, *Works and Days* 286 ff.; Aristotle's *Hymn to Virtue* 1–5.

[7] Cf. 2 Cor. 11.2.

[8] This detail would seem to refer to the parable of the Wise and Foolish Virgins: the Wise Virgins entered the marriage household before the doors were shut (Matt. 25.10).—In the description which follows it is difficult to determine whether Methodius imagined the banquet spread in the earlier fashion with three couches (*lecti*) set about a table, or in the later fashion which was becoming more common in the Christian period when diners reclined on a sigma-shaped couch (*stibadium*) which curved about the table. In the older style, the place of honor was the first place at the middle couch, whereas in the sigma-shaped type the places of honor were at the ends (*cornua*); in either case, nine was felt to be the maximum number at one *mensa*; and it may be that Methodius' choice of ten is symbolic of the perfection of which he is treating. For details on the two methods of dining, see J. Carcopino, *La vie quotidienne à Rome à l'apogée de l'empire* (Paris 1939) 307 f. At Methodius' banquet the ten virgins sat at table—in general, women did not recline—with Thecla in the place of honor; Arete does not apparently dine with the others.

[9] This description recalls the realm of the blessed as depicted in the pseudo-Platonic *Axiochus* 371 D. But the details may very well have become stereotyped; the *ekphrasis* or description of an action or a place was a regular practice in the rhetorical schools of the Empire: see Aphthonius, *Progymnasmata* 12 (46.15 Spengel), and Theon, *Progymn.* 11 (118.6 Spengel); and on the 'pleasance' in the Late Latin writers, see C. S. Baldwin, *Medieval Rhetoric and Poetic* (New York 1928) 17 f.; also E. R. Curtius, *European Literature and the Latin Middle Ages* (New York 1953) 195 ff.

[10] The sense is somewhat obscure; Clark, in his translation, speaks of the shafts of light coming in 'regular currents'; the Greek (μετὰ πολλῆς εὐταξίας) is difficult, but it would seem that Methodius is referring to the geometrical pattern made by shafts of sunlight piercing through clouds or mist.

[11] The description may be intended to suggest the spring of Gen. 2.6 and the four rivers of Gen. 2.11–14, with possible overtones of Plato, *Theaet.* 144 B, *Phaedr.* 229 B. Water is a frequent occurrence in descriptions of the place of the blessed and symbolizes, in conjunction with oil, the freshness and moistness of heaven as opposed to the dryness of death: for a discussion, see R. Onians, *The Origins of European Thought* (Cambridge 1954) 272 ff., although some of his conclusions are far-fetched. In Methodius' *Symposium* all references to liquid ultimately seem to refer to 'Immortality itself as it wells up from the pure bosom of the Almighty.'

For the imagery of the meadow filled with fragrant flowers, cf. the *Apocalypse of Peter* 5.15 f. (Klostermann): 'And the Lord showed me a very great region outside this world exceeding bright with light, and the air of that place illuminated with the beams of the sun and the earth of itself flowering with blossoms that fade not, and full of spices and plants, fair-flowering and incorruptible, and bearing blessed fruit. And so great was the blossom that the odour thereof was borne thence even unto us' (tr. by M. R. James, *The Apocryphal New Testament* [Oxford 1950] 508). For related pagan motifs, see I. A. Richmond, *Archaeology and the After-Life in Pagan and Christian Imagery* (London 1950) 26 f.

[12] The *vitex agnus castus* (Linnaeus) of the family of *verbenaceae* is sometimes called the Chaste-tree, Hemp-Tree, Monk's Pepper-Tree or Abraham's Balm. It is a shrub or small tree with a strong aromatic odor that grows in humid places along the Mediterranean from Spain to western Turkey and Persia, and has also come to thrive in the southern United States. It is usually about 10 to 15 feet high, and has digitate leaves and spikes of purplish blue (less frequently white)

flowers, which blossom from about July to September. See H. A. Gleason, *Illustrated Flora of the North Eastern United States and Adjacent Canada* (New York 1952) 3.139. It was long thought to have anti-aphrodisiac qualities if carried on the person, eaten, or brewed; see LSJ, *s.v.*; P. Wagler, 'Agnos,' RE 1.1 (1894) 832–4. For a discussion of the symbolism in Methodius and other Fathers, see H. Rahner, *Griechische Mythen* 390 ff. In Christian times, the use of sprigs of agnus castus by those who had taken a vow of chastity was perhaps also encouraged by the LXX version of the Levitical legislation in Lev. 23.40 (but not the MT) which recommended the use of agnus castus branches for the Feast of Tabernacles. The shrub would scarcely be big enough to provide shade for the ten virgins at a banquet table, but the detail is undoubtedly borrowed from Plato's *Phaedrus* 230 B, where Socrates and Phaedrus are described as resting under the shade of a plane tree and an agnus castus. For another important use of tree-symbolism, see the Parable of the Willow Tree in Hermas, *Sim.* 8; and for the use of similar symbolism in the Neo-Platonists, see E. R. Dodds, *Proclus. The Elements of Theology* (Oxford 1933) 198.

LOGOS 1: MARCELLA

[1] οὖθαρ τῆς ἐκκλησίας: so all MSS except M (which has the milder οὖθαρ τῆς ἀφθαρσίας, an obvious conjecture by the scribe of M seeing that the last word in O, from which he copied, is very indistinct). The reading is wisely adopted by Bonwetsch who departs, in this case, from the text of Allatius, Combefis (=Migne), and Jahn (whom Fendt follows). The reading of M is of course the easier one: chastity would then be the 'source (breast) of immortality, its flower, its first fruits,' and one could compare Rom. 8.23, 11.16 and 1 Cor. 15.20. If we read ἐκκλησίας, Methodius' imagery seems confused: he would be saying that chastity is at once the bosom of the Church (i.e., that men are nourished by it unto immortality: compare 'Immortality ... as it wells up from the pure bosom of the Almighty'), as well as the flower of the Church and her first fruits. But the agreement of the MSS O and P on such a peculiar reading, as well as the untrustworthiness of M, would seem to put the matter beyond all reasonable doubt. The reading is also adopted by Plumpe, *Mater Ecclesia* 110 and n. 3. The older reading is adopted by W. Völker, *Der wahre Gnostiker nach Clemens Alexandrinus* (TU 57, Berlin-Leipzig 1952) 476, but his discussion is interesting.

[2] Matt. 19.12; Methodius might have been expected to expand his interpretation of this passage, especially in view of Origen's notorious error.

[3] Greek μετοχετεύσασαι (see LSJ, *s.v.*); 'vaulting over' (Clark) would seem natural of a chariot approaching a stream, but the instances cited in LSJ will only permit the sense of 'channelling,' 'diverting,' and the like. Although the meaning is unexpected in the context, there is no reason to emend the text.

[4] This is the 'Ascent of the Soul'—a mystical imaginative vision so popular with the Neo-Platonists—modelled on Plato, *Phaedr.* 246 D ff. In Plato the souls under the leadership of the gods drive their chariots (as though in a race or a festal procession) up over the world towards the plain of truth, where they pause and contemplate the Ideas. In Plato, the chariot-driver is Judgment and the two horses are Courage and Desire. The section especially imitated by Methodius, however, is the 'Ride of the Gods,' for only the gods are able to steer their chariots correctly. As for men, only a few get a glimpse of the Ideas and only for a short time; the others lose control of their horses and fall back to earth again. For a discussion of the passage in Plato, see A. E. Taylor, *Plato: The Man and His Work* (London 1952) 307 f.

In Methodius, however, it is difficult to determine the exact meaning and tone of the passage, and this is complicated by the highly charged 'baroque' style. It would seem that by the metaphor of the Ascent, Methodius is referring to the practice of asceticism in this life with the possible connotation of mystical experience. And though there is no explicit reference to the Millennium, the Ascent may perhaps be taken to foreshadow the permanent 'leap' which the chaste make on the last day. St. Ambrose seems to echo Methodius' thought in *De virginibus* 1.3.11 (Faller), where he speaks of virginity 'quae sponsum sibi invenit in caelo. Haec nubes aera angelos sideraque transgrediens verbum Dei in ipso sinu Patris invenit, et toto hausit pectore.' On the use of the Platonic imagery by Gregory of Nyssa, see H. F. Cherniss, *The Platonism of Gregory of Nyssa* (Univ. of California Publ. in Class. Phil. 11, Berkeley 1930) 16 ff., and J. Daniélou, *Platonisme et théologie mystique* (Paris 1944) 61 ff. With the Neo-Platonists, this Ascent symbolizes the soul's gradual release from matter by the practice of interior asceticism and the quelling of the disturbances of the mind: see Plotinus, *Enn.* 2.9.18 (Schwyzer-Henry); and also by the practice of reflection or 'introversion': see Dodds, *Proclus* 202 f. In this way, the soul as it rises throws off 'impurities' and becomes 'more divine': cf. Ps.-Dionysius the Areopagite, *De eccles. hierarch.* 1.3 (PG 3.373C–376A).

What is the exact meaning of Methodius' vision of Immortality? It is perhaps inspired by the 'living water' mentioned by Jesus (John 4.10) as well as the rivers of living water (John 7.38: apparently a quotation from the Old Testament, but the source, if not e.g. Zach.

14.8 or Isa. 44.3, is difficult to determine). The Immortality which wells up from the bosom of the Father may refer to any of the following:

1. The divine nature of the Godhead. Athanasius, e.g. *Epist. ad Serap.* 19 (PG 26.573BC), uses this imagery: cf. C. R. B. Shapland, *The Letters of St. Athanasius Concerning the Holy Spirit* (New York 1951) 108 f. and notes;
2. The procession of the Son from the Father, as suggested by Ambrose, *De virginibus* 1.3.11 (Faller), quoted above; cf. also Gregory of Nyssa, *De virginitate* 2 (Cavarnos 254.17 ff.);
3. The divine nature understood in a metaphorical sense, that is, divine grace as it is communicated as 'living water' by God to the faithful Christian (and, in this case, to the virgin);
4. The virtue of chastity conceived in the perfection of its divine exemplar, somewhat in the manner of the Neo-Platonists who taught that the exemplars of all the virtues existed in *Nous*: cf. Porphyry, *Sent.* 32.1–5 (Mommert); in Methodius, however, the virtue is communicable to men through God's grace and their own *askesis.*

Our text is further complicated by Methodius' own fantasy and it is difficult to determine just how much is imaginative, but I should incline to interpretation 4. For there is no reason in the context for bringing in the doctrine of the divine processions. Moreover, our interpretation would seem to go farthest in explaining the nature of the 'gnosis' which Methodius is attempting to set forth. It is interesting to compare the Coptic *Charm of the Father* (apparently an exorcistic prayer derived from Judaeo-Christian and Gnostic sources) as quoted by E. R. Goodenough, *Jewish Symbols in the Greco-Roman Period* (New York 1953–54) 2.184 f. Here we read of 'the cup in his the Father's right hand, from which he gave the angels to drink,' and of 'water streaming from the head of the Father'—where the water seems to symbolize some communication of the divine life.

[5] Cf. John 13.5 ff.; in Methodius' view 'unwashed feet' refers to a state of imperfection due to 'baseness' (here, apparently, lack of perseverance).

[6] Clark, among others, translates as though Methodius were referring to pagan temples with their statues of the gods—and, indeed, not only is the language with him but the parallel with Plato, *Symp.* 216 E, favors his rendering. In Plato's *Symposium*, Alcibiades (215 AB) compares Socrates to a Silenus (a hollow figure of Dionysus' companion in which statuettes were enclosed as in a shrine), for despite

Socrates' rough exterior Alcibiades declares he has seen the 'statuettes within,' that is, his good qualities. On the Silenus-statues, see A. Baumeister, *Denkmäler des klassischen Altertums* (Munich-Leipzig 1888) 3.1642, where he states that Plato's text is the only evidence. Porphyry speaks of the sanctuary of a man's thoughts, in which he should keep an image of the living God: *Ad Marcellam* 11 (Nauck). And Rabelais, in the prologue of *Gargantua and Pantagruel*, compares his own book to a Silenus, which he describes as a kind of medicine cabinet with fantastic animal figures on the outside.

It is difficult to conceive of Methodius as referring here to pagan temples and idol-worship, rather than to the care and adornment of statues in Christian places of worship. But, despite the existence of some early Christian statues, the evidence is in general against a cult at this period: see E. Bevan, *Holy Images. An Inquiry into Idolatry and Image-Worship in Ancient Paganism and in Christianity* (London 1940) 103–112.

[7] Ps. 37.6; this Davidic psalm, from one of the oldest sections of the Psalter, has traditionally been one of the seven 'Penitential Psalms.'

[8] Lev. 2.13, where the priestly code sets down the ritual for bloodless offerings. Salt was regularly prescribed not only for seasoning but also, apparently, as a symbol of the permanence of the sacrifice. Cf. the 'covenant of salt' in Num. 18.19.

[9] Matt. 5.13, meaning, apparently, that the disciples were to be as a preservative for the world's righteousness.

[10] 1 Cor. 7.32–34 abridged. The passage will be treated more fully in *Symp.* 3.11.

[11] That is, our discourse is not intended for them; they ought not be allowed to listen. The section may almost be called a 'topic of exclusion' which emphasizes at the outset the seriousness of the treatise. For 'topics of the exordium' in general, see E. R. Curtius, *European Literature* 85–89. Clark's 'discrimination must be exercised with respect to these' is a misleading translation. Here it is obviously Methodius the preacher talking and the artifice of ethopoeia has momentarily lapsed.

[12] Lev. 18.9, where the prohibition expressly concerns marriage with a half-sister; brother-sister marriages are similarly forbidden in Lev. 20.17.

[13] Methodius seems to exaggerate in order to make a case. Actually there is no evidence for any extensive practice of brother-sister marriages among the Hebrews: see A. Lods, *Israël des origines au milieu du VIIIe siècle* (Paris 1932) 220. Cf. also Augustine, *De civ. Dei* 15.16, where he appeals to *melior consuetudo* and *humanus sensus* against the practice.

[14] Ecclus. 18.30.
[15] *Ibid.* 19.2.
[16] Prov. 5.18; the first part of the verse is in the Douay version translated: *Let thy vein be blessed*, etc.
[17] Jer. 5.8.
[18] Wisd. 4.3; the inspired author would seem to be referring to the marriage customs of the Ptolemaic rulers of Egypt.
[19] Ecclus. 23.1, 4, 6; the text of the LXX has been abridged and partly paraphrased. In the Douay it runs: *Give me not haughtiness of my eyes. . . . Take from me the greediness of the belly, and let not the lusts of the flesh take hold of me.*
[20] Wisd. 4.1 f.
[21] Here the Migne text (Combefis), followed by many editors, has 'of the many patriarchs and many prophets and righteous men,' but the words 'of the many patriarchs' are not in the MSS OP and derive from an insert in the text of M; that the reading has no claim to authenticity is suggested by the fact that O (from which M was copied) is at this point very faded and difficult to read.
[22] The prefix ἀρχι- (see LSJ) usually designates one who is a leader or president of a group (e.g., of officials, priests, etc.). For Christ the Archpriest or Highpriest, see Heb. 5 and *passim*. 'Archangel' may merely mean 'God's chief emissary to the world;' but it may also derive from the curious tradition of an archangel who was 'administrator-in-chief' of the world, as we find it in Irenaeus, *Dem.* 11 (Smith, ACW 16.54, with n. 68). The author of *The Shepherd* speaks of an angel named Michael 'who has power over men and governs them; wherefore he has put the law into the hearts of the faithful' (*Sim.* 8.3.3); but in another vision the archangel is spoken of as the Son of God (*Sim.* 9.12.8), and the Son seems to be confused with the Spirit in *Sim.* 5.6.5. With the passage in Methodius we may compare Gregory of Nyssa, *De virg.* 2 (Cavarnos 253 ff.).
[23] This text causes difficulty because it would appear that Methodius is denying that man was made both in the image and likeness of God (cf. Gen. 1.26). But in this Methodius is following the doctrine first reflected in Clement of Alexandria: that man, by being given intelligence, was made 'in the image' of God; only through the practice of virtue and the imitation of Christ could he achieve 'likeness': for the texts and a discussion, see H. Merki, Ὁμοίωσις Θεῷ. *Von der platonischen Angleichung an Gott zur Gottähnlichkeit bei Gregor von Nyssa* (Paradosis 7, Fribourg 1952) 83 f. It is not clear in Methodius what the relationship is between man's ὁμοίωσις and the Fall: it would appear from Methodius' general doctrine that the 'likeness' is to be merely a

restoration of what was lost—and so it seems to be taken by Merki, 107 n. 1, quoting only *De res.* 1.49.3 (Bo 303.6–9); but the truth would seem to be that Methodius did not attempt to draw all the consequences of his doctrine, or to make all his references to it consistent. See further R. Leys, *L'image de Dieu chez Saint Grégoire de Nysse. Esquisse d'une doctrine* (Brussels 1951), and H. Graef, ACW 18.184 and Index, *s.vv.* Cf. also n. 27 below.

[24] 'Spotted and stained' is difficult and is not perhaps to be pressed; it refers to the vicarious nature of Christ's Atonement (cf. 2 Cor. 5.21 and 1 Pet. 2.24) as well as His taking up of a human nature which was, in us, marred by sin (cf. Heb. 4.15). But how can we receive in turn the divine form He bore for our sake? By the divine form is apparently meant the divine nature which was, in Christ, united to the human nature; as communicated to us, however, this refers to the finite actuation of grace in us, a state, moreover, which Christ as man possessed in the highest created degree.

[25] The bracketed words are probably to be deleted; the text of Bo here is actually a conflation of the readings of O and P (depending ultimately on the Combefis-Migne text). But 'panels' which is only in P (and its copies) may well be a gloss; it could hardly have stood without some limiting word as 'just as'—and thus this has been supplied by earlier editors since Poussines.

[26] Compare the Peripatetic distinction of the three kinds of good: the morally good, the useful, and the pleasurable—as implied, for example, in Aristotle's discussion of the types of friendship, *Eth. Nic.* 8.4: 1156^b; cf. W. D. Ross, *Aristotle* (5 ed. London 1953) 190–192.

[27] Although this clause does not fit in logically with the preceding, it is consistent with Methodius' doctrine of 'likeness'; see n. 23 above. Cf. Plato, *Theaet.* 176 A: 'To fly [from the evil of the world] is a becoming like unto God so far as lies in our power.' Cf. Merki, *op. cit.* 2 ff.

[28] Apoc. 14.1–5. For Christ as the Archshepherd, see 1 Peter 5.4.

[29] ἀπάνωθεν, only here in Methodius, would seem to mean 'from above,' 'from heaven'; Combefis, however, translates it '*ab initio*' (and so Clark, 'from the beginning'), referring it perhaps to the divine predestination.

[30] Apoc. 7.9, slightly paraphrased; the Douay reads: *After this I saw a great multitude, which no man could number, of all nations, and tribes, and peoples and tongues.*

[31] And yet, later Methodius will say that the number of virgins is beyond counting—*Symp.* 7.7.

LOGOS 2: THEOPHILA

[1] Cf. Plato, *Symp.* 185 E.

[2] Nowhere in our text does Marcella say this explicitly, and it is very likely that in Marcella's discussion of continence in Logos 1, e.g. in 1.2 or 1.5, Methodius had, in the spirit of the *controversia*, put a stronger expression into the mouth of his first speaker and that this was later deleted by a later *corrector*.

[3] Methodius uses the word λόγος to mean (a) the inspired word or text of Scripture, (b) God's Wisdom as speaking in the Old or the New Testament, and (c) the Word, the Second Person of the Trinity. Often it is difficult to know the precise nuance of an individual text, but in any case the various levels of meaning are connected in the writer's mind: for it is the Wisdom of God that is revealed in the inspired text of the Scriptures and manifested in the flesh in Christ.

[4] 'This Scripture' (Clark), i.e., the book of Genesis, but it would seem that Methodius is speaking of a Scriptural argument in general and wishes to distinguish this section from the arguments which are to follow.

[5] John 5.17.

[6] Gen. 1.28.

[7] Gen. 2.23.

[8] Gen. 2.24. In this discussion Methodius has conflated many of the pre-Socratic theories on the origin of human seed. Democritus held that the seed was drawn from the entire body (Diels-Kranz[7] 2.123.31, 167.18); others connected it with bone-marrow, and Diogenes of Apollonia (fifth century B.C.) described it as the foam of the blood, a mixture of blood and air (Diels-Kranz[7] 2.57.13): see K. Freeman, *The Pre-Socratic Philosophers* (Oxford 1955) 282; also R. Onians, *Origins* 121. On anatomical knowledge during this period, see F. W. Bayer, 'Anatomie,' RAC 1.430–436.

[9] Jer. 1.5.

[10] Job 38.14 according to the LXX, not MT. Although the reference to creation is somewhat out of place in the Lord's words to Job, the LXX version is easier than the MT, which reads 'It is turned as clay to the seal; and they stand as a garment' (Jerome's Vulgate: *Restituetur ut lutum signaculum, et stabit sicut vestimentum*). The MT text would seem to be corrupt, and the reading of the LXX, however easy, does not seem to be right. On the 'hymn of glory' in Job 38, see R. H. Pfeiffer, *Introduction to the Old Testament* (London 1948) 691 f.

[11] Job 10.8.

[12] 'Witnesses' or 'martyrs'; although there is no immediate reference to persecution, both levels of meaning are perhaps present.

[13] So Matt. 24.22.

[14] Wisd. 3.16: the sense of the passage in Wisdom is that the children of such unions were doomed to a dishonorable life because of the sin of their parents. For parallel Greek ideas in the classical period, see Sophocles, *Antigone* 582–625, *Oedipus Rex* 1486–1502.

[15] Methodius' imagery seems certainly to have been inspired by the myth of Plato's Cave in the *Republic* (bk. 7) and perhaps by primitive representations of the uterus: cf. the uterine symbols on Jewish amulets in E. R. Goodenough, *Jewish Symbols* (New York 1953), plates, nn. 1174–77. It is an odd fact that the psychologist Carl Jung has suggested that Plato's Cave was an unconscious projection of womb-imagery: see R. Hostie, *Religion and the Psychology of Jung* (tr. by G. R. Lamb, New York 1957) 46, with the literature cited. Again, Methodius may have seen such shaft-caves in the mountains of Lycia, perhaps in connection with quarries, mines or pottery kilns. One might also compare the stark representation of mountain scenes in early Byzantine painting: cf. K. Weitzmann, *Die byzantinische Buchmalerei des* 9. *und* 10. *Jahrhunderts* (Berlin 1935). From the doctrinal point of view, Methodius may have been influenced by the Neo-Platonic theory of the descent of the soul—as, for example, in Plotinus, *Enn.* 4.8.1–4 (ed. Volkmann)—which apparently originated with Posidonius: see E. R. Dodds, *Proclus* (Oxford 1933) 307–8, 317.

[16] A reference to the two penalties applied in Roman law to persons of lower social rank (the *humiliores*), the *castigatio* and the *crematio* (or possibly merely torture by fire, the *quaestio per ignem*): see A. Berger, *Encyclopedic Dictionary of Roman Law* (Trans. Amer. Philos. Soc. 43.2, 1953), *s. vv.* The torture and scourging of slaves is a regular motif in the Greek novelists Chariton, Heliodorus, and Achilles Tatius: cf. H. Musurillo, *The Acts of the Pagan Martyrs* (Oxford 1954) 253.

[17] Emending the text here to ἔνδον ἡμῶν, instead of ἔνδον ἡμᾶς (Bo). On the imagery of the body as the soul's garment, see Plato, *Gorg.* 523 D, *Axioch.* 366 A; cf. also Dodds, *Proclus* 307.—The MS O inserts a long 'interpretation' on this passage immediately after the words 'descent of the soul . . .' The anonymous interpreter, who may date from the seventh century (he quotes Pseudo-Dionysius the Areopagite), defends Methodius against the charge of Origenism and suggests that the passage describing this descent may have been interpolated. In any case, by saying that souls come down from heaven, says the interpreter, Methodius means that 'the soul by its nature and substance is heavenly, and thus it is said to be a co-partner with the

heavenly spirits, for it is, like them, immortal, spiritual, and invisible.' For the entire passage, see Allatius' transcription reprinted in Migne, PG 18.223 f.

[18] This is the central idea of Methodius' treatise *On Free Will*: cf. 15.1 (Bo 183) and 18.7 (194), and for a discussion, Bonwetsch, *Die Theologie des M.* 69 ff.; also Badurina, *Doctrina* 41 ff.

[19] The evil effects of the invention of the first sword was a frequent subject in the ancient poets: see, for example, Tibullus 1.10, with the commentary by K. F. Smith, *The Elegies of Albius Tibullus* (New York 1913) 376 f., with the references there cited.

[20] There is a curious clause found here in the Migne (Combefis) edition, 'prepared channels for the blood and a tender windpipe for the breath'; but it is found only in codex M, which here offers a conjecture for words which were illegible in O, and is certainly not authentic.

Methodius' anatomical knowledge seems to have been derived directly or indirectly from contemporary medical manuals. Galen, for example, *On the Natural Faculties* 2.3.83, compares the material within the uterus to the sculptor's wax (which was, and is still, used for the preliminary stage in the casting of a bronze statue), and later mentions the possibility of the fetus drowning. Stoic philosophy laid great stress on the manifestation of divine providence in the development of the human embryo: cf. Diogenes Laertius 7.158 ff. During the patristic period, the idea of the *deus artifex*, which was perhaps a fusion of the Greek demiurge and the Jewish concept of the divine potter (Isa. 29.16, Rom. 9.20), becomes a literary commonplace: see E. R. Curtius, *European Literature and the Latin Middle Ages* (tr. by W. Trask, New York 1953) 544 ff.

[21] μεταξωγραφῶν: not listed in LSJ, but noticed from the present passage by Sophocles, *s.v.*, who renders it 'retouch'; Methodius is here attempting to render the difficult concept of Christ as the exemplary cause of our sanctification.

[22] Cf. Matt. 18.10. The word 'guardian' (τημελοῦχος) is also found in Clement of Alexandria's quotation from the *Apocalypse of Peter* (Kleine Texte 3.12.17 ff. Klostermann) in his *Eclogae* 48.1 (GCS 3.150 Stählin): 'Peter in his *Apocalypse* says that premature babies . . . are handed over to a guardian angel, that they may receive knowledge and come to a better dwelling-place, but only after suffering what they would have suffered had they lived in the body.' The doctrine here is quite unique: for a discussion see E. Schneweis, *Angels and Demons according to Lactantius* (SCA 3, Washington 1944) 72 ff., and J. Daniélou, *Les anges et leur mission d'après les Pères de l'Église* (Paris

1951) 92–110 (=Engl. trans. by D. Heimann [Westminster, Md. 1956] 68–82).

[23] F. J. Dölger, 'Das Lebensrecht des ungeborenen Kindes und die Fruchtabtreibung in der Bewertung der heidnischen und christlichen Antike,' *Antike und Christentum* 4 (1933) 50 ff., suggests that Methodius is here following the *Apocalypse of Peter*, particularly the section preserved fully only in the Ethiopic version (given by Dölger 50 f.) which describes the Last Judgment of those parents who have murdered their children by abortion, and the confrontation of parents by their children in the place of the resurrection. Since the Greek of the *Apocalypse* is not fully preserved at this point, we do not know how close Methodius' text came to the original Greek recension. See E. Hennecke, *Neutestamentliche Apokryphen* (Tübingen 1904) 213.

[24] Wisd. 4.6.

[25] Gen. 2.7. The Greek words used by Methodius for 'ageless and immortal' are used by Homer of the life of the gods in *Il.* 8.539, 12.323.

[26] Wisd. 15.10 f., of the pagan sculptors who made statues for temple worship; their beliefs, says the author of Wisdom, were far more base than the materials they used.

[27] 1 Tim. 2.4.

[28] 1 Cor. 7.38.

[29] Cf. Athanasius, *De virginitate* 7: fasting, together with virginity, puts man in the ranks of the angels. This concept of 'angelic transformation' had a great effect on ascetical theory, especially through the influence of Origen: see W. Völker, *Das Vollkommenheitsideal des Origenes* (Tübingen 1931) 25; O. Chadwick, *John Cassian* (Cambridge 1950) 92 f.; H. Musurillo, 'The Problem of Ascetical Fasting in the Greek Patristic Writers,' *Traditio* 12 (1956), esp. 11 ff.

[30] Matt. 22.30.

[31] Matt. 19.12.

[32] Ps. 44.10 and 14. Cf. also Plumpe, *Mater Ecclesia* 110. We have here the first statement in Methodius of the epithalamium-theme to be developed later on.

LOGOS 3: THALIA

[1] Gen 2.23 f., and cf. Eph. 5.31 f.

[2] But cf. *Symp.* 2.1, where she quotes Gen. 2.23 without (at least in our text) excluding a further meaning; Methodius perhaps makes his characters exaggerate in an attempt to imitate Plato's style and the tone of rhetorical debate.

[3] 'Like trees' seems illogical here, but it is perhaps a literary reminiscence of *Timaeus* 91 C (so Bonwetsch) in which the procreation of animals is compared to trees being plucked for fruit. 'Animals that they are'; ζῷον, regularly of animals, is sometimes applied as a generic term for both men and animals: see W. F. Arndt and F. W. Gingrich, *A Greek-English Lexicon of the New Testament and Other Early Christian Literature* (Chicago 1957) *s.v.* Cf. also Logos 8, n. 74 below.

[4] Eph. 5.28–32. The use of the word μυστήριον (*sacramentum*) as applied to the union of man and woman is peculiar to Ephesians: for a discussion, see M. Dibelius, *An die Kolosser, Epheser; an Philemon* (3 ed. by H. Greeven, Tübingen 1953) 84. Methodius' quotation of Ephesians here is close to the text as found in Irenaeus and in the Chester Beatty papyrus of Paul.

[5] Retaining the text ἀνδρειότερον against the commonly accepted emendation ἀκριβέστερον ('more accurately'). The entire sentence is a curious one in the Greek, and against Bonwetsch I have followed the earlier editors who have emended the text to express the subject of the infinitive and the introductory verb.

[6] This is Methodius' clear declaration against the extreme allegorism of the Alexandrian school, on which see Quasten 2.1–4, and cf. especially H. de Lubac, *Histoire et esprit. L'intelligence de l'Écriture d'après Origène* (Paris 1950).

[7] Gen. 3.19.

[8] Col. 1.15.

[9] Apoc. 2.7.

[10] See Gen. 3.22. The subsequent discussion would seem to be based on the rhetorical topic 'from contraries' given in Aristotle, *Rhet.* 2.23.23 (1400a23).

[11] The passage has been completely misunderstood by Bonwetsch, *Die Theologie des M.* 92, who thought that Methodius taught a peculiar union between the man Adam and the Logos at the beginning of the world as an anticipation of the Incarnation—a kind of hypostatic union. The same error is repeated by E. Mersch, *Le Corps mystique* (3 ed. Paris 1951) 343–347. Farges, however, in *Les idées morales* 126 ff., has understood the doctrine correctly. Methodius nowhere says that the Logos was actually united to the first man, Adam, but that in Christ, the Word, in being united to human nature, was somehow united with Adam. How this could be is explained by Methodius in §4, by the analogy of the ancient artisan's mould for casting clay figures or the technique of bronze-casting; Methodius uses both analogies indifferently. For Methodius the soft clay is man's human

nature, first modelled from the virgin earth, and then poured a second time to form Christ in the mould of the virgin's womb.

[12] The meaning of the word Aeon during this period differs widely from context to context. Sometimes it is applied to a divine emanation in the Gnostic or Neo-Platonic sense, sometimes to the Stoic or Neo-Platonic World Soul; at other times it refers to the divine attribute of Wisdom. For a discussion, see A. D. Nock and A. Festugière, *Corpus Hermeticum* 1.157, and H. Sasse, 'Aion,' RAC 1.193–204.

[13] 'Archangel' here, somewhat like Aeon, of a spiritual being intermediary between God and men. Methodius' use of the term does not, however, imply the doctrinal confusion of Hermas' *Pastor* in which the angel of repentance is at times identified with the mysterious Shepherd and at times with the 'son of God.'

[14] Methodius' imagery here shifts from sculpture to pottery against the background of the dramatic parable in Jer. 18.3 f. The ancient potter usually sat at a spindle which had two circular stones: the one at the bottom, usually heavier and of larger diameter, was spun with the foot; on the other, higher up, he placed the lump of moist clay which he worked. See G. M. A. Richter in C. Singer (and others), *A History of Technology* (Oxford 1954–56) 2.259–283. The point of the analogy in Jeremias is that the prophet attempts to console Israel by reminding it that God, the divine potter, always has the power to modify and change his creations.

[15] Cf. 2 Tim. 2.20 f.: *In a great house there are not only vessels of gold and silver, but also of wood and of earth; and some indeed unto honor,* etc. This image of the types of vases in a wealthy household is closely paralleled by the picture of the various vessels on which the potter works in Rom. 9.21; cf. also Wisd. 15.7 ff.

[16] It is clear that the womb here is like the oven of the potter's kiln which fires the various clay vases as they are taken from the wheel.

[17] The context suggests that Methodius is thinking of the process of bronze-casting and the mixture of copper and tin to produce the proper alloy; he is not therefore to be accused of adopting the later, unorthodox (Eutychian) implications of the verb 'mixing' as a description of the union of the divine and the human natures in Christ.

[18] Luke 15.4–6; Methodius' text of Luke here is closer to D (the Codex Bezae), although there are omissions and variants that are against all our known MSS. For the argument and the Christological use of the Lucan text, we may compare Irenaeus, *Adv. haer.* 3.20.3 (H), and see Bonwetsch, *Die Theologie des M.* 87 f. For a modern discussion of the parable, see J. Jeremias, *The Parables of Jesus* (tr. by S. H. Hooke, New York 1956) 28 f.

[19] John 1.1. The sudden and explicit declaration of the divinity of Christ is rather unexpected at this point and is not necessary for the general argument.

[20] Clark translates 'of the heavenly ones'; in any case, the phrase would seem to refer to the stars and planets as well as the spirits which guide them. On these guiding spirits, cf. also *Symp.* 8.15.

[21] Bonwetsch marks a lacuna here and seems to approve of Klostermann's suggestion that something like 'had a hundred sheep' has fallen out of the text. But this is quite unnecessary if we disregard the ancient paragraphing and connect (as we have done) the first sentence of §6 to the last sentence of the previous paragraph; then no further verb is necessary.

[22] Methodius pictures the ideal worship of God as a liturgical hymn of praise sung by angels and men dividing the verses antiphonally, or perhaps singing alternately strophe and refrain as do Thecla and the virgins in *Symp.* 11. Cf. Thecla's Hymn, n. 1.

[23] The verb used for 'transformed,' ἀναστοιχειόω, is also used, for example, by the Stoic Chrysippus for the resolution of the material elements of the world, and by Galen of the dissolution of the body at death: see LSJ *s.v.* Here it is a very strong expression for the physical as well as spiritual cataclysm by which man lost the gift of incorruptibility and took on, as it were, the form of death; by the death of the soul man was transformed physically so that he could die. In Origen the verb ἀναστοιχειόω is used of the complete transformation of the Christian by the grace of conversion: cf. *De princ.* 3.1.13 (GCS 218.9), *Adnot. in Deuteron.* 23 (PG 17.32D). Cf. also Sophocles, *s.v.*

[24] This image of the Good Shepherd coming down from the mountains of heaven to the lowlands of earth in quest of His lost sheep is also found in Origen, e.g., *In Gen.* hom. 9.3 (GCS 29.92 ff.). See also the Inscription of Abercius 3 f., with the remarks of J. Quasten, *Monumenta eucharistica et liturgica vetustissima* (Flor. Patr. 7.1, Bonn 1935) 22. Cf. also F. J. Dölger, ΙΧΘΥΣ 2 (2 ed. Münster i. W. 1928) 464–468.

[25] 1 Cor. 15.22 (cf. Rom. 5.15 ff.). This sentence with the one following makes it admirably clear that Methodius' theory of the union of the Logos with Adam refers to the Incarnation.

[26] For the Christian origins of the clothing symbolism, see Rom. 13.14, Gal. 3.27, and cf. Arndt and Gingrich, *A Greek-Christian Lexicon of the New Testament, s.v.* ἐνδύεσθαι. For the concept of Christ 'dressed in mankind,' see also Origen, *Comm. in Matth.*: fr. 392 f. ([GCS 41.31] with the reference to Zach. 3.3), and cf. also perhaps fr. 48. The image is also perhaps implicit in *Comm. in Ioann.* 6.56

(GCS 165), the garments of the Word dyed red in the wine press, on which see J. Daniélou, *Origène* (Paris 1948) 269, with the discussion of Origen's Christology.

[27] The terminology has a certain basis in Plato, *Phaedo* 93 E; but in what follows Methodius has changed Plato's discussion of participation and communication (between the Ideas and material objects) into the perhaps less meaningful analysis of man bending or inclining towards either side of a contradiction. It is such passages as this that suggest that Methodius had not really assimilated Platonic doctrine.

[28] Cf. Gen. 2.9.

[29] 1 Cor. 15.22; in the Pauline text, however, the verb is in the present; in Methodius it is in the future against all the MSS.

[30] Cf. Plato, *Lach.* 188 D; there Laches, discussing the role of the intelligent philosopher, compares him with the musician who plays 'neither the lyre nor any other instrument for amusement, but modulates his own life with the harmony of words and deeds, following not the Ionic, the Phrygian, or the Lydian mode, but the only authentic Greek mode, the Doric.' In Methodius the imagery seems somewhat poorer by comparison.

[31] Following Bonwetsch's correction of the MSS συμφωνήσῃ (subj.) to συμφωνῆσαι (opt.), which fits in better with the preceding ἄν.

[32] The imagery here is extremely bold and recalls the realistic expressions of Origen's commentary *On the Canticle*, on which see Quasten 2.98–100, with the literature cited. It should also be remarked that the more mystical branch of the Neo-Platonic school fancied images connected with procreation: cf. Pseudo-Dionysius, *Caelest. hierarch.* 15.6 (PG 3.357 DE).

[33] Eph. 5.27, 26.

[34] Gen. 1.28. In the sentence which follows, the expression 'memorial (ἀνάμνησις) of His Passion' probably refers to the primitive Christian liturgy. For a different use of the term, see Logos 8, n. 37 below.

[35] Titus 3.5.

[36] ἵνα χωρηθῇ κατὰ τὴν ἀνακεφαλαίωσιν τοῦ πάθους. On the 'comprehension of the Word' (χωρεῖν τὸν Λόγον), see in general the discussion of the *commixtio Dei et hominis* (man's divinization-union with God) in Irenaeus by J. Lawson, *The Biblical Theology of Saint Irenaeus* (London 1948) 157–161, and cf. also A. Houssian, *La christologie de Saint Irénée* (Louvain-Gembloux 1955) 56.

In our present text, the 'recapitulation' (ἀνακεφαλαίωσις) of the Passion would seem primarily to refer to the 'completion' or consummation of the Messianic mission which reached its climax in the

Passion and Death. But in Irenaeus, to whom Methodius is indebted, the concept of 'recapitulation' is extremely rich and complex, and the two most important levels of its meaning are: (1) in Christ the divine plan is fulfilled perfectly by His restoration of what man had been before the Fall (here the ideas of 'restoration' and 'consummation' are very close); and (2) Christ's work is a recapitulation or a 'compendium' of God's entire plan for the salvation of men. For the most important passages in Irenaeus, see the list in Plumpe, *Mater Ecclesia* 113 n. 11; for *Adv. haer.* book 3, see the listing by F. Sagnard, SC 34.456 (col. 2), and add also *Adv. haer.* 4.11.2 (H), 5.19.1 (H) and 5.29.2 (H). For a discussion, see Lawson, *op. cit.*, esp. 140–150, and Houssian, *op. cit.*, 216 ff.; cf. also H. Bettenson, *The Early Christian Fathers* (London 1956) 110–111. For the literature (besides the authors already cited) see also Quasten, *Patrology* 2.132.

[37] οἱ πεφωτισμένοι, the regular name for the newly baptized, for (a) they had been enlightened in the truths of the faith by the completion of the catechumenate, and (b) they had in baptism received the *Spirit of Truth* (John 15.26) with Christ, the Light. See *Symp.* 8.8. Cf. F. X. Dölger, *Sol Salutis. Gebet und Gesang im christlichen Altertum, mit besonderer Rücksicht auf die Ostung in Gebet und Liturgie* (Liturgiegesch. Forsch. 4/5, 2 ed. Münster i. W. 1925) 364–379.

[38] The Greek here is very ambiguous; I take κεκοιμημένου (if the reading of OP is correct) as a pass. participle modifying ὕπνου, 'a slept sleep,' therefore, 'a deep sleep.'

[39] The so-called seven gifts are, since Justin Martyr, traditionally based on a passage in proto-Isaias describing the virtues of the Messias (Isa. 11.2 f.): *And the spirit of the Lord shall rest upon Him: the spirit of wisdom and of understanding, the spirit of counsel and of fortitude, the spirit of knowledge and of godliness. And He shall be filled with the spirit of the fear of the Lord.* So the Vulgate here (following the LXX); but the MT omits *and of godliness* (or 'the gift of piety'), and indeed this would appear to be merely an expansion of the idea of fear of the Lord; similarly, the traditional qualities of good rulers, wisdom and understanding, would appear to form really one virtue. In any case, the prophet is thinking of the Messias as the perfect ruler of Israel and describes his personal holiness as well as his ability to guide His people. Thus the actual number of the virtues is not to be stressed.

[40] In Methodius we may distinguish the following levels of meaning in his concept of the Church:

1. *The generic concept of the Church*, as the actual multitude of all the faithful (and here the criterion would appear to be supernatural faith);

2. *The specific concept*: which is divided into two groups,
   (a) *The 'more perfect'* (the κρείττονες or τελειότεροι): all those who have perfect faith and are purified from the evils of the flesh; these constitute the Church in its strictest sense, the virgin Spouse and Mother, the helpmate of Christ. It is they who preach to 'the imperfect' and 'bring them forth' as true members of the Church by virtue and holiness.
   (b) *The 'imperfect'* (the ἀτελεῖς): those who have made only a beginning in the way of salvation and who become members of the Church in its strict sense only when they are 'brought forth' by the more perfect. Only then may they co-operate with the rest of the Church in preaching (κήρυγμα) to others.

Methodius' thought is striking, but difficult to comprehend. Among the imperfect are apparently (as the example of St. Paul's own conversion suggests) those who are converted but not yet baptized. By analogy, one might include among the imperfect all those who, though baptized, are still without perfect faith (however Methodius might define this) and are still subject to the 'absurdities of the flesh.' Though the perfect preach to the others, there is no proof that this group is restricted to the hierarchy; they recall somewhat Clement of Alexandria's 'true gnostics,' and thus might include pious monks, laymen, and consecrated virgins. But see Plumpe's discussion of the passage, *Mater Ecclesia* 115–117, with the literature there quoted. See also G. Müller, *Lexicon Athanasianum* (Berlin 1952), *s. vv.* ἀτελής, τέλειος.

[41] 2 Cor. 11.2: *I have espoused you to one husband that I may present you as a chaste virgin to Christ.*

[42] For a slightly different version, see Plumpe, *Mater Ecclesia* 115: 'And those who are still imperfect and only beginners are borne to the salvation of knowledge and formed as by mothers in travail. . . .'

[43] Cf. Col. 1.28.

[44] Acts 9.17 f.

[45] Gal. 4.19.

[46] 1 Cor. 4.15.

[47] Cf. Eph. 5.32. Methodius' Greek literally means: 'it has been established that the proposition (theorem) with regard to Eve is truly to be connected with Christ and the Church.' It is Methodius' *Q. E. D.*, but one should not here press the mathematical terminology too far.

[48] From the two accounts of the creation of man, (a) Gen. 1.28, and (b) Gen. 2.24.

[49] The Greek word used here, ἐνθωπεύω (neither in LSJ nor in Sophocles) is found three times in Methodius' works. θωπεύω means 'caress,' 'flatter,' and in the compound form, the ἐν would seem to be slightly intensive.—The reference in the passage is perhaps to a group of local Asiatic Christians who decried the practice of celibacy, rather than to any heretical sect. In any case, the answer seems to lie in Thalia's suggestion in *Symp.* 3.1 that these adversaries were using the Genesis passage to praise the married state to the detriment of virginity; and, she suggests, one answer to this group is to point out that the 'physical' or obvious meaning of Genesis is not the only one; in fact, the second or spiritual sense is far more important. Thalia does not, however, bring the argument to a point, save to remark that the bride of Christ is a virgin; and that all the faithful are intended to become the 'bride of Christ' by perfection. How far perfection will involve the actual practice of celibacy, will be explained farther on.

[50] Eph. 5.25 f.

[51] The Greek, κατὰ κρατός, is ambiguous; the construction is perhaps ἀπὸ κοινοῦ, e.g., 'Paul, desiring *with all his might* that the faithful practice chastity *so far as possible.*'

[52] 1 Cor. 7.1.

[53] Methodius' view here would seem to be excessive, for he suggests that marriage is permissible only by way of exception, to avoid greater evil. The analogy from fasting, even though it primarily refers here to second marriages, makes this clear: just as the fast is a universal precept, allowing an excuse or a dispensation only in the case of those who are sick, so too the precept of chastity is binding on all, though entailing an excuse for those who are morally weak. At the same time, the tenor of Methodius' remarks in 2.1 f. should indicate that this severity is not so much doctrinal as pedagogic, i.e. to urge as many as possible to take up the life of celibacy. Another factor that should be considered here is the possible influence of the declamatory debate-style, in which pros and cons are deliberately pointed and exaggerated.

[54] 1 Cor. 7.5. On the text, see the following note.

[55] 1 Cor. 7.1–6. Methodius' text here is eclectic, in general close to A, but sometimes following the readings of P^{46} (the Chester Beatty papyrus).

[56] This is a complete distortion of the obvious sense of the Pauline text. The last verse picks up the 'it is good' of 7.1; in the question of marriage and the abstinence from marital duties—just as in the question of virginity (7.5)—Paul is obviously offering a counsel, not enjoining

a divine commandment; whereas Methodius curiously takes celibacy as the 'commandment' and marriage as the 'indulgence' or concession. But Methodius is not alone in misinterpreting the passage: see Augustine, *De peccato originali* 38 (CSEL 42.201), with the discussion by F. Prat, *The Theology of St. Paul* (tr. by J. L. Stoddard, Westminster, Md. 1952) 1.108 n. 1; and for the historical background of Augustine's viewpoint, see V. J. Bourke, *Augustine's Quest of Wisdom* (Milwaukee 1945) 191 f.; see also M. Pontet, *L'Exégèse de S. Augustin prédicateur* (Paris 1944) 163 n. 39, and W. J. Dooley, *Marriage According to St. Ambrose* (SCA 11 Washington 1948) 47.

[57] 1 Cor. 7.8 f.

[58] In suggesting that Paul was a widower, Methodius reflects a tradition which we also find in Eusebius, *Hist. eccl.* 3.30 (GCS 2.202). Some scholars, e.g. Prat, *op. cit.* 107, would prefer to hold that Paul never married, but there is obviously no conclusive evidence for either side. See also W. P. Le Saint, ACW 13.142 n. 67. There may be a hint here that Methodius himself was a widower at the time he wrote the *Symposium*.

[59] The text of this sentence is very corrupt, but the general sense is clear.

[60] Methodius here seems to take the verb 'to burn' (1 Cor. 7.9) as referring to actual impurity, although it may mean merely to experience the passion of love (see LSJ, *s.v.* πυρόω).

[61] 1 Cor. 7.25–27.

[62] 'In accordance with the soul's free choice,' which would seem to contradict the view expressed in §12, unless that position is, as we have suggested, rather pedagogic than doctrinal.

[63] It is not clear that Paul, in the text, has modified his position; and Methodius himself may have realized that he has gone too far as he resumes his thought in the following sentence. This Pauline passage was a favorite with Tertullian: see *De monog.* 3, *De exhort. cast.* 3, with the notes of Le Saint (ACW 13) *ad loc.*

[64] The passage is difficult, and though the general tenor is clear, our text may be corrupt. To what abuse does Methodius refer? Perhaps (a) to the view that the conjugal act is somehow sinful in itself; (b) to lack of moderation in the exercise of marital rights, though the act itself be not sinful; or (c) to certain deviations among the married which may have been current in Asia Minor. It would seem that (b) fits in better with Methodius' context, and possibly (c). Cf. also Logos 9, n. 36 below.

[65] 1 Cor. 7.29.

[66] 1 Cor. 7.32–34; for verse 34 Methodius follows a text not un-

common among the Fathers: see the editions of Merk (Rome 1951) and Nestle (Stuttgart 1954) *ad loc.*

[67] 1 Cor. 7.35.

[68] 1 Cor. 7.36.

[69] Cf. 1 Cor. 7.37.

[70] In the Greek we have a complete line and a half of iambic trimeter (up to the caesura of the second); the lines may be borrowed from a lost tragedy or perhaps they are Methodius' own. The word εὐεξάλειπτος ('easily erased') is rare in classical Greek (see LSJ, *s.v.*: found only in prose), and Methodius does not usually quote from the tragedians: see the bare reminiscences in Bonwetsch's Index.

LOGOS 4: THEOPATRA

[1] Heb. 1.1, one of Methodius' favorite Pauline texts.

[2] In the Greek, ἀποκατάστασις; but for Methodius it is the juridical restoration to mankind of the power of attaining heaven, in virtue of the Atonement, and not the Origenistic *apokatastasis*, by which, as some held, all souls, even of the devils and of the damned, would one day be permitted to enter heaven. On the Origenistic doctrine, see Quasten, *Patrology*, 1.87–91, with the literature there cited, and J. Daniélou, *Grégoire de Nysse: La vie de Moise* (SC 1 bis, Paris 1955) 54 n. 1. See also Logos 8, n. 52 below.

[3] αἱ αἰσθήσεις τῆς ψυχῆς, 'the senses of the soul,' but not here in the mystical sense as we find it used by Origen, e.g., *Comm. in Cant. Cant.* 2 (GCS 33.167.25 f. Baehrens)=ACW 26.162, where also see n. 221 and the Index, 'senses of the inner man.'

[4] One may translate 'the *entire* ship,' as here, or 'they become *entirely* darkened'; the Greek is ambiguous.

[5] The symbol of the world as a river goes back to the philosopher Heraclitus (see K. Freeman, *The Pre-Socratic Philosophers: A Companion to Diels* [Oxford 1949] 115), and recurs with added significance in the Stoics: see, for example, Marcus Aurelius 5.23, 7.19; and we find the metaphor of the soul in the body as a ship at sea developed in Maximus of Tyre, *Diss.* 40.5. The image in general fitted in with the Stoic concept of apathy, wherein the mind was to preserve its calm and inner 'liberty' despite the storms of the passions which came from without.

[6] Ps. 136 (MT 137), from the fifth book of Psalms, is set dramatically during the period of the Babylonian exile. Written by a pious Jew it is a beautiful, mournful lyric put into the mouth of the Jewish exiles who were probably doing forced labor by the streams between

the Tigris and the Euphrates. The fact that their harps are hung on nearby trees (and these would be perhaps Euphrates poplars or Mesopotamian aspens) is a symbol of their sorrow and inability to sing in the land of their pagan captors. For Methodius, the stream is the river of the world, the mourning of the Jews a symbol of the chastity of the faithful soul.

[7] Literally, 'the river,' but obviously the Nile is meant. Cf. Exod. 1.16, 22 for the Pharaoh's directions to the midwives, and see P. Heinisch, *History of the Old Testament* (tr. by W. Heidt, Collegeville 1952) 77 f. The allegorical interpretation of the slaughter of the males is Alexandrian and recurs in Origen and Gregory of Nyssa: see J. Daniélou, *Grégoire de Nysse: La Vie de Moise* 32 n. 2.

[8] Cf. Rom. 5.14.

[9] Ps. 136.1 f.

[10] Homer, *Od.* 10.510, where ὠλεσίκαρποι is usually translated 'fruit-losing': the willow was thought to drop its fruit before it was fully developed. The willow tree, in ancient Greek as well as early Christian writers, is symbolic of both life and death: see the discussion by H. Rahner in his *Griechische Mythen in christlicher Deutung* (Zurich 1945) 861–413 (390 quotes the present passage from Methodius). For the tree as a symbol of chastity, see also Rahner, 'Die Weide als Symbol der Keuschheit in der Antike und im Christentum,' *Zeitschr. f. kath. Theol.* 56 (1932) 231–253.

[11] Isa. 44.4, from the LXX (with a few inversions). Compare the MT version of the text: '... spring up as amid the grass, as poplars by the watercourse.' The Biblical tree was quite certainly not the willow, but rather a variety of poplar or aspen.

[12] λόγοις, that is 'with (sacred) doctrine.' This 'doctrine' (such as Methodius himself teaches, based on the Scriptures) together with the practice of chastity forms the chief means by which, in his view, the Christian becomes perfect.

[13] Here paraphrasing Plato, *Symp.* 180 B.

[14] The commandment is most probably Deut. 6.7 (*Thou shalt love the Lord thy God*, etc.), as quoted in Luke 10.27 and elsewhere.

[15] In Hebrew the name *Ṣîôn* referred specifically to the southern part of Jerusalem's eastern hill, and came early to be applied to the city itself. The Hebrew for 'watch-tower' is *migdāl*, and of the various Hebrew words for 'ordinance' none would seem to justify this etymology. Although the etymology of 'Sion' is disputed, the derivation given by Methodius (and frequently elsewhere: see Wutz, *Onomastica sacra*, vol. 2 Index p. 1149 *s.v.*) cannot be right.

[16] Ps. 136.4.

[17] See Eph. 6.12, and cf. Origen, *Sel. in Ps.* 136 (13.137 Lommatzsch).

[18] See Matt. 7.6.

[19] Amos 4.5, according to the LXX; the MT, followed by Jerome's Vulgate, has 'and offer a sacrifice of praise with leaven.'

[20] An allusion to Titus 1.16.

[21] Cf. Matt. 24.35, 2 Peter 3.10.

[22] Ps. 136.5 f; that is, 'the choicest [*rôš*: head] of my joys,' 'my greatest joy.'

[23] The chalice-image is perhaps derived from Our Lord's prediction in Matt. 20.22 f. made to the mother of James and John; the austerity of the drink refers to chastity, and the draught itself would appear to be connected, in symbolism, with the water of immortality welling up from the bosom of the Father in *Symp.* 1.1. Cf. also Thecla's Hymn, n. 12 below.

[24] 2 Cor. 11.2.

[25] Wisd. 4.2.

[26] Isa. 60.1.

[27] Methodius would here appear to be abandoning, against his own principles, all literal sense. The passage here seems to mean that during the Millennium, the final reign of Christ, the virgins will occupy a special place 'in the front rank'; they will then proceed to the 'pure habitation of innermost light.' The light symbolism here is correlated with the white garment of purity (a reminiscence of the wedding garment of the parable in Matt. 22.11), and may be in turn related to the robe of light which we find in Hellenistic-Jewish art: cf. Goodenough, *Jewish Symbols* 1.28 f., 2.27 f.

[28] ἐκτόποις, 'strange,' or 'foreign,' that is, anything, sinful or not, which would distract from the main effort of salvation.

[29] Jer. 2.32, with inversion of the subjects: literally, in the Hebrew, 'can a maid forget her ornaments, a bride her sashes (*qiššrîm*)?' The sashes or *qiššrîm* (apparel that is bound on) is translated by the LXX as στηθοδεσμίς, 'a breast-band,' and it is from this word that Methodius draws his tropological exegesis.

LOGOS 5: THALLUSA

[1] On the motif of collecting one's thoughts before speaking, see L. Arbusow, *Colores rhetorici: Eine Auswahl rhetorischer Figuren und Gemeinplätze als Hilfsmittel für akademische Übungen an mittelalterlichen Texten* (Göttingen 1948) 97; cf. also the so-called 'affected modesty' formulae in E. R. Curtius, *European Literature* 83 f.

[2] Num. 6.1 f., introducing the Nazarite law (see below, n. 18).

[3] Gen. 15.9.

[4] To understand the symbolism one must recall that the ancients divided the hours from dusk to dawn into four watches, each lasting about three hours. Thus we have the parallelism in this passage and in what follows:

heifer = the soul = childhood = 1st (evening) watch
goat = the flesh = adulthood = 2nd watch
ram = the mind = old age = 3rd watch.

Note that the number three (and the age of the animals) becomes symbolic of 'the perfect knowledge of the Trinity.' But Methodius does not work out all the details and may have left this section incomplete.

[5] See Luke 12.35–38. For a discussion of Messianic sense of the parable, see J. Jeremias, *The Parables of Jesus* 46, 73 f.

[6] τὸ ἡγεμονικόν, translated by Jerome and Rufinus, when the word occurs in Origen, as *principale cordis* (*animae*). A. Lieske, *Die Theologie der Logos-Mystik bei Origenes* (Münster i. W. 1938) 103, translates the term as 'Seelengrund,' 'Tiefengrund der Seele.' Cf. also J. J. O'Meara (ACW 19.173) on Origen, *Exh. ad mart.* 33: 'the higher part of the soul.' See also R. P. Lawson (ACW 26.64, *passim*) for Origen, *Comm. in Cant. Cant.* 1, etc., and cf. *ibid.* 324 n. 10. In Methodius, however, the term does not seem to have the same theological depth as it does in Origen.

[7] Lam. 3.27.

[8] An adaptation of Jer. 17.5 and 6.8.

[9] Here by a modification of the Platonic image (*Phaedr.* 254 E, 247 B), the driver of the chariot (or νοῦς) becomes Christ (and, later, chastity itself), and instead of the two horses of Plato (θυμός and ἐπιθυμία, 'spirit' and 'desire') we have the single horse, the faithful soul.

[10] The Nazarite vow of Num. 6.2 ff. See n. 18 below.

[11] 1 Cor. 7.34 partly paraphrased.

[12] Ps. 44.2, from the great Hebrew epithalamium which will play such an important role in Methodius' imagery later on.

[13] Cf. Rom. 8.2.

[14] Isa. 8.1. Literally (in the MT) the verse means: 'Write in it: belonging to *Maher-šālāl-ḥāš-baz*,' that is, 'Haste-booty-speed-spoil,' which is the name of the child to be born.

[15] Col. 3.1. And on the thought of the passage, cf. the Epistle of James 1.16 ff.

[16] In the Greek, the words, 'where malefactors are born' (or, simply, 'where men are malefactors'; see LSJ *s.v.* τελέθω), form a metrical colon, a catalectic anapaestic pentameter, but the source (if any) has not been determined. For the idea, cf. Plato, *Theaet.* 173 D.

[17] Reminiscences, perhaps, of Ps. 1.2 and Ecclus. 6.37.

[18] Num. 6.1–4, following the LXX where here varies slightly from the MT. Verses 1–21 reflect the ancient legislation of the Priestly Code with regard to the so-called Nazarite vow (from Hebrew *nāzar*, to separate apart): see R. H. Pfeiffer, *Introduction to the Old Testament* (London 1953) 255 ff. The vow was usually taken for a period of thirty days at a time by both men and women—though some seem to have taken it permanently—and the chief practices entailed were abstention from alcoholic drinks, allowing the hair to grow, and omission of the customary ritual mourning for the dead. The vow was taken by Samson (cf. Judges 13.4 ff.), St. Paul (Acts 18.18, 21.24), James the Less (Eusebius, *Hist. eccl.* 2.23.3), and others, including Julia Bernice, the sister of Agrippa II (Josephus, *Bell. Iud.* 2.15.1). Among the Fathers and early theologians, the vow assumes an importance as a symbol and a foreshadowing of Christian asceticism: see, for example, Gregory of Nazianzus (*Or.* 43.28), Gregory the Great (*Mor. in Iob* 32.22), Thomas Aquinas (*Summa theol.* II–II q. 186 a. 6). For the literature, see H. Lesêtre, 'Nazaréat,' DB 4.1015–20; H. Strathmann, *Geschichte der frühchristlichen Askese* (Leipzig 1914) 50 ff.; J. Bonsirven, *Le judaisme palestinien au temps de Jésus-Christ* (Paris 1935) 2.165 f.; E. Zolli, *The Nazarene: Studies in New Testament Exegesis* (tr. by C. Vollert, St. Louis—London 1950) 36 ff.

[19] It would seem that Methodius does not wish his virgins to forego all wine—surely this would appear strange and unhealthy in an Asiatic Greek community—but rather merely to avoid excess and to abstain from stronger intoxicants as, for example, the σίκερα or *šēkār* referred to in the Nazarite legislation. The Stoics (e.g., Epictetus, *Diss.* 4.2.7) had discussed the two effects of alcohol, οἴνωσις which was licit, and μέθη ('drunkenness') which was disapproved of; and this distinction was taken over by Philo of Alexandria: see E. Bréhier, *Les idées philosophiques et religieuses de Philon d'Alexandrie* (Paris 1925) 257 ff.; see also H. Lewy, *Sobria ebrietas* (Giessen 1929), and H. Preisker, in TWNT 4.550–554. On intoxication as a symbol of emotion or passion, see Basil, *De ieiun.* 1.10. *The Testament of the Twelve Patriarchs*, Judas 4.16 (PG 2.1080A), speaks of the 'four evil demons of wine: concupiscence, passion, lust and hardness of heart.' Wine as a symbol of the supernatural is also found in Pseudo-Dionysius, *Epist.* 9.4 (PG 3.112 A).

[20] A conflation of John 15.1 and 5.

[21] Deut. 32.32 f., from the canticle of Moses: he is here speaking of the enemies of Israel.

[22] Cf. Rom. 1.26; and for Noe and Cain in what follows, see Gen. 6.12 f. and 4.8.

[23] According to the early Stoics (cf. Diogenes Laertius, *Zeno* 7.111 ff.), the four great classes of passions were grief, desire, pleasure, and fear; and these with their subordinate species were the cause of that spiritual disturbance which Stoic *askesis* attempted to overcome in order to live only according to the 'indifferent things' of life and thus arrive at 'apathy.' But it must be recalled that in the early Christian period, from the formation of the Alexandrian school down to the fifth century, this doctrine was hardly the unique property of the Stoic school through the process of cross-influence and levelling in the various philosophical schools, with the result that the moral doctrines taught by many different philosophers had much in common. On this philosophical syncretism, especially on the practical moral level, see E. Bréhier, *Les idées philosophiques et religieuses de Philon* 253 f.; G. Highet, *Juvenal the Satirist* (Oxford 1954) 248, in the note on Juvenal, *Sat.* 1.81–87; and A.-J. Festugière, *Personal Religion Among the Greeks* 157 n. 27. It is precisely this levelling effect that is sometimes overlooked, for example, by G. Fritschel, *Methodius von Olympos und seine Philosophie* 37, and Bonwetsch, *Die Theologie des M.* 157 ff.

[24] Literally, τῷ λόγῳ, 'for the Word' (so Clark and Fendt), or, as I prefer to take it, 'with (by means of) the Word,' that is, the revealed doctrine as found in the Scriptures and (as so often in Methodius) communicated by the official teaching; for Methodius this Word would also include his own private instruction on chastity and the Millennium.

[25] Luke 21.34; the last words, 'as a snare,' are assigned by a number of MSS and Scriptural witnesses to the following verse.

[26] Greek σίκερα (Hebrew *šēkār*), 'fermented liquor' (LSJ), usually of other than vinous liquors and of a higher alcoholic content.

[27] A reminiscence of the food prohibitions of the Priestly Code as contained in Leviticus 11. The prohibition of hyena flesh is not in the MT or the LXX as we have them today; but it is found, for example, in the *Epistle of Barnabas* 10.7 (on which see J. A. Kleist, ACW 6.177 n. 119), and may be due to Rabbinical exegesis of Hellenistic times. Just as the Jews were forbidden to avoid unclean animals and also many others because of a resemblance (though this is not explicit in Leviticus), so too the virgin must avoid both actual sin and all that resembles it, that is to say, the proximate occasions, as is clear from the context.

[28] For the symbol of the altar as used of holy widows, see Polycarp's *Epistle to the Philippians* 4.3, with the note of J. B. Lightfoot, *The Apostolic Fathers* 2.3 (2 ed. London 1889) 329 f.; also Kleist, ACW 6.189 f.; and for the entire complex of images, see Nugent, *Portrait of the Consecrated Woman* 97.

[29] Exod. 30.1, 3, 6–9, slightly modified and abridged, from legislation of the Priestly Code dealing with the construction of the Tabernacle. The setim-wood would appear to be acacia and suggests the vicinity of Mt. Sinai. Cf. n. 36 below. Methodius skips the dimensions; for the rest of his variations he largely follows the readings of the Alexandrian MS of the LXX.

[30] The entire passage, containing reminiscences of Rom. 7.14, Heb. 10.1, and 2 Cor. 3.6, 16, is important for an understanding of Methodius' fusion of Platonism and Alexandrian allegorism. The following scheme of relationships is suggested, although they are not always so clear in Methodius:

Shadow	*Image*	*Reality*
the Tabernacle	the Church	Heaven
Moses' exemplar (of the Tabernacle)	our idea of Heaven	Heaven

For Methodius the final revelation of the Reality will begin with the Millennium, after the resurrection of the body. Compare here Origen's contrast between the spirit and the letter of the Law in *De princ.* 4.2.4 f., and cf. Bonwetsch, *Die Theologie des M.* 169.

[31] Cf. Exod. 25.40.

[32] In the doctrine of Plato the so-called metaphysical objection to artistic creations (poetry, painting, music, etc.) is that they are mere imitations of material things, which are, in their turn, imitations of the 'ideas'; hence they are at three removes from reality: cf. Plato, *Rep.* 10.599 D.

[33] Heb. 11.10.

[34] Cf. 1 Cor. 13.12.

[35] Methodius' emphasis on the dignity of widows suggests that the community he is addressing (that is, the Lady of Termessus and her associates) included a number of these holy women. Concerning the office and duties (mainly ascetical) of widows in the early Church (cf. 1 Tim. 5.9–13), see K. Bihlmeyer—H. Tüchle, *Kirchengeschichte* 1 (15 ed. Paderborn 1951) 107 f.; also Kleist, ACW 6.189 f. (n. 37). Methodius seems confused on the location of the various altars of the Temple. The altar of holocausts, to which he compares the holy

widows, was within the Court of Men before the steps which led up to the Temple proper; leaving the porch, one entered the Holy Place, which contained the altar of incense. Now the Holy Place was separated from the Holy of Holies by a curtain (or veil); and within the Holy of Holies was kept the Ark, whose cover (the so-called 'mercy-seat' or propitiatory) was of pure gold. Methodius, in our text, has apparently confused the altar of incense, which stood in the Holy Place, with the mercy-seat on the Ark within the Holy of Holies. For the various types of sacrificial offering in the Temple, see R. K. Yerkes, *Sacrifice in Greek and Roman Religion and Early Judaism* (New York 1952) 115 ff.

[36] The translation cannot capture the play on words here: 'not liable to decay,' is also the word used by the LXX for the acacia wood used in the building of the Tabernacle: on this species (*acacia tortilis*, or another similar), see H. N. and A. L. Moldenke, *Plants of the Bible* (Waltham, Mass. 1952) 24 f.

[37] Cf. Eph. 5.2. Once again, Methodius is referring to the altar of incense within the Holy Place; see n. 35 above.

[38] Cf. Apoc. 5.8.

Logos 6: Agathe

[1] Methodius here compares God's activity in creating the human soul with the function of the demiurge in *Timaeus* 29 A ('If then this world is beautiful and the demiurge good,' says Plato, 'then it is clear that he looked towards what was immortal'). In view of the present passage as well as the discussion of the divine Craftsman in *Symp.* 2.4, it is difficult to understand how C. H. Moore could have said: 'Methodius' view of the human soul as material shows in part the persistent influence of Stoic doctrine'; see his *Ancient Beliefs in the Immortality of the Soul* (Our Debt to Greece and Rome 27, New York 1931) 177.

There is, however, a serious difficulty in Methodius' conception, namely, with regard to the nature of the 'form' by which the soul reflects the divinity. If this form refers to supernatural grace, when was the soul created with it? And if the image refers merely to man's rational qualities, how could this form be lost? There would seem to be a confusion here between the soul of Adam, created in God's image and likeness, and the souls of men born after Adam; in any case, Methodius seems to be speaking of the soul before it comes into contact with *actual* sin; this 'sinlessness' is the beauty it should preserve by resisting temptation and by the practice of asceticism. The problem of the transmission of Adam's sin is not envisaged in the context.

[2] On God as light, cf. John 1.4, 1 John 1.5, James 1.17, Eph. 5.8, and elsewhere. Imagery involving luminosity and beauty is common in Hellenistic mysticism. With Plato, *Symp.* 210 D ('the vast sea of beauty') and *Phaedr.* 250 C, compare Plotinus 3.8.11 (411.28 Henry-Schwyzer); and for the passages in the *Hermetic Corpus,* see Festugière, *Personal Religion Among the Greeks* 137 f. On the dualism of Light and Darkness in the Dead Sea Scrolls, see M. Burrows, *The Dead Sea Scrolls* (New York 1956) 338, and T. H. Gaster, *The Dead Sea Scriptures in English Translation* (New York 1956) 328 f.

[3] Suggesting that Methodius took the 'image' and 'likeness' of Gen. 1.26 as synonymous terms; for his place in the tradition of image-theology, see W. J. Burghardt, *The Image of God in Man According to Cyril of Alexandria* (SCA 14, Washington 1957) 19.

[4] Eph. 6.12.

[5] Jer. 3.3, from one of the early exhortations to North Israel as the faithless wife: see Pfeiffer, *Introduction to the Old Testament* 502.

[6] The word here used for statue (ἄγαλμα) often refers to the statue of a god, as opposed to ἀνδριάς, the statue of a man; the reference further on to the effect of blackening may refer to the smoke of ancient temples from oil lamps and sacrifices with its consequent effect on the cult statues.

[7] Methodius combines the commands of Luke 12.35 with the parable of the Ten Virgins; on the messianic interpretation of the parable see Jeremias, *The Parables of Jesus* 41–43.

[8] At this point, Methodius begins his instruction in *Zahlensymbolik* or numerological exegesis, which will become more important as he proceeds. The basis of this exegesis was to interpret any given number as the product or sum of numbers whose symbolism was accepted, as, for example, 1 of unity, 3 of the Trinity, 4 of the points of the compass, 7 of the branched candlestick or the days of Creation, 12 of the Apostles, and so on. Now the numbers 1, 3, 7, 10, and 12 were all considered as symbols of totality or completeness. Note also that the number '10,' besides the obvious connection with the fingers as the basis of reckoning, can also be presented as a perfect triangle, thus:

•
• •
• • •
• • • •

As E. Bréhier has pointed out, the Alexandrian use of numbers in exegesis should not strictly be derived from the Pythagorean doctrine of number as the form of ultimate reality; for Philo and those who followed him, numerical symbols were hardly more than convenient and 'mystical' ways of representing the allegorical sense which they felt had to underlie the prosaic references to numbers and quantities in the Scriptures. See Bréhier, *Les idées philosophiques* 43 f.; and on numerology in the Scriptures and the Fathers, see J. Lesêtre, 'Nombre,' DB 4.1677–97; O. Zöckler, *Die Tugendlehre des Christentums mit besonderer Rücksicht auf deren zahlensymbolische Einkleidung* (Gütersloh 1904); J. Sauer, 'Zahlensymbolik,' LTK 10 (1938) 1025 ff.; Curtius, *European Literature* 501 ff. See also Logos 8, nn. 53, 56 below.

[9] Cf. Plato, *Symp.* 212 A.

[10] The Greek letter 'I,' the ordinary symbol for the number 10, does not, I think, stand for Ἰησοῦς as Coxe takes it; indeed, the very shape of the letter seems to suggest for Methodius the singleness of purpose with which all ten virgins set out.

[11] The Greek text is corrupt here. Bonwetsch, following Wendland reads αἱ ⟨δέκα⟩, but we should perhaps emend this to ⟨αὗται⟩ αἱ.

[12] So, in the Greek, 'are strengthened,' though Clarke translates, '(our habits of good and evil) are confirmed.' But there is no question of habits in the text, but merely the fact that our senses are involved in all external actions.

[13] Luke 12.49.

[14] Literally, σκηνώματα, 'tabernacles'; cf. above, 4.3.

[15] Matt. 5.16. On the symbolism of oil in the ancient world, see Onians, *The Origins of European Thought* 188 ff. In the second century novel by Chariton, *Chaereas and Callirhoe* 1.1.15 (ed. Blake, Oxford 1938), Callirhoe, recognizing her lover's kiss, is 'like the light of a lamp, which, when it is about to go out and oil is poured in, flares up again and is even bigger and brighter than before.' Unless this comparison had already become a commonplace by the third century, it is possible that Methodius had read Chariton.

[16] Lev. 24.2 f., with a reminiscence of Exod. 27.20.

[17] Cf. Deut. 32.9 and Ps. 104.11.

[18] Mal. 4.2.

[19] The imagery seems to begin with a succession of maidens each lighting her lamp from the fire of the one preceding; it then changes to a kind of relay race from heaven to earth as though with lighted torches. The idea of bringing fire to earth is reminiscent of the symbolic act of Prometheus.

[20] That is, the *Parousia*, a word used in pagan literature of the advent or visitation of an important personage or of a god (see LSJ, *s.v.*); for Christian literature, see Prat, *The Theology of St. Paul* 2.370–382, and Arndt and Gingrich, *A Greek-English Lexicon of the New Testament*,

s.v.; O. Cullmann, *The Early Church* (tr. by A. J. B. Higgins, London 1956) 141–164. In Methodius (as with the other Chiliasts) the *Parousia* of Christ will inaugurate the final millennium of His reign upon earth: for a discussion, see the Introduction.

[21] Cf. Exod. 11.4, 12.23.

[22] Matt. 25.6.

[23] Allusions to 1 Thess. 4.15 f.

[24] See *ibid.* Note the omission in v. 16 (so also in MS G and in Tertullian) of 'we who are alive.' For the doctrine, cf. also 1 Cor. 15.51–54. The 'mystery' St. Paul attempts to reveal is the different effect the *Parousia* will have on the dead and the living: see Prat, *The Theology of St. Paul* 364 ff.; K. Barth, *Die Auferstehung der Toten* 4 ed., Zürich 1953) 125 f.; K. Rahner, 'Auferstehung des Fleisches,' *Schriften zur Theologie* (2 ed. Einsiedeln 1956) 2.211–226. However, Methodius' interpretation of the Pauline passage is quite unique.

[25] One would expect the trimming of the lamp to refer to the keeping of the end of the wick out of the oil and removing the burnt portion; Methodius, however, here writes as though the trimming (κοσμέω) also referred to actual ornamentation.

[26] The language (e.g. τὰ ὄργια, 'secret rites,' especially of Dionysus) here seems obviously borrowed from the pagan mysteries, but it is not clear what exactly is referred to in the passage. Here it would appear to be the parable of the Virgins in its allegorical meaning, the espousals of the faithful virgins with Christ and their procession to meet Him at His final coming.

[27] Cf. Wisd. 4.2. The Book of Wisdom had a great influence upon Methodius' thought, as it did upon the epistles of St. Paul. For recent discussions of the book, see R. Pfeiffer, *History of New Testament Times with an Introduction to the Apocrypha* (New York 1949) 313–351; and for the development of the concept of Wisdom in the Scriptures see Heinisch, *Theology of the Old Testament* 106–115. Methodius is chiefly interested, as here, in Wisdom's teaching that a virtuous life is more precious than all earthly rewards. On the problem of the canonicity of the book in Origen, see ACW 26.317 f.

[28] Another allusion to Wisd. 4.2.

[29] Cf. 1 Tim. 6.16, and on the light-symbolism, cf. n. 6 above. Here the mystical lights are the five senses, filled as it were with the oil of justice and the grace of Christ.

[30] Cf. Apoc. 14.3 f.

[31] 'I swear it, etc.' is an hexameter line in the Greek; it would seem to be a fusion between a fragment of a Pythagorean verse preserved in Aetius (Diels-Kranz[7] 1.445.9) and a line of Xenophanes

(Diels-Kranz[7] 1.130.19) which reads: 'Now I shall turn to another argument and show its path.'

LOGOS 7: PROCILLA

[1] Literally, 'she spoke as an equal,' but the sense in the context is clear. In the position which Procilla takes up, 'in front of the entrance (gate),' G. Lazzati sees a reflection of the primitive Christian non-liturgical synaxis, which Methodius may have been thinking of when he portrayed his maidens as preaching: for Lazzati's evidence, inadequate as it is, see 'La tecnica dialogica nel Simposio di Metodio d'Olimpo,' *Studi Ubaldi* (Milan 1937) 117 ff.

[2] Cf. Eph. 3.10.

[3] Cf. Wisd. 7.22. For the Greek πνεῦμα meaning both 'spirit' and 'wind' we have no single word; the German translator, Fendt, however, ventures *Geisteswind* for νοερὸν πνεῦμα.

[4] The testimony of witnesses is a regular topic in the progymnastic writers of the Roman period (Theon, Hermogenes, and Aphthonius), especially in the development of the encomium, the *chreia* and the diatribe. Cf. Aphthonius, *Progymn.* 3 (24 f. Spengel). That the authorities should be eminent seems obvious, but I know of no rhetorician who puts the rule precisely in this way, and it is more reminiscent of the Aristotelian principle of efficient cause.

[5] The prophets here referred to would seem to be Christians of the Apostolic period who enjoyed charismatic gifts: see Acts 15.32, 1 Cor. 12.28 f.

[6] Despite the slightly Subordinationist tone of the passage, this sentence is clear testimony to Methodius' belief in the divinity of Christ. The argument is the same as that in Heb. 1.1–13.

[7] Cf. John 14.28.

[8] Cant. 2.2. Methodius adopts a straightforward allegorical interpretation of the Canticle in accordance with Alexandrian theory; but his contribution was that in addition to the more traditional view which took the bride of the Song to stand for the Church (or, as in Origen, for the individual soul), he applied it to the consecrated virgin or widow. For Origenist influence on Methodius, see Bonwetsch, *Die Theologie des M.* 168 ff., and see our Introduction. For the more recent literature on the problem of the Canticle and its interpretation, see R. Pfeiffer, *Introduction to the Old Testament* 708–716; O. Rousseau, *Origène: Homélies sur le Cantique des Cantiques* (SC 37, Paris 1953); R. E. Murphy, 'Recent Literature on the Canticle of Canticles,' *Cath. Bib. Quarterly* 16 (1954) 1–11; and cf. ACW 26 *passim.*

[9] Cant. 4.9–12 with a few minor variants. The sense is that one glance of the maiden's eyes (and here she is called 'my sister'), one chain of her necklace, have charmed the king. Gregory of Nyssa has a long exegesis of the same passage in his *In Cant. Cant.* hom. 8 (PG 44.945 D–949 B).

[10] The Greek verb ἐποπτεύω was used in reference to the final revelation of the mystery religions; cf., e.g., Plato, *Phaedr.* 250 C, and see LSJ *s.v.* See also Logos 6, n. 26.

[11] The Greek of the LXX is ἔνθεμα which Jerome in the Vulgate translates *crinis*; but Methodius as well as Gregory of Nyssa (see n. 9 above) both explain the word in a sense closer to the Hebrew word which means a chain or a necklace.

[12] Literally, σωμασκέω, 'exercise the body,' 'practice wrestling.'

[13] Perhaps a reminiscence of Homer, 'The generation of men is like to that of leaves,' *Il.* 6.146; cf. also Mimnermus 2.1 f. (Diehl).

[14] Ps. 44.14, though the exact meaning of the verse has been disputed. Cf. NP: *Tota decora ingreditur filia regis*; there may perhaps be a reference to the beautiful inner lining of the queen's robe. The psalm itself is an epithalamium on the occasion of a royal wedding, and was included in the Elohistic psalter: see T. E. Bird, in the *Catholic Commentary on Holy Scripture* 347 d; R. Pfeiffer, *Introduction to the Old Testament* 631. It is interesting to note how close the psalm is, in conception, to the Hellenistic rules for composing a wedding hymn as given in the *De arte rhetorica* 4, a work attributed to Dionysius of Halicarnassus.

[15] Cf. Rom. 12.6.

[16] 1 Cor. 15.41 f.

[17] That is, in the Beatitudes, e.g., Matt. 5.3 ff.

[18] Here the theme of virginity as a type of martyrdom is suggested but left undeveloped. Cf. Nugent, *Portrait of the Consecrated Woman* 102 f. For other statements of the connection between martyrdom and asceticism, see the *Barlaam and Joasaph*, attributed to St. John Damascene, especially 12.101–108; and for a discussion, see my 'Problem of Ascetical Fasting in the Greek Patristic Writers,' *Traditio* 12 (1956), esp. 55–62 ('The Martyrdom of Asceticism'), with the literature there cited.

[19] Cant. 6.7 f. The meaning would seem to be that though some Semitic princes might have in their harems sixty queens (or wives with primary rights) and eighty concubines (perhaps those with secondary rights), the King of the Canticle has but one queen who is especially beloved.

[20] Cf. Isa. 26.18.

[21] Literally, 'the prophetic souls,' but referring to all those who lived during this second period.

[22] Cf. Luke 15.23.

[23] Here 60 is considered as the product of 10 (that is, symbolic of any large group, complete of its kind) and 6. For the general principle of numerological exegesis, see Logos 6, n. 8 above.

[24] Cf. Heb. 12.23.

[25] If this passage is pressed, there would seem to be no trace in Methodius of the doctrine of a *limbus patrum* or *sinus Abrahae* ('the bosom of Abraham'), as a place of natural beatitude in which the just of the Old Testament awaited the Atonement; on this see E. Mangenot, 'Abraham (Sein d'),' DTC 1 (1903) 111–116.

[26] Such phrases as this lend a Subordinationist tone to Methodius' Christology.

[27] The passage may be corrupt or the result of incomplete revision by the author; the general sense, however, is clear. The Old Law is implied in the circumcision; and since the number 8 can be taken as a symbol of circumcision (since this was required of male Jews eight days after birth), 8 can also stand symbolically for the Old Law. Further, in what follows, the number 8 is associated with Sunday, the day of Christ's Resurrection which occurred on the day following the sabbath or seventh day of the week. Thus, by the principle mentioned above (n. 23), the period of the prophets can be designated by the number 80 (that is, 10×8).

[28] Luke 10.23 f.

[29] Cant. 6.7 f.

[30] On the spotless flesh of Christ, cf. also Hermas, *Pastor* Sim. 5.6.7; on His flesh as the bride, Tertullian, *De res. carn.* 63.

[31] Ps. 44.9.

[32] *Ibid.* 44.14, in the NP: *texturae aureae sunt amictus eius.* The 'varieties' (NP: *amictu variegato*) of the queen probably refer to embroidery, and the 'golden borders' perhaps to cloth-of-gold edging or tassels. Cf. Logos 2, n. 32 above.

[33] Perhaps a reminiscence of 1 Peter 4.8.

[34] Literally, 'the enthronement . . . of the man (ἄνθρωπος) whom the Word assumed.' On the enthronement of Christ, cf. Acts 2.33, Heb. 1.3.

[35] Ps. 44.15 f.

[36] Literally, 'inscribed on a *stele* (or stone slab),' a metaphor from ancient parliamentary procedure, especially in cases where a speech was connected with official public legislation: cf. M. N. Tod, *A Selection of Greek Historical Inscriptions* 1 (Oxford 1946²) 38 ff.

LOGOS 8: THECLA

[1] In Greek, ἐγκυκλίου παιδείας, the general education given at the ancient Greek universities (Alexandria, Athens, Antioch, etc.) prior to professional studies. With Thecla, the dramatic date of the *Symposium* as imagined by Methodius, would be contemporary with the life of St. Paul. The historical existence of Thecla has been doubted in recent times; the main source is the so-called *Acta Pauli et Theclae* (on which see Quasten 1.131), an edifying story composed about the middle of the second century in the manner of a Hellenistic romance. Tertullian, *De bapt.* 17, tells us that the cleric who composed it 'out of love for Paul' was later deposed. According to the tradition, Thecla was a Greek girl of Iconium in Lycaonia who was converted by Paul and became a devoted fellow missionary; despite torture and persecution, she finally escaped and retired to Seleucia. Her cult has spread over East and West, she is the patroness of the cathedral of Milan, is mentioned in the canon of the Ambrosian Mass as well as in the Litanies for the Dying in the *Roman Ritual*; her feast is commemorated in the Roman Martyrology on Sept. 23. J. Stiltinck, of the early Bollandists, in ASS 6 (1867) 546 ff., accepted Thecla's existence chiefly on the testimony of the Fathers (e.g., Gregory of Nyssa, Ambrose, Chrysostom) who mentioned her; but in recent times the tradition with regard to Thecla's life has been rightly suspected by, among others, H. Delehaye in ASS: *Propylaeum Decembris* (1940) 412 f. (Sept. 23, no. 2).

[2] Not in the Greek, but implied from the change in speakers.

[3] Methodius' use here of etymological exegesis combines the ancient practice of popular etymology (cf., e.g., Plato's *Cratylus*) and the rhetorical Aristotelian topic, 'from etymology': see Curtius, *European Literature* 495 ff. Our Greek text here, however, is uncertain. For the second word, which we have printed as *partheia*, the MSS disagree, and the ultimate choice appears to be between παρθεία (O), which I have adopted in my text, following Bonwetsch, and πανθεία (P). In either case there is reference to the divinizing effect of chastity; but in the first reading the meaning would be 'next (παρά) to the divine,' but the word occurs nowhere in Greek; in the second reading we have a Greek cult-title meaning 'the all-embracing divinity' (see LSJ *s.v.*), but we must note that not only has a letter been dropped, as the text tells us, but there is also a displacement of the *v*.

[4] Again the language of the mystery religions; the initiation here is the revelation of the meaning of virginity as explained by Methodius' allegorical interpretation. See Logos 6, n. 26, and Logos 7, n. 10, above.

[5] For the imagery cf. Plato, *Phaedr.* 246, 248 f.; and compare the mystical ascent of the soul in Pseudo-Dionysius, *Caelest. hierarch.* 13.4 (PG 3.304 D), and *Eccles. hierarch.* 1.3 (PG 3.373 C–376 A).

[6] Diogenes Laertius (8.1.8) preserves the tradition that Pythagoras compared life to a *panegyris* or festal assembly at which some compete, others merely look on, and still others are busy hawking their wares. The comparison of life to a theater, however, seems to have been a regular motif of the Cynic diatribe: see Horace, *Serm.* 1.1.15–19, and for the literature on the subject, A. Oltramare, *Les origines de la diatribe romaine* (Lausanne–Geneva 1926) 53, and Curtius, *European Literature* 138 ff.

[7] σχήματα, literally, 'shapes,' with the suggestion of 'pomps,' pretence.' The charm of the demons' καλλιφωνία suggests Homer, *Od.* 12.39–54.

[8] Filling in the lacuna with διὰ τὸ εἶναι ἀρεστήν; so too cf. the modern etymology of ἀρετή from the root 'to be pleasing' in J. B. Hofmann, *Etymologisches Wörterbuch des Griechischen* (Munich 1950) *s.v.* ἀρέσκω. Klostermann, following an early suggestion by Poussines, had suggested διὰ τὸ εἶναι αἱρετήν (and cf. Plato, *Cratylus* 415 D); Bonwetsch abandons the text as a *locus desperatus.*

[9] The drama here refers to the 'things performed' by priests for those initiated into the mystery religions; in a Christian sense the words might be taken to refer to the performance of the Liturgy.

[10] Literally, the 'supramundane place of life'; 'life' here would seem to mean the material, worldly existence which the virtuous soul is said to transcend.

[11] Cf. 1 Cor. 13.3, where Paul may be thinking of the gymnosophists or other pagan 'heroes' who immolated themselves by leaping into fire; cf. F. J. Dölger, 'Der Feuertod ohne die Liebe. Antike Selbstverbrennung und christlicher Martyrium-Enthusiasmus. Ein Beitrag zu I Korinther 13,3,' *Antike u. Christentum* 1 (1929) 254–270. Methodius, however, is obviously thinking of the Roman forms of torture and execution, condemnation to the beasts and *crematio*, which Christians might perhaps pray for.

[12] For ancient imagery in connection with the air and ether, see W. K. C. Guthrie, *The Greeks and Their Gods* (London 1952) 207 ff., and J. H. Waszink, 'Aether,' RAC 1.150–158 (with a reference to the present passage on 157).

[13] On the angelic life, see n. 27 on Logos 2.

[14] That is, εὐφημία, perhaps of the solemn silence observed during religious rites (cf. LSJ *s.v.*), and this would fit Methodius' general use of terminology taken from the mystery religions. However, Clark's

translation, 'with much rejoicing,' and Fendt's 'mit viellieblichen Gesang,' suggest that the Greek may be ambiguous.

[15] This phrase perhaps tends to cast doubt on the view that the ascent of the soul, as described by Methodius, was a truly mystical experience. Indeed, it is difficult to explain the exact function of these imaginative descriptions of the soul's rise to the heavenly regions and the contemplation of the eternal realities. If this is all to take place by 'picturing them in the imagination (φαντασία) from afar,' then Methodius' discussion would amount to little more than an outline of a method of prayer. We may note that Methodius' treatment of the imagination is more Aristotelian; that of Gregory of Nyssa, for example, is more Platonic: cf. his *De vita Moysis* theor. 2.23 (SC 1 bis. 38) on the role of the imagination in error. For Aristotle's theory of the imagination, see W. D. Ross, *Aristotle* (London 1953) 142–145; and for a discussion of the different ancient theories on the imagination, see M. N. Bundy, *The Theory of the Imagination in Classical and Mediaeval Thought* (Univ. of Illinois Stud. in Lang. and Lit. 12, Urbana 1927).

[16] The verb used here, ἰνδάλλομαι (see LSJ, *s.v.*) regularly means 'appear,' or 'resemble' (with the dative), but here it would seem to be governing an accusative, τὰ θεῖα; but ἴνδαλμα can mean a 'mental image,' and thus I have taken the verb to mean 'form a mental image.'

[17] ἐκεῖ, 'there,' is often used by Plotinus of the intelligible world of ideas within *Nous* or Mind; in Methodius it designates the heavenly dwelling-place of God surrounded by the divine meadows of immortality.

[18] For the language, cf. Plato, *Phaedr.* 250 B.

[19] That is, ἐν τῷ ὄντι. Clark, however, translates, 'In Him whose name is I AM,' and I am not sure that the Old Testament revelation (Exod. 3.14) is not perhaps implied. It is here that Methodius comes closest to uniting the Christian and Platonic notions of heaven.

[20] On the tree of life in Paradise, see Apoc. 2.7.

[21] Baruch (often quoted as Jeremias) 3.14 f., with a few variations from our LXX text. God's law, says the author, is the only source of man's happiness; if man will have peace in this life, he must seek Wisdom, that is, keep the commandments. For a discussion of recent theories on Baruch, see R. H. Pfeiffer, *History of New Testament Times* (New York 1949) 409–425.

[22] Referring perhaps to the sub-tropical Asiatic climate, in which brilliant light can hardly be thought of without oppressive heat; the passage may be another indication that Methodius' origins are to be sought for in the southernmost parts of Asia Minor and not in Macedonia.

[23] The reference here is not, I think, to persecution, but rather to the difficulties which young women of the Greek-speaking world would experience in practicing perfect chastity. It is perhaps Methodius' clearest reference to the opposite side of the picture.

[24] Apoc. 12.1–6, following S and P[47] in some of the variants.

[25] Cf. John 5.39 which Methodius obviously takes as a command.

[26] Isa. 60.1–4.

[27] 'By baptism' is only in MS O but has been adopted, perhaps rightly, by Bonwetsch.

[28] Or perhaps 'in quest of resurrection,' and so Plumpe has taken it in *Mater Ecclesiae* 118.

[29] Cf. Ps. 103.2. And for the context, cf. also Hippolytus, *De anti-Christo* 61, and see F. J. Dölger, *Die Sonne der Gerechtigkeit und der Schwarze* (Münster i. W. 1919) 105 f.

[30] That is, πνεύματος, which is Bonwetsch's emendation for πατρός, the reading of the MSS.

[31] Here following P, which is closer to Plato, *Rep.* 7.532 D.

[32] Rom. 11.25.

[33] That is, from 'natural' or 'unspiritual' (ψυχικός) men they become 'supernatural' (πνευματικός): cf. 1 Cor. 2.14 f. These adjectives, first used by St. Paul in this sense, have an ethical dimension: the opposition is between those who are worldly-minded and still lead pagan lives and those who have been quickened with the grace of the Spirit: see F. Prat, *The Theology of St. Paul* 2.172 f., 404 f.; and cf. also M. Zerwick, *Analysis philologica Novi Testamenti* (Rome 1953) 365.

[34] The verb, 'take refuge in,' seems out of place and destroys the underlying image of natural procreation; one would have expected a much bolder phrase, and it is not unlikely that the text has been tampered with.

[35] The text has λουτρόν, 'washing,' 'bath,' and it is difficult to grasp Methodius' meaning; unless, as Plumpe has privately suggested, we are to take the whole expression as meaning 'presiding over the washing,' we may perhaps emend the noun to a form of λούτριον (see LSJ, *s.v.*), 'bathing-tub,' referring in this case to an early baptismal font.

[36] The derivation of σελήνη from σέλας can also be seen in Hofmann, *Etymologisches Wörterbuch des Griechischen s.v.* σελήνη. On moon-symbolism in the Fathers, see Rahner, *Griechische Mythen* 215–224: 'Der Ostermond.'

[37] The periodic representation or memorial (ἀνάμνησις) of the Passion would appear to be the liturgy of the primitive Christian Holy

Week. Cf. J. Quasten, *Monumenta Eucharistica* 161 n. 2, 223. Cf. Logos 3, n. 34 above.

[38] Cf. Plato, *Laws* 10.898 C.

[39] For the tradition that the reference in the Apocalypse is to the flight of the Holy Family into Egypt (Matt. 2.13 ff.), see Arethas, *Comm. on the Apoc.* 33 (PG 106.664D).

[40] Or perhaps, as Fendt takes it, 'on His flesh.'

[41] Isa. 66.7 f. This section in Deutero-Isaias speaks of the prosperity of Sion once God has eliminated the apostate Jews.

[42] Cf. Gal. 4.19.

[43] Ps. 104.15. 'Anointed' is, in Greek, χριστῶν—hence the interpretation.

[44] Eph. 3.14–17, with a few minor deviations from the NT.

[45] Actually Ps. 2.7 instead of the words as they are given in Matt. 3.17 (spoken to the crowd) or in Mark 1.11, Luke 3.22 (spoken to Christ).

[46] This entire paragraph, though in the MSS and quoted substantially by Photius *Bibl.* cod. 237, ought perhaps to be reconsidered from the viewpoint of authenticity. Methodius' language on the problem of the generation of the Word elsewhere is most often apt to have a slightly Subordinationist tone; such a clear statement of what was to be the orthodox theological solution is quite unique in his writings so far as they are extant. The ostensible purpose of the passage is to distinguish between the birth of Christ by faith in our hearts and His historical birth in time; this point brings in the theological discussion on the eternal generation of the Son from the Father. Of six important words used to describe this, three (προγεννάω, υἱοθεσία and, following P and Photius, προϋπάρχω) are not found elsewhere in Methodius, and three others (ἀόριστος, ἄχρονος, and πρόειμι) are indeed used by him but not with a Trinitarian connotation. Though the point is not completely convincing, it is interesting to note that these terms become far more common at the time of the Arian controversy: see, for example, G. Müller, *Lexicon Athanasianum*, *s.vv.* ἄχρονος and προϋπάρχω. For ἄχρονος of the generation of the Son, see also Gregory of Nazianzus, *Orat. theol.* 3.2 (75 f. Mason). As the text stands, however, we cannot completely rule out the possibility that the passage comes from the hand of Methodius himself.

[47] Apoc. 12.3.

[48] That is, τὰ ἐκεῖ; see n. 17 above.

[49] The heresy-catalogue which follows is found in all the MSS (Photius does not quote the section); but it is omitted by Andreas and Arethas. Andreas, in quoting this and the following paragraphs, goes

directly from 'one of the numbers of the Trinity' to (§11) 'and the wilderness into which our Mother the Church comes,' without any indication that material has been skipped: see Cramer, *Catenae* 8.355 (=PG 106.321 C). Arethas, however after the words 'numbers of the Trinity,' immediately adds: 'just like Arius and Macedonius' (PG 106.662 D). If the heresy-catalogue is interpolated, it may be that the first sentence of §11, which attempts to resume the thread of the discussion, is to be rejected as well.

As for the heretics mentioned, Sabellius was an Egyptian priest who was excommunicated by Pope Callistus about A.D. 220. Artemas recalls the disciple named in Titus 3.12, but the name (being a shortened form of Artemidorus) was common enough. Those who claimed that Christ became manifest in appearance only were, of course, one of the various sects of the Docetes: cf. Houssian, *La Christologie de Saint Irénée* 155. The Ebionites were a heretical Judaeo-Christian sect which was split into various factions. Marcion, one of the most famous and formidable of second century heretics (see Tertullian's treatise against him), was excommunicated in 144. Valentinus flourished at Rome around 136–160 after having preached Gnosticism in Egypt; Elchasai was a self-confessed Jewish Gnostic prophet who founded the Elchasaite sect around A.D. 101. On the entire period, see F. C. Burkitt, *Cambr. Anc. Hist.* 12 (1939) 467 ff.; E. C. Blackman, *Marcion and His Influence* (London 1948); E. Evans, *Tertullian's Treatise against Praxeas* (London 1948) 18 ff.; E. Peterson, 'Gnosi,' EC 6 (1951) 875 ff.; Quasten 1.256 ff.; H. E. W. Turner, *The Pattern of Christian Truth* (London 1954) 117 ff.

[50] Cant. 4.16, where it is the north wind that is bidden to rise and the south wind to blow.

[51] 'Here,' that is, in the garden of Virtue, symbolic now of the knowledge of the mysteries through revelation as opposed to the direct vision of heaven. Thus the 1260 days of Apoc. 12.6 are taken to be the period of the Church on earth before the Millennium; during this time the faithful grow in the knowledge of the Father, Son and Spirit until the final culmination.

[52] The 'restoration' (ἀποκατάστασις) here seems to refer to the era beginning with the Second Coming of Christ and the Millennium. There is no evidence that Methodius believed in the *apocatastasis* in the sense of a restoration of the damned to heaven after a certain period. See also Logos 4, n. 2, and Thecla's Hymn, n. 19 below.

[53] According to Euclid, a perfect number is equal to the sum of its factors other than itself; and the ancients knew four of these 6, 28, 496 and 8128. 'Over-perfect' (ὑπερτέλειος) numbers, on the other

hand, were those the sum of whose factors is greater than the original number; a third class were called 'less than perfect' (ὑποτέλειος) or defective. See LSJ, *s.vv.*, and also M. R. Cohen and I. E. Drabkin, *A Source Book in Greek Science* (New York 1948) 10–12. It should be noted that Methodius speaks of two kinds of perfect numbers: those like 6 in the strict mathematical sense; others, like 3 and 10, in the allegorical sense. See Logos 6, n. 8 above.

[54] Phil. 2.7.

[55] Exod. 20.11.

[56] The Greek text of Bo (following O) has: 'the number 6 by which *the Trinity* is productive of bodies;' but I omit the words 'the Trinity' following P, since the words do not seem relevant here; they may well have come from a marginal gloss that pointed to the parallelism between the three dimensions of a body and the three Persons. The connection between the two 'perfect' numbers 6 and 3 as given here (that is, 3=a triangle, and 6=2×3) is not convincing and Methodius wisely abandons it. For the Neo-Pythagorean view of the number 3 and the triangle, see F. E. Robbins, *Ptolemy: Tetrabiblos* (Loeb Library 1940) 83 n. 2.

[57] See Ezech. 17.3.

[58] Cf. Eph. 6.11 ff.

[59] The five lines of poetry are adapted from Homer, *Il.* 6.181–183. Lines 1–3 follow the Homeric text with the exception of a change (in line 183) from 'the gods' (omens)' to 'His Father's (omens).' The fourth line is a completely original hexameter, and the last line is a pentameter of the sort that closes the elegiac distich; these last two lines have not been identified and may well be Methodius' own composition.

[60] There are seven contests because of the seven heads of the Beast in Apoc. 12.3, though it is said to have ten crowns in Apoc. 13.1. The reference to St. Paul must mean the armor passage of Eph. 6.12 ff.

[61] Methodius does not give the complete list of the seven contests. They are, together with their rewards or crowns: (1) Incontinence and luxury: the diadem of temperance; (2) cowardice and weakness: the diadem of martyrdom; (3) folly and disbelief: (no reward mentioned); (4–7) 'the fruits of wickedness': their 'respective rewards.' Neither, in the subsequent passage, does he develop fully the meaning of the Beast's ten horns, which refer to the sins against the Commandments, but he mentions fornication, adultery, lying, covetousness, theft, and 'the related vices.' The idea is also developed by Arethas, *Comm. on the Apoc.* (PG 106.661 C).

[62] Cf. Deut. 6.5 and Mark 12.30.

[63] The connection between this sentence and what follows is difficult and Bonwetsch has rightly indicated a lacuna. But the trouble is more deep-seated, for the subsequent paragraph beginning 'For of all the evils,' would seem to resume from 'to Fate or to the whims of Fortune'; hence the entire sentence, 'So that each one of us,' etc., if it is part of the authentic text, may well have been dislocated.

[64] Referring really to the astrologers. On astrology in the ancient world, see F. Boll and C. Bezold, *Sternglaube und Sterndeutung. Die Geschichte und das Wesen der Astrologie* (4 ed. by W. Gundel, Leipzig 1931); W. Gundel, 'Astrologie,' RAC 1.817–831; M. P. Nilsson, *Geschichte der griechischen Religion* 2 (München 1950) 256–267; U. Riedinger, *Die heilige Schrift im Kampf der griechischen Kirche gegen die Astrologie von Origenes bis Johannes von Damaskos: Studien zur Dogmengeschichte und zur Geschichte der Astrologie* (Innsbruck 1956) with the literature cited on 9–12. The *Tetrabiblos*, most probably by the astronomer Claudius Ptolemaeus, was perhaps the most influential astrological treatise in Christian times; the author attempts to utilize the findings of astronomy in order to put both diagnostic and prognostic astrology (i.e. the techniques of casting a horoscope and of predicting the future) on a more scientific basis. The occasion for Methodius' discussion here would appear to be the references to the stars in the Apocalypse; but his attack on astrology would appear to reveal a lack of a first-hand acquaintance with the astrological manuals and the technique of diagnosis and prognosis, and may well derive from earlier pagan or Christian manuals: see, in this connection, D. Amand, *Fatalisme et liberté dans l'antiquité grecque* (Louvain 1945) 238. A more detailed account of the ancient technique of casting a horoscope can be found in the fourth chapter of Hippolytus, *Refutatio* (GCS 26.32 ff.), wherein Hippolytus gives lists of characteristics of persons born under each of the twelve signs of the Zodiac. But part of the horoscope, in addition to noting the constellation under which the person was born, was also the position of the planets with respect to one another, their 'applications' or 'conjunctions' (or coming together) and their 'separations' (moving away from one another); for the astrologer's method of handling this, see Clement of Alexandria, *Exc. ex Theod.* 69–71, especially with the commentary of F. Sagnard (SC 23, Paris 1948); for Basil's treatment of astrology, see Y. Courtonne, *Saint Basile et l'hellénisme. Étude sur la rencontre de la pensée chrétienne avec la sagesse antique dans l'Hexaéméron de Basile le Grand* (Paris 1934) 99–110.

[65] Homer, *Od.* 1.34, a favorite passage with Methodius (cf. below,

§16) because it supports, to an extent, his view of the will and the origin of moral evil. After Plato, Homer is the most frequently quoted pagan author in Methodius (the *Iliad* eight times, the *Odyssey* seven). For the problem connected with the abnormal theological views expressed in *Od.* 1.28–43, see D. Page, *The Homeric Odyssey* (Oxford 1955) 168 f.; for a general discussion of morale in the Homeric poems, see M. I. Finley, *The World of Odysseus* (London 1956) 119–157. On Fate in general, cf. Onians, *Origins of European Thought* 390–394.

[66] One would have expected a reference here to the 'obligatory' instead of the 'expedient'; but Methodius apparently distinguished only two sorts of moral objects of choice, the pleasant and the expedient (which would, of course, also include the obligatory); cf. also his discussion in *De res.* 1.44 (Bo 294.5).

[67] Here MS O has 'Chaldaeans' (which Bo follows), P has 'Egyptians,' and M has the obviously conflated reading 'Egyptians and Chaldaeans.' The Chaldaeans traditionally laid the foundations for European astronomy and astrology; but during the Hellenistic period, Egypt, and especially the school at Alexandria, became very prominent. Cf. W. J. W. Koster, 'Chaldäer,' RAC 2.1009–1018.

[68] Rom. 1.21.

[69] Perhaps a reminiscence of 1 Cor. 14.20; cf. also Gal. 4.9.

[70] That is, τοῖς οὐρανίοις (following O), which may perhaps here mean 'heavenly phenomena;' see LSJ, *s.v.* MS P, however, has 'to the heavens,' and this is followed by Combefis and Jahn.

[71] That is, the physical movement of the various planets, as well as their influence upon men, were explained by reference to the mythological stories or deities the planets and constellations were supposed to represent. For example, Mars suggests strife, Jupiter suggests extravagance, Venus indolence and luxury, and so on; these are referred to as the 'signatures' of the planets, or their influence upon men's characters. Cf. Ptolemy, *Tetrab.* 1.13.5 (Robbins). This is perhaps Methodius' strongest argument for the refutation of astrology.

[72] Methodius use of astronomical terms is fairly accurate; the various circles which he describes, though they originated with the Greek geocentric theory of the solar system, are still the basis of our division of the heavens. Considering the earth as a sphere, the line (or circle) which goes directly over the North Pole and the South Pole, or the circle which passes through the Sun at noon, is called the meridian; the horizon is the circle which cuts the meridian at right angles, and is sometimes called the equinoctial circle or the celestial equator. What Methodius calls the 'equinoctial' (ἰσημερινός) is really the ecliptic, or the circle made by the apparent path of the sun around

the earth; this cuts diagonally across the celestial equator, going through the points known as the Vernal Equinox, the Summer Solstice, the Autumnal Equinox and the Winter Solstice. The circles parallel to the equator which pass through the two solstices are called the tropic of Cancer and the tropic of Capricorn. On the Zodiacal circle, see n. 74 below.

[73] The story (cf. Apollodorus 1.9.1) was that Nephele, the wife of Athamas, son of Aeolus, tried to save her two children Phrixus and Helle with the help of a golden-fleeced ram given her by the god Hermes. Helle, however, fell into the strait later called the Hellespont, and only Phrixus came safely to Colchis. But these aetiological tales are not to be found in the more serious astrological works like Ptolemy's *Tetrabiblos*.

[74] From Leo (the Lion) to Aquarius (the Water Carrier), Methodius enumerates the twelve signs or constellations of the Zodiac, but not in the correct order (as though he were reading from some sort of chart). The others, from Perseus to Draco (the Dragon) are constellations which are visible at some time of the year in the northern hemisphere. If Methodius had given us more exact information, we might have determined whether he had merely obtained the information from the existing manuals or had actually observed them himself, and from what part of the world. From the geocentric point of view—as the Babylonians and the Greek astronomers conceived it—the sun's apparent path around the earth, called the ecliptic, seems to pass in front of twelve constellations as the twelve months of the year pass by. This, the so-called Zodiac (because all the constellations, except Libra the Balance are ζῷα or 'living beings') extends 8° above and below the ecliptic; and each sign is contained within 30°, making up the full 360° of a circle. From the astrologer's point of view, each person's character depends upon the particular sign of the month under which he was born. The complete horoscope (or, in Greek, γένεσις, 'nativity' and hence 'fate') would consist in plotting the position of sun, moon and planets with respect to the particular constellation of the Zodiac at the moment of his birth.—In the first section of Methodius' argument, which is more directly aimed at astrology, we have translated γένεσις as 'horoscope(s),' but in the latter part, where the discussion deals with determinism in general, we have translated it as 'fate.' For the term as used in astrology, see LSJ, *s.v.* II 2, and cf. Ps.-Clement, *Hom.* 14.3 (PG 2.348 A), with the discussion by G. L. Prestige, *God in Patristic Thought* (London 1952) 52–54.

[75] The Age of Gold is the first of the five ages of mankind as given by Hesiod, *Works and Days* 109–201. In the Golden Age, under Cronos,

gods and men lived together without pain or toil, and the earth yielded fruit of itself; next came the Silver Age, under Zeus, when men's impiety began; third was the Age of Bronze, marked by primitive savagery; fourth was the Heroic Age, when Thebes and Troy fell; and last was the Iron Age, Hesiod's own; for a discussion, see T. A. Sinclair, *Hesiod: Works and Days* (London 1932) 15–17; Guthrie, *The Greeks and Their Gods* 297 f. Cf. also the *Saturnia regna* of Vergil, *Eclogues* 4.6.

[76] Cf. Gen. 1.16.

[77] Unless Methodius is here merely assuming the astrologers' position for the sake of argument, it is possible that he believed that the celestial bodies were moved by some sort of (angelic) spirit.

[78] ἀπορροίας καὶ κινήσεως, perhaps also, 'their separations (i.e. opposite to conjunction) and their changes.'

[79] This syllogism, or rather sorites, seems defective as it stands. In the first premiss, the 'act' in question must surely refer to human actions, and immediately the problem arises of the analogy between human and divine action. The form, however, is valid:

All A is B,
all B is C,
but no D is C;
therefore no D is A.

But the conclusion should be: what is divine cannot act (i.e. in a human way). How then does 'experience of evil' get into the conclusion? One suspects that something may have happened to the text; the first premiss may well have been: 'no *evil* act can occur without a desire.' But even granting this, we might reasonably deny that there cannot be an evil desire without a need. For surely one can desire, wrongfully, what one does not need—unless the words 'desire' and 'need' are meant to be equivalent terms, in which case the premiss is invalid. If, however, Methodius means that the sinful desires of human beings imply a fundamental imperfection in their natures (and an imperfection which the divine cannot have), his argument would be far more subtle and would take many pages to develop cogently.

[80] Ptolemy divided astrology into four general types: (1) *universal* (affecting communities and groups); (2) *individual*; (3) *diagnostic* or descriptive, in which the 'nativity' or horoscope determines actual character, temperament and activity; (4) *prognostic*, or the technique of predicting future events. Methodius seems to be mainly concerned with the diagnostic type of astrology, especially insofar as it was linked to a Stoic or deterministic view of Fate. In strict logic, however,

belief in astrology need not be connected with a denial of free will.

[81] Here begins the discussion which is basic to Methodius' entire refutation of the astrologers: the concept of God and human freedom as held by the Christians must necessarily contradict the doctrines of astrology. But Methodius does not attempt to prove his concept of God, and his argument is therefore more theological than strictly philosophical: it merely supports the traditional Christian view of the relationship between man and God based on moral responsibility.

[82] Since the argument now becomes more general, I have translated γένεσις here as 'destiny' instead of 'horoscope': the Greek word, of course, means the individual destiny as determined by the horoscope cast at one's birth. See n. 74 above. Methodius' syllogisms, or sorites, are expressed in the regular form developed by Aristotle; on the Aristotelian form, see W. D. Ross, *Aristotle* 32–38 ,and also J. Lukasiewicz, *Aristotle's Syllogistic from the Standpoint of Modern Formal Logic* (Oxford 1951).

[83] For the tradition of this moral refutation of determinism, which probably goes back to Carneades, the founder of the New Academy who flourished in the middle of the second century B.C., see D. Amand, *Fatalisme et liberté dans l'antiquité grecque* 62 ff. Methodius' treatment, however, is somewhat deficient from a logical point of view. The ancient determinists (like their modern counterpart) distinguish between actions which are designated 'good' and 'evil'; but these terms refer rather to the good or evil effects of the act and not to the element of culpability; they would not therefore deny that virtue and vice are distinct so far as their external effects are concerned. For an attempt to reconcile ethical theory with Determinism, see, for example, W. D. Ross, *Foundations of Ethics* (Oxford 1951) 208–251.

[84] Homer, *Od.* 1.34. See n. 65 above.

[85] For the argument of the passage, cf. Alexander of Aphrodisias, *De fato* 116 (209 Bruns). For a discussion of the problem of responsibility in Greek law, see J. W. Jones, *The Law and the Legal Theory of the Greeks: An Introduction* (Oxford 1956) 261–273.

[86] 'And Rhadamanthys' is found only in Photius' quotation of the passage (against the MSS and Bo); it is natural that he should be mentioned with Minos as the two were believed to be the judges in the Lower World, and the name might have been lost in some of the mediaeval MSS. Lycurgus was an early Spartan legislator, whose existence is doubted by some; Zaleucus of Locri flourished in the seventh century B.C.; Draco (7th cent. B.C.), Solon (5th cent. B.C.), and another Lycurgus (4th cent. B.C.) were famous Athenian legislators. The list is probably a traditional one: lists of lawgivers were used

as a motif in the rhetorical schools in the argument from authority—see Theon, *Progymn.* 12 (123 Spengel). Though Methodius' argument as stated does not logically stand up, it implies the more cogent principle that the making of laws presupposes man's common conviction that he is endowed with free will.

[87] Clark's translation, 'rape,' may be right, but in the context seems less likely.

[88] This abridged argument probably means: whether sin is due to education and habit (as the present adversaries hold) or to man's passions (governed by his free will, as Methodius holds), in either case God is not to blame. On any interpretation, however, the logic of the dilemma is very confused, and the argument may well have been derived from an earlier treatise without being fully assimilated. On the passage, see also Farges, *Les idées morales* 100 ff.

[89] Though logically circular, the argument up to this point may be interpreted as an exposition of the common-sense argument in favor of man's freedom: that is, the persistent impression that men traditionally have had that good and evil are, at least sometimes, under their control. This argument, reinforced by the data of revelation on the nature of God and the universe, is Methodius' strongest point; and it is perhaps from this conviction of man's freedom that Methodius' interest in virginity ultimately derives. In his view men have the ability, with God's assistance, to transcend the limitations of the flesh.

Logos 9: Tusiane

[1] Lev. 23.39–43. This section of Leviticus incorporates the regulations, from the ancient ritual code, for the celebration of the Feast of Tabernacles (*ḥag hassukkôṯ*) during the month of Tishri.

[2] *Ibid.* In v. 40, Methodius, of course, follows LXX in his reference to the chaste-trees (ἄγνος=*agnus-castus*) against the MT.

[3] That is, ψυχία (see LSJ, *s.v.* ψυχή VI), 'little souls,' of butterflies or moths; but these do not, as we know, limit their activity to the leaves of plants; what is meant, perhaps, is that the Christian should imitate rather the purposeful honey-gathering of the bee.

[4] Cf. Heb. 10.1.

[5] From here on the meaning of Methodius' Chiliasm becomes clear. The seven days of creation are a symbol of the ages of the world; the seventh day is the period of the Millennium, and the eighth refers to heaven. Men will rest during the period of the seventh day, and there will be no marriage during the Millennium. Cf. also Methodius, *De res.* 2.21, and see Bonwetsch, *Die Theologie des M.* 124 f.

[6] Cf. Apoc. 21.4.

[7] Gen. 2.1 f.

[8] Cf. Ps. 103.31.

[9] Cf. Gen. 1.11–21.

[10] Literally, 'be applauded in common.'

[11] Prov. 1.5 f., omitting the second half of v. 5.

[12] A reflection of some of the stock charges against the Jews during the Roman empire; see, in general, I. Heinemann, 'Antisemitismus,' RE Suppl. 5.3–43, and J. Leipoldt, 'Antisemitismus,' RAC 1.469–476.

[13] The 'seal' here refers strictly neither to baptism nor to membership in the Church, but to the designation of the elect. Cf., in this context, G. W. H. Lampe, *The Seal of the Spirit* (London 1951) 255.

[14] In accordance with the doctrine enunciated in *Symp.* 5.7. In the sentence which follows, the words 'which will be fulfilled . . . Christ' are preserved only in Photius, but they should be retained as being closer to Methodius' doctrine of the Second Coming.

[15] Cf. John 14.6; 1 Cor. 13.9, 12.10.

[16] Literally, 'purely,' or 'truly'; for Methodius this implies not only truth but the absence of sensual or worldly elements.

[17] On the doctrine that the purpose of death is to destroy sin, see also Theophilus, *Ad Autol.* 2.26 f., and Irenaeus, *Adv. haer.* 3.35.2 (2.128 f. Harvey); and for the parallels in Ambrose, see T. Thompson and J. H. Srawley, *St. Ambrose: On the Sacraments and On the Mysteries* (London 1950) 65 n. 4.

[18] 'There,' that is, perhaps (a) in the Gospels, (b) in Methodius' text, *Symp.* 6.3, or (c) in heaven.

[19] Lev. 23.40, with an omission and minor variants.

[20] Cf. Jer. 9.26, Ezech. 44.7, and Acts 7.51 (the speech of Stephen). 'Circumcision of the heart' referred to the proper internal disposition towards God of which the external circumcision was only a sign: cf. also Rom. 2.29.

[21] Isa. 40.16, with an inversion of the text. Methodius' discussion may reflect a contemporary controversy among Christians on botanical exegesis.

[22] Cf. Apoc. 20.6.

[23] Cf. Ecclus. 1.4 and Prov. 8.22.

[24] Prov. 3.18.

[25] Ps. 1.3.

[26] That is, τὴν ἀρχήν, 'the beginning,' with a reminiscence perhaps of Apoc. 22.13.

[27] Cf. Ps. 44.3.

[28] Cf. John 1.17.

[29] Lev. 23.40.

[30] That is, ἄσκησις, by this time a technical term. On the development of asceticism, cf. M. Viller and K. Rahner, *Aszese und Mystik in der Väterzeit* (Freiburg i. Br. 1939); H. v. Campenhausen, *Die Askese im Urchristentum* (Tübingen 1949); H. Strathmann—P. Keseling, 'Askese II (christlich),' RAC 1.758–795; H. Musurillo, 'The Problem of Ascetical Fasting in the Greek Patristic Writers,' *Traditio* 12 (1956) 1–64.

[31] Cf. Matt. 12.44 and Luke 15.8.

[32] Methodius confuses the story of the widow's mite (Luke 21.2) with that of the woman and the lost drachma (Luke 15.8). On the latter, see J. Jeremias, *The Parables of Jesus* 106 f.

[33] 1 Cor. 13.2 f., but the clause 'sell my goods and give to the poor' is a faulty intrusion from Mark 10.21 (or parallel passages).

[34] Isa. 44.4. Cf. *Symp.* 4.3.

[35] Lev. 23.40. See also Origen, *In Exod. hom.* 9.4 (GCS 29.16 ff.).

[36] Literally, 'without distinction,' apparently referring to the same lack of moderation in the use of marital privileges as Methodius mentions in *Symp.* 3.13, but the exact meaning remains obscure. Cf. Logos 3, n. 64.

[37] 1 Cor. 7.29.

[38] For the language, cf. Plato, *Symp.* 212 B.

[39] That is, *Sukkôṯ*, as a place-name in Num. 33.5, Ps. 59.8 (=Ps. 107.8).

[40] Cf. Heb. 4.14. For Methodius, the Millennium is not only the seventh 'day' of the world, but can also be considered as seven 'days' in length. See *Symp.* 9.1.

[41] Ps. 41.5.

LOGOS 10: DOMNINA

[1] Following the reading of Bo; the Greek of MS P could mean 'nodded (or assented) with difficulty.'

[2] Avoidance of the rules of τάξις (*dispositio*, rhetorical order) seems to have been a strong point with Methodius, and this may reflect an oblique attack on the excessive amplifications of contemporary Asiatic rhetoric.

[3] Here chastity seems to be identified with the *gratia Christi*, the grace of the new dispensation, whose effects Paul describes in Rom. 5.14–21. The note on this passage in A. D. Caillau and M. N. S. Guillon, *Collectio selecta SS. Ecclesiae Patrum* 16 (Paris 1829) 346, has 'Dura haec, nec ita ut sonant admittenda.'

[4] The technique, that is, of debating or of dialectic: cf. Aristotle's definition of dialectic, 'to reason from probable premisses without error,' *Top.* 1.1: 100a18.

[5] The parable of Joatham to the Sichemites, Judges 9.8–15; Methodius' text agrees in general with MS A, with some variants. For a discussion of this folk fable, see Pfeiffer, *Introduction to the Old Testament* 330. Relying mainly on an interpretation of this fable, G. Kretschmar, in *Studien zur frühchristlichen Trinitätstheologie* (Beit. z. hist. Theol. 21, Tübingen 1946) 95–97, 103–105, attempts to derive from Logos 10 evidence for an earlier tradition of Trinitarian theology that saw in the Word and the Holy Spirit two co-equal (angelic) powers before the Father.

[6] For the image, see also *Symp.* 6.3.

[7] Gen. 3.7.

[8] Gen. 9.21 f.

[9] The 'inheritance' for the Israelites was, of course, to live happily in the Promised Land under the constant guidance of Yahweh and the prophets.

[10] Not perhaps any specific command (as, for example, the one recorded in Matt. 28.19), but rather the general mandate or deposit of Christian revelation (cf. 1 Tim. 6.20).

[11] There may have been different popular names for the chaste-tree (or agnus castus) then, as now; but Methodius perhaps exaggerates in order to make his allegorical interpretation easier.

[12] 3 Kings 19.1 ff.

[13] *Ibid.* 4, but the tree was not a bramble; the 'juniper tree' under which the prophet rested has now been identified as the white broom tree: see H. N. and A. L. Moldenke, *Plants of the Bible* (Waltham, Mass. 1952) 201.

[14] That is, ἀθετησάντων, following P rather than the emendation of Combefis, 'were unable' (to save). See LSJ, *s.v.* ἀθετέω.

[15] Cf. the parable, Judges 9.15, and n. 5 above. For Methodius the reference would appear to be to the Last Judgment and the pains of the damned; but his eschatology is not always clear.

[16] For a similar idea, cf. Tertullian, *De exhort. cast.* 13, with the notes of W. LeSaint, ACW 13 *ad loc.*

[17] 2 Cor. 11.14. We have here the beginnings of the ascetical doctrine of the devil's illusions and his ability to cause a counterfeit of true piety: cf. Nilus (5th cent.), *De diversis malis cogitationibus* 25 (PG 79.1229B–C) and *Ep.* 3.46 (PG 79.413D).

[18] Jer. 24.3.

[19] Ps. 103.15.

[20] Deut. 32.33. In the following sentence the Greek for 'the true olive and' is bracketed by Bo, but, I think, without sufficient warrant.

[21] Joel 2.21–23, in which the prophet (whose date is disputed) declares Yahweh's promise of protection and material blessings. In the text Methodius has an inversion in v. 22 (following MS A); in 23, it should be noted, the MT has 'he hath given you the former rain moderately.'

[22] Matt. 21.19.

[23] Cf. Joel 2.23.

[24] Cf. 4 Kings 20.7; the story is told again in Isa. 38.21.

[25] Gal. 5.22 f. In this text the Greek NT lists nine (though a few witnesses have ten, adding chastity); the Vulgate has twelve (adding *longanimitas, modestia* and *castitas*); Methodius gives only eight, omitting goodness (ἀγαθωσύνη).

[26] Mich. 4.4.

[27] A reminiscence perhaps of John 14.27.

[28] Zach. 4.1–3, with omissions as indicated. This is the fifth of the eight great visions of Zacharias: the golden candlestick, with seven lamps each of which has a pipe, with two olive trees at the sides. The seven lamps are meant to symbolize God's knowledge; the two olive trees, God's anointed servants, Josue and Zorobabel; and the vision predicts the successful restoration of the Temple.

[29] Zach. 4.11 f.

[30] Zach. 4.14.

[31] Literally, 'are spearmen.'

[32] The sense seems to be that the oil is somehow pressed from the branches and then flows through them.

[33] Perhaps a reference to the slippery quality of an oily branch, but the imagery and typology have become too intricate for analysis.

[34] Gen. 3.19.

LOGOS II: ARETE

[1] The MSS only give headings for Discourses 1–10; Combefis was the first to insert at this point 'The Discourse of Arete: XI.'

[2] That is, ὑπόμνημα, a 'memorial,' or (in a scientific sense) a 'treatise.'

[3] Cf. Matt. 23.25.

[4] Wisd. 7.9.

[5] In other words, the virgin must *be holy both in body and in spirit* (1 Cor. 7.34); for the development of this Pauline view in the Fathers, see Viller-Rahner, *Aszese und Mystik in der Väterzeit* 58 and n. 58.

[6] τῷ ὄντι τῷ ἀγαθῷ, which can also mean, '(opposed) in truth to the good.'

[7] A reflection perhaps of the tensions which must have existed among various groups of ascetics in the early Church; on abnormalities in the practice of asceticism, see my monograph, 'The Problem of Ascetical Fasting in the Greek Patristic Writers,' *Traditio* 12 (1956) 24–32.

[8] Literally, 'in the form of a chorus (choir),' which may have been a set position for solemn hymns and invocations. Thecla stands at Arete's right, the position of honor (Krumbacher, *Gesch. der byz. Lit.* 653, has misunderstood the arrangement), with the ten other virgins in a circle, thus:

•
• •
• •
Arete Thecla
• •
• •
•

Thecla's Hymn

[1] On the epithalium of Thecla, see W. Christ and M. Paranikas, *Anthol. graeca carminum christianorum* (Leipzig 1871) 33 ff.; W. Meyer, 'Anfang und Ursprung der lat. und griech. rhythmischen Dichtung,' *Denkschr. der kön. bay. Akad. der Wiss.*, Phil.-philol. Kl. 17.2 (Munich 1885) 309 ff.; L. Havet in *Étude sur les origines du rhythme tonique* (Nîmes 1886) 126 ff.; J. Farges, *Les idées morales* 60 ff.; F. Dölger, *Die byzantinische Dichtung in der Reinsprache* (Berlin 1948) 29, with the bibliography cited.

In form the hymn is an acrostic of twenty-four stanzas with a refrain in the manner of the ancient *cantus responsorius* of the Western Church, in which the solo voice of the precentor sings the stanzas or strophes, with the rest of the congregation repeating a regular responsion or refrain: see, for example, H. Vroom, *Le psaume abécédaire de Saint Augustin et la poésie latine rhythmique* (Lat. chris. prim. 4, Nijmegen 1933). Thus it is to be distinguished from the *cantus antiphonalis* and the *cantus directaneus* (where all sing every verse). In the Eastern Church, a similar form can be seen in the Syriac *madrasha*, seen at its best in the poetry of St. Ephraem, which later developed into the acrostic Greek hymn called the *kontakion*; on this see E. Wellecz, 'Early Christian Music,' in *Early Mediaeval Music up to 1300* (ed. by Dom Anselm Hughes, Oxford 1954) 1–13. Methodius' hymn is written in predominantly iambic metra, with resolutions and syncopation, without accurate correspondence from strophe to strophe. Each strophe begins with a letter of the alphabet in order; most stanzas have four lines, but three have five lines. In the refrain we have:

∪ — — — | — — ∪ — | ∪ — ∪ —
∪ — ∪ — | ∪ (∪) ∪ — | ∪ — —

But the text and metric of the hymn still remain very unsatisfactory. It is not unlikely that Methodius also composed music for the hymn, for the use of his benefactress, the Lady of Termessus, and perhaps a community of consecrated women. In this case, the style of the music might explain the numerous departures from regular metrical structure.

In form, Thecla's Hymn is a symbolic marriage hymn to Christ, in which Thecla speaks on behalf of all the virgins. The setting is the Day of Resurrection, the first day of the Millennium, when Christ comes as the Bridegroom to His Spouse the Church. After recounting her own sufferings, Thecla gives a long list of *exempla* of Christian fortitude and chastity, and then concludes with an exultant song of joy, in which the virgin choir is pictured as escorting the King and Queen in a mystical marriage procession towards the Gates of Life. Methodius here reiterates some of the motifs he has previously employed from the Apocalypse, the Canticle of Canticles, and Ps. 44; and in general he follows the techniques suggested by the *De arte rhetorica* attributed to Dionysius of Halicarnassus (cc. 2 and 4) for the development of the 'nuptial oration'—the use of *encomium*, *ecphrasis* (picture of the occasion, of future happiness) and *exempla*.

[2] That is, κρατοῦσα, 'holding,' with the sense of 'guarding,' 'preserving' (in this case, the 'lamps' of the senses).

[3] For the cry announcing the coming of the bridegroom in the parable, cf. Matt. 25.6; cf. also the trumpet and the voice of the archangel in 1 Thess. 4.15. Cf. also Logos 6 n. 23 above.

[4] Reflecting the tradition that Christ's final coming would be from the east: cf. Luke 1.78 ('the Orient from on high'). The east has a wide sphere of symbolic significance in the manner of burial, in primitive Christian prayer and liturgy: see especially F. J. Dölger, *Sol Salutis* esp., for the present hymn, 126 n. 1, 132 n. 1, 378, 390 n. 3, 399 n. 4.

[5] The text is corrupt at this point, but the general sense seems clear.

[6] A reference to Thecla's trials and sufferings as recounted in the apocryphal *Acta Pauli et Theclae* 28 ff. (255 ff. Lipsius); see the translation by M. R. James, *The Apocryphal New Testament* (Oxford 1924) 278 ff.; cf. also Ambrose, *De virginibus* 2.19–20 (Faller).

[7] Referring perhaps to Thecla's travels as a disciple of St. Paul, but symbolic also of the virgin's retreat from the world.

[8] Literally, φρύαγμα, 'wanton behavior,' 'insolence' (see LSJ, *s.v.*), but this ill accords with the tone of the passage; hence the meaning must perhaps be extended to include a sense such as 'freedom,' 'gay abandon,' or the like.

[9] On the title, cf. F. J. Dölger, 'Lumen Christi,' *Antike und Christentum* 5 (1936) 8–11, and Rahner, *Griechische Mythen* 215–221.

[10] On the 'open doors' cf. the parable of the Ten Virgins, Matt. 25.10; but the detail is here symbolic of the bounty of Mother Church —and she is the Queen here addressed—who receives all men of good will.

[11] Literally, in the Greek, 'in like robes,' and it is not clear from the text whether the virgins are pictured as (a) all dressed alike, (b) dressed like Christ (as Clark and Fendt take it), or finally (c) dressed like the Queen. The last possibility seems the more likely, and so we have translated it.

[12] Cf. Alcaeus, fr. 346 (Lobel-Page). Here the nectar—the divine equivalent for wine among the ancient Greeks—must be related to the draught of immortality of *Symp.* 1.1. On the symbolism of nectar, see Onians, *Origins of European Thought* 296–299.

[13] Gen. 4.8, and for the use of this as an *exemplum.* see Nugent, *Portrait of the Consecrated Woman* 74.

[14] See Gen. 39.7 ff.

[15] The 'judge' Jephte slew his only daughter in fulfillment of a vow: see Judges 11.30–40, especially 11.39.

[16] Judith 13.8; cf. also Ambrose, *De virginibus* 2.24.

[17] Literally, 'the fair form of Susanna's web' (ὑφῆς); it is difficult to understand the meaning of ὑφή, but the sense of the text is perhaps very close to 'the woven (ὑφαντόν) form of the limbs' which we find in Timotheus, *Persae* 148.—The *exemplum* is taken from the so-called Susanna-story in the LXX version of the Book of Daniel, ch. 13. See Pfeiffer, *History of New Testament Times* 448–454.

[18] The epithet 'woman-mad' is applied to Paris in Homer, *Il.* 3.39; cf. also the Greek saying, 'All barbarians are woman-mad,' Chariton 5.2.6 (Blake).

[19] The punishment here is called 'eternal' (αἰώνιος); thus there is no evidence that Methodius taught the restoration (ἀποκατάστασις) of the damned in the Origenistic sense. See also Logos 4, n. 2, and Logos 8, n. 52 above.

[20] On the reason for John the Baptist's death, St. Ambrose clearly states: 'Causa illius passionis certe haec fuit: Non licet, inquit, tibi

eam uxorem habere,' *De virginitate* 3.11; cf. also *De virginibus* 5.29–31. See Mark 6.22 ff., Matt. 14.1 ff., and Josephus, *Ant. Iud.* 18.5, with the discussion of the problem by D. Papebroch, ASS June 4 (1867) 589 ff. If Methodius' text seems to suggest that John's chastity was the reason for his death, this ought perhaps to be interpreted as referring to John's preaching of chastity, especially to Herodias and Herod, grandson of Herod the Great. The view that Herodias had tempted John seems to be merely a modern fiction: cf. Oscar Wilde's play, *Salomé* (1893) which served as the basis of Richard Strauss' opera of the same name.

[21] Following the emendation of S. G. Mercati, *Didaskaleion* 2 (1927) 25–29, I read μομφὴν ὑπέσχεν, 'was under suspicion,' instead of the reading of the MSS and Bo, μορφὴν ὑπέσχεν, 'underwent the form' (?). Mercati's suggestion seems almost certainly right.

[22] There are several levels of meaning here. 'He who was cast out' is, of course, Adam, and, by implication, all men; the one who now lives in Paradise, 'incorruptible, blessed,' is the new Adam, Christ, and, again by implication, all those who are saved through Him.

[23] Cf. Apoc. 5.9.

[24] The Greek text is very uncertain here, and Meyer's suggestion, φῶς ὅλη, has been provisorily adopted.

[25] In Greek, παῖς, referring to Christ: cf. also the *Didache* 9.2, with the note of J. A. Kleist, ACW 6.160 n. 56. Methodius is using, it would seem, a deliberately archaic term.

Epilogue

[1] The Greek word *Telmesiake* (Τελμησιακή) has previously been taken as a woman's name, but the position of the article before it and its derivation suggest rather that it is an adjective meaning 'from Telmessus' (or, by interchange of -l- and -r-, Termessus). We know now that the once prosperous city of Termessus (now represented by the little village of Telnesin) in S.W. Pisidia in Roman times came under the administration of the province of Lydia and Pamphylia, and its ruins (a theater, temples, and gymnasia) are still visible, not far from the modern Güllük. Termessus was important enough to have its own bishop, Euresius, as early as A.D. 325. See R. Heberdey, RE 2 R. 9 (1934) 732–775; R. Paribeni, *Enc. ital.* 33 (1937) 556 ff.; D. Magie, *Roman Rule in Asia Minor to the End of the Third Century after Christ* (Princeton 1950) 1136.

The peculiar nature of the references to the Lady and Methodius suggests that it was intended as a kind of 'seal' (σφραγίς) or signature on the work; and the Lady from Termessus, who is pictured as running 'like a bird in search of food,' was perhaps a benefactress of Methodius, and may well have been the moving spirit of a household of women consecrated to chastity, somewhat like Olympias, the friend of Gregory of Nyssa and John Chrysostom.

[2] There is a gap in the thought here and there may be a lacuna.

[3] This entire clause is missing from the MSS, but this or something similar must have been lost by homoioteleuton. Throughout this section, which closely imitates the Platonic dialectic technique of the *elenchos* (or demonstration, by a series of questions, that the opponent's position is absurd), the argument seems to imply several points at issue: (a) whether concupiscence is an evil in itself, (b) the providential role of concupiscence in the world, and finally (c) whether the essence of all virtue actually consists in perseverance (or 'fortitude') in the struggle against concupiscence. Moreover, in Methodius' entire discussion, it is not completely clear whether by concupiscence (ἐπιθυμία) and the passions (πάθη) he is referring to all instinctive drives and impulses or merely to those which tend towards sinful or immoral activity; it would seem, however, that only the latter sense is intended. For a discussion of the problem in the Fathers, see A. Chollet, 'Concupiscence,' DTC (1908) 803–814.

[4] For the language of the reply, cf. Plato, *Hipp. Mai.* 287 A.

[5] A strong expression (presumably for Matt. 5.8: 'they shall see God') and the text may be corrupt.

[6] Or just possibly, 'looking in all things towards Christ'; the verb ἀνανεύω may have either meaning.

[7] See Matt. 7.24.

[8] Or, perhaps, 'luxurious,' 'voluptuous.' Thus the 'dry' body, through fasting and bodily penance, is easier to control. Cf. also *Symp.* 8.4. In some way the ancients felt that drying up the bodily humors prevented impure thoughts; but it is not clear exactly how this was connected with the theory of the four humors: cf. Athanasius, *De virginitate* 7: 'Consider the effects of fasting: it cures disease, dries up the bodily humors, puts demons to flight, gets rid of impure thoughts'; and the Abbot Nilus of Sinai: 'The mind is sober when it has a dry diet; a liquid one plunges the soul into the depths. The prayer of him who fasts flies like the eaglet, but the prayer of the dissipater, weighted down with satiety, drags along the ground,' *De octo spiritibus malitiae* 1 (PG 79.1145 A). But see the discussion in 'The Problem of Ascetical Fasting in the Greek Patristic Writers,' *Traditio* 12 (1956) 16–19. And for a discussion of the four qualities (or δυνάμεις) of the body—dry, moist, hot, and cold—and the four humors in the development of ancient medical theory, see George Sarton, *A History of Science: Ancient Science through the Golden Age of Greece* (Cambridge, Mass. 1952) 338–9.

[9] That is, presumably, under normal human conditions, granting the world as it is. But the argument is ultimately sophistical; for it would logically imply that man's condition could not be improved if he were free from concupiscence, or an inclination to sin. Further, Methodius' view would also imply that anyone who had received, by special privilege, the gift of 'integrity' or freedom from concupiscence in this life, would be inferior from the viewpoint of moral virtue. Methodius' almost semi-Pelagian concept of virtue and its 'force' (δύναμις) in this section somewhat mars the conclusion of the *Symposium.*

[10] That is, it is now late and Gregorion must go home for dinner. There follows, at the end of the text in MS B (16th/17th cent.) the subscription: 'The end, and glory be to God'; and in V (15th/16th cent.): 'The end of the Symposium on Chastity by St. Methodius, Bishop of Patara.' It would, of course, be in accord with ancient practice to mark the close of a work by giving the title and author, but we cannot be sure that either of these subscriptions, both from late manuscripts, have any claim to authenticity.

INDEX

ANCIENT CHRISTIAN WRITERS

THE WORKS OF THE FATHERS IN TRANSLATION

Edited by

J. QUASTEN, S.T.D., and J. C. PLUMPE, PH.D.

1. THE EPISTLES OF ST. CLEMENT OF ROME AND ST. IGNATIUS OF ANTIOCH. Trans. by JAMES A. KLEIST, S.J., PH.D. Pages x + 162. 1946.
2. ST. AUGUSTINE, THE FIRST CATECHETICAL INSTRUCTION. Trans. by JOSEPH P. CHRISTOPHER, PH.D. Pages vi + 176. 1946.
3. ST. AUGUSTINE, FAITH, HOPE, AND CHARITY. Trans. by LOUIS A. ARAND, S.S., S.T.D. Pages vi + 165. 1947.
4. JULIANUS POMPERIUS, THE CONTEMPLATIVE LIFE. Trans. by SR. MARY JOSEPHINE SUELZER, PH.D. Pages vi + 220. 1947.
5. ST. AUGUSTINE, THE LORD'S SERMON ON THE MOUNT. Trans. by JOHN J. JEPSON, S.S., PH.D. Pages vi + 227. 1948.
6. THE DIDACHE, THE EPISTLE OF BARNABAS, THE EPISTLES AND THE MARTYRDOM OF ST. POLYCARP, THE FRAGMENTS OF PAPIAS, THE EPISTLE TO DIOGNETUS. Trans. by JAMES A. KLEIST, S.J., PH.D. Pages vi + 235. 1948.
7. ARNOBIUS, THE CASE AGAINST THE PAGANS, Vol. 1. Trans. by GEORGE E. MCCRACKEN, PH.D. Pages vi + 372. 1949.
8. ARNOBIUS, THE CASE AGAINST THE PAGANS, Vol. 2. Trans. by GEORGE E. MCCRACKEN, PH.D. Pages vi + 287. 1949.
9. ST. AUGUSTINE, THE GREATNESS OF THE SOUL, THE TEACHER. Trans. by JOSEPH M. COLLERAN, C.SS.R., PH.D. Pages vi + 255. 1950.
10. ST. ATHANASIUS, THE LIFE OF SAINT ANTONY. Trans. by ROBERT T. MEYERS, PH.D. Pages vi + 155. 1950.
11. ST. GREGORY THE GREAT, PASTORAL CARE. Trans. by HENRY DAVIS, S.J., B.A. Pages vi + 281. 1950.
12. ST. AUGUSTINE, AGAINST THE ACADEMICS. Trans. by JOHN J. O'MEARA, D.PHIL. Pages vi + 213. 1950.
13. TERTULLIAN, TREATISE ON MARRIAGE AND REMARRIAGE: TO HIS WIFE, AN EXHORTATION TO CHASTITY, MONOGAMY. Trans. by WILLIAM P. LESAINT, S.J., S.T.D. Pages viii + 194. 1951.
14. ST. PROSPER OF AQUITAINE, THE CALL OF ALL NATIONS. Trans. by P. DE LETTER, S.J., S.T.D. Pages vi + 234. 1952.
15. ST. AUGUSTINE, SERMONS FOR CHRISTMAS AND EPIPHANY. Trans. by THOMAS C. LAWLER. Pages vi + 249. 1952.
16. ST. IRENAEUS, PROOF OF THE APOSTOLIC PREACHING. Trans. by JOSEPH P. SMITH, S.J. Pages viii + 233. 1952.
17. THE WORKS OF ST. PATRICK, ST. SECUNDINUS, HYMN ON ST. PATRICK. Trans. by LUDWIG BIELER, PH.D. Pages vi + 121. 1953.
18. ST. GREGORY OF NYSSA, THE LORD'S PRAYER, THE BEATITUDES. Trans. by HILDA C. GRAEF. Pages vi + 210. 1954.
19. ORIGEN, PRAYER, EXHORTATION TO MARTYRDOM. Trans. by JOHN J. O'MEARA, D.PHIL. Pages viii + 253. 1954.
20. RUFINUS, A COMMENTARY ON THE APOSTLES' CREED. Trans. by J. N. D. KELLY, D.D. Pages viii + 166. 1955.
21. ST. MAXIMUS THE CONFESSOR, THE ASCETIC LIFE, THE FOUR CENTURIES ON CHARITY. Trans. by POLYCARP SHERWOOD, O.S.B., S.T.D. Pages viii + 285. 1955.
22. ST. AUGUSTINE, THE PROBLEM OF FREE CHOICE. Trans. by DOM MARK PONTIFEX. Pages vi + 291. 1955.
23. ATHENAGORAS, EMBASSY FOR THE CHRISTIANS, THE RESURRECTION OF THE DEAD. Trans. by JOSEPH H. CREHAN, S.J. Pages vi + 193. 1956.
24. TERTULLIAN, TREATISE AGAINST HERMOGENES. Trans. by J. H. WASZINK. Pages vi + 178. 1956.
25. ST. CYPRIAN, THE LAPSED, THE UNITY OF THE CATHOLIC CHURCH. Trans. by MAURICE BÉVENOT, S.J. Pages vi+133. 1957.
26. ORIGEN, THE SONG OF SONGS: COMMENTARY AND HOMILIES. Trans. by R. P. LAWSON. Pages vi+385. 1957.
27. ST. METHODIUS, THE SYMPOSIUM, A TREATISE ON CHASTITY. Trans. 1958. by HERBERT MUSURILLO S.J., D.Phil. (Oxon)., Pages vi+249.